METHLAND

By the Same Author

The Last Cowboys at the End of the World

METHLAND

THE DEATH AND LIFE OF AN AMERICAN SMALL TOWN

NICK REDING

BLOOMSBURY
New York   Berlin   London

Published by Bloomsbury USA, New York

Some of the names in this book have been changed.
All of the events portrayed are completely factual.

All papers used by Bloomsbury USA are natural, recyclable products made from wood grown in well-managed forests. The manufacturing processes conform to the environmental regulations of the country of origin.

LIBRARY OF CONGRESS CATALOGING-IN-PUBLICATION DATA

Reding, Nick.
Methland : the death and life of an American small town / Nick Reding.—1st ed.
p. cm.
Includes bibliographical references.
ISBN-13: 978-1-59691-650-0 (hardcover)
ISBN-10: 1-59691-650-8 (hardcover)
1. Methamphetamine abuse—Iowa—Oelwein.
2. Methamphetamine—Iowa—Oelwein.   I. Title.

HV5831.I8R43   2009
362.29'9—dc22
2008045398

First U.S. Edition 2009

1 3 5 7 9 10 8 6 4 2

Typeset by Westchester Book Group
Printed in the United States of America by Quebecor World Fairfield

To my wife and my son

For most of those which were great once are small today; and those which used to be small were great in my own time ... Human prosperity never abides long in the same place.

—Herodotus, *The Histories*

CONTENTS

CONTENTS

PROLOGUE

HOME

As you look down after takeoff from O'Hare International Airport, headed west for San Francisco, California, it's only a few minutes before the intricate complexity of Chicago's suburban streets is overcome by the rolling swell of the prairie. The change is visceral as the plane's shadow floats past houses hidden within protective moats of red cedar and evergreen shelter belts. The land unfolds a geometric sweep of corn and switchgrass. Grain elevators shine like tiny pieces in a diorama; next to them, venous brown-water creeks extend their fingers warily onto the negative space of the prairie. And if you look closely as the plane climbs past Mississippi Lock and Dam Number 10, on the Iowa side of the river, you'll see a little town called Oelwein, population 6,772. You'll see, for a few ascendant moments, every street, every building, and every pickup truck in brittle, detailed relief. Briefly, you can look at this photographic image of a town, imagining the lives of the people there with voyeuristic pleasure. And then Oelwein (along with your curiosity, perhaps) is gone.

Such is the reality of thousands of small communities dotting the twenty-eight landlocked states of the American flyover zone. Lying beneath some of the most traveled air routes in the world, they are part of, and yet seemingly estranged from, the rest of the country. In many ways, it's easier to get from New York to Los Angeles, or from Dallas to Seattle, than it is to get from anywhere in America to Oelwein, Iowa. Yet much of what there is to know about the United States at the beginning of the new millennium is on display right there, gossiping at the Morning Perk café, waiting for calls at Re/Max Realty, or seeing patients in the low brick building occupied by the Hallberg Family Practice. In their anonymity, and perhaps now more than ever, towns like Oelwein go a long way toward telling us who we are and how we fit into the world. Who we are may well surprise you.

Look again, then, this time from the window of a commuter flight from Chicago as it descends into Cedar Rapids, Iowa, on a clear May morning. Follow the gentle arc of I-380 north, over the Cedar River and past the red-and-white-checked logo of the Purina plant, which bathes everything for miles around in the sweet smell of breakfast cereal. What appears from the plane window to be only a few inches is really an hour's drive to the junction of Highway 150, a no-nonsense two-laner that eschews the complexity of cloverleaf exits and overpasses. Every twenty miles or so, the speed limit drops from fifty-five to twenty-five as Highway 150 bisects another cluster of three- and four-story buildings bookended by red-brick churches and bright metallic water towers. The names of the towns are as companionable and familiar as the country is harsh: Bryantsburg, Independence, and Hazleton accompany the road all the way to where the Amish homesteads sit kitty-corner from the Sportsmen's Lounge. There, just across the Fayette County line, is Oelwein, pronounced *OL-wine*.

Like most small towns in Iowa, Oelwein's four square miles are arranged on a grid system divided into quadrants. At what would be the intersection of the x and y axes is the central feature of Oelwein's architecture and economy: the century-old Chicago Great Western roundhouse, where trains were once turned back north or south and where entire lines of railroad cars could be worked on without regard for the often-brutal weather outside. An enormous brick and steel structure the size of three football fields, the round-house, like the town it long supported, is the biggest thing for many miles. Amid the isolation, Oelwein's very presence defines the notion of somewhere.

On the surface, Oelwein would appear to be typical in every way. Driving into town from the south, you first notice the softening profile of the maples and oaks that fill out the middle distance of an otherwise flat landscape. Once you are inside the city limits, Oelwein's skyline is divided between the five-story white spire of the Sacred Heart Catholic Church and, six blocks farther north, the four-story red bell tower of Grace Methodist. Between them is a jewelry store, a sporting goods shop, two banks, a florist, a movie house, and four restaurants, all housed in turn-of-the-twentieth-century brick and stone buildings. Across the street from Las Flores Mexican Restaurant, there's a clothing boutique, a photography studio, and a crafts store. There are almost as many bars in Oelwein (eleven) as there are churches (thirteen). The biggest congregations are Lutheran and Catholic, owing to the two separate movements of immigrants into the county: Scandinavians and Bavarians at the end of the nineteenth century; Irish and Italians at the beginning of the twentieth. Von Tuck's Bier Haus generally sees the high-end clientele, which is likely to stop in following a lasagna supper at Leo's Italian Restaurant, the newest incarnation of a business that Frank Leo began as a grocery store in 1922, shortly after arriving from Italy. The Do Drop Inn, on the other hand, is Oelwein's seediest and most eclectic watering hole. Run by Mildred Binstock, the Do Drop, as it's known, is decorated in what Mildred terms "High Amish Kitsch," a smorgasbord of lace doilies, mismatched wooden chairs, and all manner of antique farm equipment washed in the harsh reds and soft greens of year-round Christmas lights.

Heading south on Main Street, back toward Hazleton, you'll find a Dollar General, a Kmart, and a Kum and Go gas station. For the most part, though, things in Oelwein are still owned by the same families that have owned them forever. There is no Starbucks, and there are no plans for one. This is not a town that thrives on fanfare. Luxury is not a word that comes to mind inside either of Oelwein's clothing stores, VG's and Sam's, where wool dominates the fabrics of the men's suits and the ladies' dresses alike. Practical, on the other hand, is a word that applies at nearly every turn. Even the photography studio, despite its large picture window full of high school vanity shots, has a decidedly utilitarian feel, owing in part to the long shadow cast by the wide aluminum awning—a necessary accoutrement in an area of the Midwest that sees three feet of rain and five feet of snow in a normal year.

The closest thing to opulence in Oelwein comes in the predictably reserved form of a coffee shop, the Morning Perk. There, members of Oelwein's professional class gather each morning around an antique oak dresser featuring brushed aluminum carafes of both regular and flavored coffee. Next to the carafes, a wicker basket is filled with containers of liquid creamers in hazelnut, amaretto, and cinnamon flavors—this in a state (and a region) where packages of granulated nondairy creamer are de rigueur. Their husbands off to work, the wives of Oelwein's best-known men (the mayor, the high school principal, the police chief, and the Methodist minister) linger on big couches and in stiff-backed chairs to gossip and make collages. Later, it's off to the Kokomo to have their hair and nails done.

How and where you drink your coffee speaks volumes about who you are and what you do in Oelwein. Three doors away from the Morning Perk is the Hub City Bakery, a leaner, more hard-edged sibling of its sophisticate sister. Painted a dirty, aging white, and with a long, family-style folding table covered in a paper tablecloth, Hub City looks less like a café and more like the kitchen of a clapboard farmhouse. There is no focaccia or three-bean soup. In fact, there's not even a menu. Instead, there's a plastic case of doughnuts and a two-burner gas stove where the cook and owner fries eggs destined for cold white toast on a paper plate. Not that the old men mind as they linger at the table, layered in various forms of Carhartt: their discussions of corn prices and the relative merits and deficiencies of various herbicides are ongoing, if not interminable. A refined palate is not a prerequisite for entry at what is referred to by regulars as simply "the Bakery," though it helps to be short on appointments and long on opinions. Questioning the cook, like taking your coffee with cream, amounts to something like a breach of etiquette.

Together, the separate constituencies of Oelwein's two cafés give a sense of the pillars on which society in that town is built. Life in a small midwestern town lingers in the bars and passes weekly through the church sanctuaries. But it's rooted in the stores that line Main Street, and on the green and yellow latticework sprawl of the farms that begin just feet from where the pavement ends. The fit is symbiotic, though not always seamless. Without the revenues generated by the likes of the 480-acre Lein operation—a sheep and corn farm twelve miles north of town—Repeats Consignment Store and Van Denover Jewelry Plus would be hard-pressed to stay in business. As life in the fields and along the sidewalks goes, so goes the life of the town, and along with it, the life of the hospital, the high school, and the local Christmas pageant, for which Oelwein is known throughout at least two counties.

And yet, things are not entirely what they seem. On a sultry May evening, with the Cedar Rapids flight long gone back to Chicago, and temperatures approaching ninety degrees at dusk, pass by the Perk and Hub City on the way into Oelwein's tiny Ninth Ward. Look down at the collapsing sidewalk, or across the vacant lot at a burned-out home. At the Conoco station, just a few blocks south of Sacred Heart, a young man in a trench coat picks through the Dumpster, shaking despite the heat. Here, amid the double-wides of the Ninth Ward, among the packs of teenage boys riding, gang-like, on their Huffy bicycles, the economy and culture of Oelwein are more securely tied to a drug than to either of the two industries that have forever sustained the town: farming and small business.

This is the part of Oelwein, and of the small-town United States, not visible from the plane window as the flat stretch of the country rolls by. After sundown in the Ninth Ward, the warm, nostalgic light that had bathed the nation beneath a late-afternoon transcontinental flight is gone.

Against the oppressive humidity, the night's smells begin to take shape. Mixed with the moist, organic scent of cut grass at dew point is the ether-stink of methamphetamine cooks at work in their kitchens. Main Street, just three blocks distant, feels as far away as Chicago. For life in Oelwein is not, in fact, a picture-postcard amalgamation of farms and churches and pickup trucks, Fourth of July fireworks and Nativity scenes, bake sales and Friday-night football games. Nor is life simpler or better or truer here than it is in Los Angeles or New York or Tampa or Houston. Life in the small-town United States has, though, changed considerably in the last three decades. It wasn't until 2005—when news of the methamphetamine epidemic began flooding the national media—that people began taking notice. Overnight, the American small town and methamphetamine became synonymous. Main Street was no longer divided between Leo's and the Do Drop Inn, or between the Perk and the Bakery: it was partitioned between the farmer and the tweaker. How this came to be—and what it tells us about who we are—is the story of this book. And this book is the story of Oelwein, Iowa.

By the time I went to Iowa in May 2005, I'd already spent six years watching meth and rural America come together. The first time I ran across the drug in a way that suggested its symbolic place in the heartland was not in Iowa but in Idaho, in a little town called Gooding. I went to Gooding in the fall of 1999 to do a magazine story on that town's principal industry, ranching. At the time, I didn't know what meth was; it was completely by accident that I found myself in a place overrun with the drug, though the obviousness of meth's effects was immediate. That first night in Gooding, I went to have dinner at the Lincoln Inn, a combination roadhouse and restaurant. On Friday nights, the road crews who'd busied themselves all week paving and grading the county's few byways descended on the Lincoln to drink beer. An inordinate number of them, it seemed to me, were also high on meth. When the sheriff and a deputy drove by in the alley around midnight, they stopped to look in through the back door. Then they got back in their cruiser and drove away. What could they do, the two of them, faced with a room full of crank users? Two nights later, I was in the bunkhouse of a nearby ranch when three Mexicans drove up in a white Ford F-150. They were meth dealers, and the oldest among them, a nineteen-year-old who gave his name as Coco and said he'd been deported three times in the last four years, explained the crank business to me this way: "At first we give it away. Then the addicts will do anything to get more." Meth, it seemed, was just a part of life for the 1,286 inhabitants of Gooding, Idaho.

Back in 1999, very little was being written about the drug, with the exception of a few newspapers on the West Coast and a smattering of smaller ones like the Idaho *Mountain Express*. At the time, I was living in New York City. To read the *New York Times*, the *Washington Post*, and even the *Chicago Tribune* was to be largely unaware of methamphetamine's spread throughout the United States. When I talked to friends about what I'd seen in Gooding, no one believed it. That, or they dismissed crank as one more unseen, unfathomable aspect of life in The Middle: as prevalent as corn, as inscrutable as the farm bill, and as tacky as evangelical theology. Whether I traveled to Ennis, Montana, to Merced, California, or to Canton, Georgia, local consciousness of the drug was invariably acute, even as meth somehow avoided coherent, national scrutiny. For four years, wherever I went, there meth was, as easy to discount as it was to discover; once I was back in any major American city—be it New York or Chicago—whatever I'd seen or heard lost all context. I even began to get the feeling that the drug was somehow following me around. I tried and failed on numerous occasions to convince my agent and several magazine and book editors that meth in American small towns was a major issue. Eventually, I tried to forget about it and move on. But I couldn't ignore what I saw in November 2004, five years after being in Idaho, which is that meth had become a major feature in the landscape of my home.

I grew up near St. Louis, Missouri. Fifty-five miles away, near the town of Greenville, Illinois, is a wetland complex that is one of the more important stopover points in North America for what is annually the world's most concentrated migration of waterfowl. I've duck-hunted there for much of my life, and consider Greenville to be a part of the place, largely defined, from which I come. Like St. Louis, Greenville sits in the midst of the bluff prairies and timbered hollows that once stretched along the Mississippi Valley from east-central Missouri down to Kentucky. Together, this area is a discrete subset of the southern Midwest, unified by a geography, an accent, an economy, and a cultural sensibility that is an elemental part of who I am. Hunting ducks each autumn at Carlyle Lake has always served as an annual exploration of my family's history, for the birds that hatch on the prairies of northwest Iowa and the Dakotas migrate south, like my father did six decades ago, down the Missouri River toward the promise of St. Louis. There, they meet with great masses that have moved north along the Mississippi River, just as thousands of people have done, my grandmother included: she left an Ozark mountain subsistence farm along Ebo Creek, Missouri, and came looking for a better life on the fertile floodplain that surrounds St. Louis. Not far from where the two strands of my family came together, there's Carlyle Lake, and the little town of Greenville, where I have always felt at home. Somehow, despite having run across meth in small towns all over the Mountain and Middle West, I had persisted in thinking that the area where I grew up was somehow immune to its presence. That all changed one night in Greenville.

I was in Ethan's Place, a bar to which I've retired for many years after duck hunting. There, I met two men whom I'll call Sean and James. Sean was a skinhead. He'd just a few days earlier been released from the Illinois state penitentiary after serving six years for grand theft auto and manufacture of methamphetamine with the intent to distribute. He was a thin and wiry six feet one, 170 pounds, with a shaved head and a predictable mixture of Nazi tattoos. He was twenty-six years old. James was black, twenty-eight years old, and a heavily muscled six feet three. His frame was less sturdy, it seemed, than his burden, for James moved with a kind of exhausted resignation, like someone who suffers from chronic pain. For the last six years, James had been serving with the Army Airborne, first in Afghanistan, where he participated in the invasion of that country; then in Iraq, where he was also a member of the initial offensive; and finally, as a policeman back in Afghanistan, where he'd found himself in the curious position of protecting people who had been shooting at him a couple of years before. Like Sean, James had been in a sort of prison, and he was finally home.

Shared history is stronger than the forced affiliations mandated by jail or the military, and pretty soon James and Sean, the black and the neo-Nazi, talked amiably about all the people they knew in common. They drank the local specialty, the Bucket of Fuckit, a mixture of draft beer, ice, and whatever liquor the bartender sees fit to mix together in a plastic bucket. As they played pool, James stalked around the table, shooting first and assessing the situation later, each time hitting the balls more aggressively. The contours of his face formed themselves into a look of desperate perplexity beneath the shadow of his St. Louis Cardinals cap. Why, he seemed to be thinking, will the balls not go in?

Sean, too, moved around the table with a kind of pent-up aggression. Whereas James's muscular shoulders sagged in defeat beneath his knee-length Sean John rugby shirt, Sean's movements were fluid and decisive inside his Carhartts. His confidence was palpable. The enormous pupils of his blue eyes brimming with lucid possibility, Sean easily crushed James in the game of pool. Sean was riding the long, smooth shoulder of a crank binge.

As I shot pool and talked with James and Sean over several nights, it hit me with great force that meth was not, in fact, following me around. Nor was it just a coincidental aspect of life in the places I'd happened to be in the last half decade, in Gooding or Los Angeles or Helena. Meth was indeed everywhere, including in the most important place: the area from which I come. There, it stood to derail the lives of two people with whom, under only slightly different circumstances, I could easily have grown up.

Meeting Sean and James took away the abstraction that I'd felt regarding meth since 1999. In the wake of what I'd seen in Greenville, writing a book about the meth epidemic suddenly took on the weight of a moral obligation. Around that same time, after a decade in New York City, I'd begun yearning to return to the Midwest. My desire to understand the puzzle of meth had now conspired with an instinct to view the fullness of the place I'd left when I was eighteen. So, too, was the need to consider both parts of the puzzle growing more urgent. By mid-2005, meth was widely considered, as *Newsweek* magazine put it in its August 8 cover story, "America's Most Dangerous Drug."

In the end, meth would have a prolonged moment in the spotlight during 2005 and 2006, which can in some ways be traced to a late-2004 series called "Unnecessary Epidemic," written by Steve Suo for the *Oregonian*, an influential newspaper in Portland. In all, the *Oregonian* ran over two hundred and fifty articles in an unprecedented exploration of the drug's ravages. Following the cover story in *Newsweek*, a *Frontline* special on PBS, and several cable television documentaries, the United Nations drug control agency in late 2005 declared methamphetamine "the most abused hard drug on earth," according to PBS, with twenty-six million addicts worldwide. Even as global awareness of the drug grew, meth's association with small-town America remained strongest. The idea that a drug could take root in Oelwein, however, was treated as counterintuitive, challenging notions central to the American sense of identity. This single fact would continue to define meth's seeming distinctiveness among drug epidemics.

In 2005, after six years of trying, I got a contract to write this book under the assumption that meth was a large-scale true-crime story. In that version of the meth story, the most stupefying aspect is the fact that people like Sean could make the drug in their homes. Or that Coco, the Mexican teenager I'd met in 1999, would risk deportation for a fourth time in order to come to Gooding, Idaho, to sell the drug. By 2005, many law enforcement officers were being quoted in newspapers predicting that the state of Iowa would soon take over from my native Missouri as the leading producer of so-called mom-and-pop methamphetamine in the United States. For this reason, and because Sean and James had made it clear that they did not want to be written about, I'd been focusing my research on the state from which half my family comes, and which seemed poised to become the newest meth capital of America. One day, while poring over archived newspaper articles in the *Des Moines Register*, I came across an interesting quote made by a doctor in the northeast part of the state. I called the doctor one afternoon from my apartment in New York City. We talked for an hour and a half, during which the doctor began to change my thinking about meth as a crime story to one that has much more pervasive and far-reaching implications. What struck me most was his description of meth as "a sociocultural cancer." Later that day, I spoke at length to the doctor's twin brother, who was the former county public defender, and then to the assistant county prosecutor. The doctor lived in Oelwein. I made the calls on a Saturday. The following Wednesday, I was driving north on Highway 150, following flights from New York to Chicago to Cedar Rapids.

The doctor's name is Clay Hallberg. Doctor Clay, as he's known around town, is Oelwein's general practitioner and onetime prodigal son. As his father had done before him for forty-five years, Clay has for two decades delivered babies, overseen cancer treatments, performed surgeries, and served as proxy psychologist, psychiatrist, and confidante to Oelwein's wealthy farmers and poor meatpackers, to its Mexicans and Italians and Germans, its Catholics and Lutherans and evangelicals. Oelwein, replete with its humdrum realities and unseen eccentricities, passes daily through Clay's tiny, messy office across the street from Mercy Hospital, one block north of the senior high school. Clay grew up in town and had come back following medical school and a residency in southern Illinois. He raised three children there with his wife, Tammy, all the while living down the street from his parents and his two brothers. Really, I went to Oelwein for the reason that Clay and his hometown seemed inseparable to me, in the same way that hometown America was becoming inseparable with meth. I thought Clay could explain to me how that had happened.

By May 2005, Oelwein was on the brink of disaster. As I stood on First Street in front of the post office, the signs of entropy were everywhere, and hardly less subtle than those in East New York, Brooklyn, or in Compton or Watts, in Los Angeles. The sidewalks were cracked, half the buildings on Main Street stood vacant, and foot traffic was practically nonexistent. Seven in ten children in Oelwein under the age of twelve lived below the poverty line. Up at the four-hundred-student high school, on Eighth Avenue SE, 80 percent of the students were eligible for the federal school lunch program. The principal, meantime, was quietly arranging with the local police to patrol the halls with a drug-sniffing dog—essentially, to treat the high school as a perpetual crime scene. The burned-out homes of former meth labs dotted the residential streets and avenues like open sores. At the same time, the Iowa Department of Human Services, whose in-home therapists serve as one of the only realistic options for dealing with a mélange of psychiatric ailments, drug addiction, and all manner of abuse in Oelwein, was cutting 90 percent of its funding to the town. The meatpacking plant was on the verge of closing its doors. The industrial park sat unoccupied. Unemployment was pegged at twice the national level. For Larry Murphy, Oelwein's embattled second-term mayor, the question was this: How would he keep his town from literally vanishing into the prairie?

The afternoon that I arrived in Oelwein, Clay Hallberg's friend Nathan Lein met me at the Super 8 motel. For forty years, Nathan's parents have farmed and raised livestock on 480 acres north of town. Following law school in Indiana, Nathan returned home to take the job of assistant Fayette County prosecutor. On our way to the police station, Nathan drove by what he described as several working meth labs on the pretty, oak-lined streets that fill out Oelwein's residential neighborhoods, where the hand-laid stone houses date back in some cases 120 years. We passed Amishmen coming to town in their buggies, the Rent-a-Reel movie rental store, and the farm co-op. Two blocks farther on, Nathan pointed out his favorite restaurant, a drive-in burger joint called EI-EI-O's, which had recently closed. On the boarded-up windows, the owner had scrawled in red spray paint, "Make Offer—Please!"

The Oelwein Cop Shop, as the police station is known, is a nondescript 1960s-era brick building by the railroad tracks, one block north of the Chicago Great Western roundhouse. Inside, past the blue-lit dispatch station, Nathan introduced me to the new chief of police, Jeremy Logan. Logan had recently been promoted from sergeant by Mayor Murphy with mandates to clean up a force with a reputation for impropriety and to spearhead a desperate effort to get Oelwein's small-time meth manufacture under control. Sitting in his windowless office wearing a bulletproof vest, Logan scrolled through mug shots of Oelwein's best-known crank dealers and most notorious addicts, one of whom had recently been taken from his home along with fifteen assault rifles and thousands of rounds of ammunition—all while his fifteen-year-old daughter watched.

Many of Oelwein's addicts and dealers, said Logan, hung out at the Do Drop Inn. The idea was that I would go there and, with the blessing of Logan and Nathan Lein, have free range to meet whomever I could. The further hope was that I would get the stories of several addicts and dealers and, with luck, be allowed to follow their lives for the next two years.

It didn't take long. Two days later, I was in the dank living room of Roland Jarvis's small house, watching TV with the shades drawn against the bright May sunlight. Jarvis, a thirty-seven-year-old former meatpacking worker, had just smoked some crystalline shards of crank heated on a small piece of tinfoil, the vapor of which he sucked through a glass pipe. As we settled in for the denouement of the mobster movie *Goodfellas*, Jarvis told his story, principally about the night he blew his mother's house up while cooking a batch of meth. That night had earned him three months in the burn unit at the University of Iowa Hospital in Iowa City, and had melted most of his hands and face off.

Clay Hallberg is Roland Jarvis's doctor. Nathan Lein put Jarvis in jail. On the frigid winter night in 2001 when Jarvis blew up the house, he ran screaming onto the street, begging then-sergeant Jeremy Logan—with whom Jarvis had gone to Oelwein High School in the 1980s—to shoot him. Such was the pain of burning alive. And so, too, is this just a small part of the difficulty caused a tiny rural community by the specter of a drug epidemic, which directs life there in a thousand unseen ways. Nathan Lein and his girlfriend, a caseworker with the Department of Human Services, hardly ever went out to dinner anymore, for fear of seeing people that Nathan had put in jail, or whose children his girlfriend had recommended be taken away by the state. Of Roland Jarvis's four children, one, at thirteen, already needed a kidney transplant, a defect that Jarvis blames on his and his wife's intravenous meth use while the child was in utero. Summing up the damage done to Oelwein one morning at the Perk, Tim Gilson, the former principal of the nearly bankrupt high school, was almost driven to tears remembering the harsh metrics of the job from which he'd recently resigned in order to finish his Ph.D. in education. "We just didn't have the money and the staff to help the kids that needed the most of it," Gilson said, describing the events leading up to asking the police to patrol the halls. "On the one hand, I had an obligation to my teachers, who were frightened of their students. On the other hand, is there anything worse than calling the cops on your own children?" He went on, "We're in Iowa, for God's sake. We don't *do* that."

And yet, he did.

The notion that bad things don't—or shouldn't—happen in small towns is not uncommon. What Tim Gilson's disbelief suggests is that nowhere is that conceit more prevalent than in the small towns themselves. By 2005, meth was not just challenging Oelwein's sense of itself; it had destroyed it. Gilson had much from which to draw for his incredulity. That same year, an analysis by Slate.com showed that U.S. newspapers had used the title "Meth Capital of the World" to describe no less than seventy different American towns, cities, states, and counties, from California to Pennsylvania. Several meth-related murders had become national news, most notable the murder of a nine-year-old girl in Cruthersville, Indiana, who'd inadvertently found a neighbor's meth lab and was subsequently beaten to death.

Throughout its history, America has panicked over narcotics perhaps more often and more extravagantly than any nation in the world. Measured by its habitual recurrence, drug addiction is our defining morality play. The first act dates to the late 1700s, when alcohol consumption was blamed for everything from sloth to moral incertitude in the new and largely rural nation. Ever since then, most drugs and drug epidemics have been associated with urban life, whether expressed by the Prohibition raids of Chicago and New York speakeasies, LSD in San Francisco in the 1960s, or Wall Street's and South Beach's cocaine excesses of the 1980s.

What set meth apart was not only the idea that one could make it in the bathtub, but also that the people doing so were poor or working-class rural whites. In that way, the meth epidemic appeared to have neither analog nor precedent in any time since the Revolution.

In truth, all drug epidemics are only in part about the drugs. Meth is indeed uniquely suited to Middle America, though this is only tangentially related to the idea that it can be made in the sink. The rise of the meth epidemic was built largely on economic policies, political decisions, and the recent development of American cultural history. Meth's basic components lie equally in the action of government lobbyists, long-term trends in the agricultural and pharmaceutical industries, and the effects of globalization and free trade. Along the way, meth charts the fears that people have and the vulnerabilities they feel, both as individuals and as communities. The truly singular aspect of meth's attractiveness is that since its first wide-scale abuse—among soldiers during World War II—meth has been associated with hard work. For seventy years, the drug more commonly referred to as crank has been the choice of the American working class. It's in this way more than any other that the story of meth is the story of Oelwein, Iowa, along with that of Roland Jarvis and Tim Gilson and Jeremy Logan. It is also the story of the remarkable, even heroic lengths to which people and communities will go in order to fix themselves.

Some of the deeper meanings of this drug's hold on America had been evident back in 2004, in Greenville, Illinois. Since the farm crisis of the 1980s, many of the farmers there had long since foreclosed on their land. People left in large numbers. According to Sean and James, in nearby Hagarstown, Illinois, there is but one resident who remains. By 2004, many of the employment opportunities in Greenville and the surrounding area were half-time, with no benefits. Out by Interstate 70, just a couple hundred yards from Ethan's Place, there were no fewer than seven major chain motels, none of which contributed more than a few minimum wage jobs to the town's economy. Greenville, once a proud, vigorous farm town, now depended in part on reluctant passersby moving between St. Louis and Indianapolis in order to survive.

Soon enough on the night that Sean and James played pool with each other, they were talking about job opportunities. There were construction gigs closer to St. Louis, in Belleville, Illinois, or even farther still, forty miles beyond the Missouri line, in St. Charles, sixty miles from Greenville, one way. There was a night-watch job across the street from Ethan's at the Super 8, a position held at the time by a forty-year-old divorced mother of two who was heading to Chicago to try her luck. And there was some work at Wal-Mart. James, who'd entered the Army a grunt and left it six years later a proud staff sergeant, was not enthused by these options.

Sean just laughed. He knew what he was going to do: make meth. The money was good, the drugs were good, and it garnered him access to all kinds of women who, once they smoked a foil or two, would do anything for more. Sean clearly didn't give a shit about the consequences. The way he saw it, life in Greenville was a prison anyway. It was better to live well for a time and go back to jail than to pretend to make ends meet on two hundred dollars a week and no health insurance that Sean said a job at Wal-Mart would get him.

That night, it was unclear whether James was buying it. But it was impossible not to wonder at what point he would start seeing things through Sean's eyes. After all, they'd immediately been able to overlook their immense surface differences: black skin, white skin; shaved head, military crew. On a deeper level, there existed a stronger, and ultimately more enduring, foundation: they were united by history. Life in Greenville had, in the course of their lives, changed fundamentally. And yet here they were together, finally home. If James planned to stay, how long could it be before crank, and Sean, seemed like his best option?

That's not a question I will ever be able to answer directly, for in all the times I've been back to Greenville, Illinois, I've never seen

James or Sean again. The nights I spent talking to them in 2004, though, drove me in my attempt to understand meth in small-town America. Along the way, I began to understand how greatly life in those towns has changed in the past thirty years. Oelwein is a simulacrum for Greenville, and by extrapolation, for the great expanse of the rural United States. Beginning in Oelwein, one can follow meth's currents backward to the thousands of disparate sources from which it flows. From May 2005 until June 2008, I went back many times to Oelwein; I went to California, Idaho, Alabama, Georgia, Illinois, and Missouri, to big cities and small towns alike, in an attempt to put the events in that small Iowa town into some kind of large-scale perspective. Eventually, the story I'd once viewed through the lens of homespun crime became one that stretched from the Czech Republic to China to Washington, D.C., and involved not just addicts and prosecutors and public defenders, but also congresspeople and governors and U.N. officials; neuropharmacologists and macroeconomists; rural sociologists and microbiologists; and drug lobbyists and pharmaceutical company executives.

What it took three and a half years to fully understand (nine if I count back to my trip to Gooding, Idaho) is that the real story is as much about the death of a way of life as it is about the birth of a drug. If ever there was a chance to see the place of the small American town in the era of the global economy, the meth epidemic is it. Put another way, as Americans have moved increasingly to the coasts, they have carried with them a nostalgic image of the heartland whence their forebears came, as worn and blurry as an old photograph. But as the images have remained static, the places themselves have changed enormously in the context of international economics, like an acreage of timber seen in two photos, one in spring, the other in winter. Really, what James and Sean were confronted with that November night back in 2004 was nothing short of finding a place for themselves in a newly unfamiliar world.

PART 1

2005

CHAPTER 1

KANT'S LAMENT

Nathan Lein, the assistant Fayette County prosecutor, is twenty-eight years old. He has a bachelor's degree in philosophy from Luther College in Iowa, a law degree from Valparaiso State University in Indiana, and a master's in environmental law from the Vermont Law School. The latter two degrees he completed in an astonishing three years by attending Valpo, as it's called, in the fall, winter, and spring and then transferring credits to Vermont in order to get his master's after only three summers' worth of study. Meantime, Nathan, a white farm kid from rural Iowa, financed all of it by working as a bouncer in an all-black strip club in the industrial wasteland of Gary, Indiana.

Nathan is six feet nine inches tall and weighs 280 pounds. He moves with surprising grace around his tiny, four-room house in Oelwein's Ninth Ward. What evidence there is of the great burdens of Nathan's life is limited to a habit of slowly raising his hand to his face and then rubbing the tip of his nose in one quick motion, as if to remove a stain that only he can perceive. Perhaps knowing that his size will lend extra weight to whatever he says, Nathan fashions his sentences from the leanest fibers. It's a habit that underscores the gravity of the contradictions by which his life is defined.

Despite his size, Nathan—a card-carrying Republican—drives

the same white diesel Volkswagen Jetta that he has been driving for 177,000 miles, or the rough equivalent of seven circumnavigations of the globe, most of it logged within the confines of a single Iowa county. To court up in the town of West Union, he wears a gray suit, a white shirt, a blue tie, and a ring on each thumb. His hair is dark blond and is short on the sides and longer on top, where Nathan, aided by the stiffening properties of hair gel, arranges it in a way that looks like neat, stubbled rows of winter wheat. The name Lein is Norwegian; beneath a wide forehead, Nathan's eyes are sled-dog blue. On one window of Nathan's Jetta is a sticker for the hallucinogenic-hippie band Widespread Panic, whom Nathan goes to see whenever they are within a reasonable driving distance, which for him means about 400 miles. Nathan has been to nineteen shows to date. In the trunk of the Jetta, there is a hunting vest in Mossy Oak camouflage, the pockets of which are stuffed with shotgun shells and wooden turkey calls; a cardboard crate of police reports and depositions; and a twelve-gauge semiautomatic Winchester X2 shotgun.

It's mid-May 2005, and in the wake of a front that blew out of Regina, Saskatchewan, and overshot the Dakotas, the sky above Oelwein is gray and roiling. As there is more rain in the forecast, Nathan's father will be planting corn till long past dark on the farm where Nathan grew up, twelve miles outside town, hoping to get the year's crop seeded before the soil is too wet to plow. Meantime, there are plenty of chores to be done, most of which revolve around the fifty or so Lincoln long-wool and Corriedale sheep that Nathan's parents raise: sweeping the pens, freshening the water, feeding hay to the rams and ewes. Changed from his suit, in ruined duck-cloth bibs and size 15 work boots, Nathan pilots the white Jetta north along Highway 150. He passes Grace Methodist, somber and maroon-red in the long, sunless dusk, then turns west on Route 3. The late-day smells of cut grass and wet pavement are underlain with the sultry, textured scent of pig shit. Twenty miles distant, the western sky is bruised black and green in a way that has the Amish urging their Clydesdales onward at a trot along the shoulder of the road, the plastic rain-doors already zipped tight on their buggies.

The house where Nathan was born and raised is a white-clapboard three-bedroom that sits on a slight rise in the prairie at the end of a gravel road. It was built in 1910. The yaw in the place is visible, two or three degrees measured foundation to rooftop, northwest to southeast, as meaningful a testament as there is to the prevailing ferocity of the prairie wind. The views are stunning, as much for the austere grandeur as for the suffocating sense of desolation. From the driveway, mile after mile of newly planted corn and soybeans spread in every direction, interrupted now and again in the shifting line of sight by an evergreen shelterbelt or an anemic finger of timber. The maples and oaks, like the farmhouses, have taken their chances against the weather for as long as anyone can remember. Out here, it seems, stubbornness is just a part of the landscape.

As is frugality. Inside the farmhouse, Nathan's mother and father stand in the kitchen, next to the sink. The rest of the room consists of a tiny four-burner stove, one bank of white wood cabinets, an Amish table with two chairs, and a small refrigerator. Stacked in piles throughout the room are dozens, if not hundreds, of agricultural bulletins, almanacs, magazines, and foldouts that the Leins pore over in an attempt to anticipate sheep and crop prices—*Wallace's Farmer*, *Today's Farmer*, *Sheep* magazine, the *Corn Producer*, the Iowa Farm Bureau *Spokesman*. There is no Internet and no computer, no fax machine or BlackBerry. The only nod to modern technology aside from the wall-mounted phone is a small TV on the counter, on which Nathan's father watches (and talks back to) the two hosts of *Market to Market* every Friday night on PBS at eight P.M.

Every decision made by the Leins—how much seed to buy, and from whom; when to harvest; how long to hold the crop—is arrived at from a process of superimposition of dated economic information onto subtle, veinous changes of seasonal matter. What to do tomorrow depends on this week's weather relative to last year's yield, or on how today's futures markets at the Chicago Board of Trade relate to anticipated trends in Australian or Canadian wool production. In this way, the Leins are less like farmers and more like mystics clinging to belief in a hazy vision born not just of weather and organic chemistry, but of a hundred other unseen and uncontrollable forces. To look at them, leaning against the counter in the tiny kitchen, is to understand the connection between farming, itself an act of blind faith, and religion. If you can believe in a year's worth of corn or beans, it seems, you can believe in anything.

Nathan's father, James, is sixty-nine years old. His hair is short and black, and his glasses are broken. Standing somewhat off-kilter from a bad back, in a red and blue work shirt, jeans, and sneakers, he looks fifty. His mother, Donna, who is seventy, has shoulder-length brown hair that is going gray. Dressed in jeans and a light gray wool sweater, she, too, looks younger than her years, though the arthritis from which she suffers is readily apparent in her hands, which are bent and knobbed at the joints like a bird of prey's claws. And though neither parent is short (James stands six feet, Donna five seven), it's unclear whence Nathan got his tremendous size. Ducking as he entered the kitchen, with its low ceiling and peeling linoleum floor, Nathan immediately fills the room, even as his parents seemed to shrink. The weight of his presence makes it odder still that the Leins barely take notice of their son, who now stands next to the refrigerator. It's as though Nathan has just briefly come in from the barn for a glass of water; no one says a word. Then, with a nod, Nathan goes outside to see about the sheep. With a storm coming and the tractor awaiting his father's return, there's no time for talk.

Farming is still, as it has always been, the lifeblood of Fayette County—and by extension, of Iowa. Nathan goes to his parents' place at least three times a week. During spring planting, from late

April till mid-May, he's there every night, as he is during the hay cutting and baling season of late summer, the corn harvest in the fall, and when the ewes lamb-out in the winter. Thanks in part to this, the Lein operation is a successful one. The fecundity of the land helps, too. With soil that boasts a corn sustainability rating (CSR) of 75 to 85 out of 100, the land in Fayette County has remained exceptionally rich for the 150 years that people have farmed it. Annual rainfall here averages three feet, and farmers here, unlike those in many places in the United States, needn't bother with irrigation, thereby saving themselves untold thousands of dollars each growing season. Though they have a 50 percent rotation of soybeans, the Leins make their bottom line most years off row crops alone, raising hay just to keep the sheep fed. Selling wool, lambs, and the occasional ram or ewe is predominantly a labor of love—or what Nathan's ascetic parents consider an indulgence, and one for which the Leins have won prizes as far away as Maryland and Colorado. All together, it's a formula that James and Donna Lein have applied with good success for almost forty years.

Unfortunately for many farming families around Oelwein, the Lein place is an anomaly. Since the early 1980s, three out of four farms in Fayette County have gone out of business, in a trend reflected everywhere in the rural United States. In their stead, many family farms have become add-ons to the ever-increasing holdings of private corporations like Cargill and Archer Daniels Midland (ADM). That, or free-falling land and corn prices have forced smaller places like the Leins' into bankruptcy, making them easy targets for the few families who control the bulk of land in rural counties like Fayette. With their land sold and no jobs, large numbers of people have left the farm belt in the last two and half decades. Oelwein is typical: between 1960 and 1990, the population fell from eight thousand to just over six thousand, a decline of nearly 25 percent. Along with this came a decline in education and employment. Of those who remain in rural America, only one in ten men over the age of twenty-five have at least two years of college education.

Unemployment averages one and a half times that of the urban United States. That is to say that the lifeblood of Fayette County, as in most farming areas, now sustains far fewer lives than it did just twenty years ago.

Out of respect for his parents, Nathan does not use the word *poverty* when describing the circumstances of their lives, though any qualitative analysis would hardly fail to label his parents as poor. Only one side of the Leins' century-old farmhouse has siding, despite the ruthless weather systems that pound northern Iowa. As a child, Nathan wore clothes from Goodwill. Christmas was for praying, not for gift giving, less for reasons of religious stricture, Nathan says, than for the financial constraints endemic to a seat-of-your-pants farming existence. Donna, whose parents were new German immigrants from over by Waverly, Iowa, has lived here since the 1960s. In 1968, Donna's first husband was killed in a car accident. She married James, the first-generation auto-mechanic son of a Norwegian day laborer, in 1972, after having kept the farm going by herself for four years. Back then, with crop prices good, the average size of a farm in Fayette County was still 250 acres— that's all it took to make a living. Since then, the 480-acre Lein place has become an artifact of a different time. Many neighbors farm ten times that much land, and planting is done with quarter-million-dollar machinery, guided by GPS. Meanwhile, says Nathan, the equipment his father uses has been largely relegated to museums.

Whether Nathan will take over his parents' place one day is one of the defining questions of his life, and one that, for now, remains sorely unanswered. No one understands the ins and outs of the Lein place like Nathan. Nor is there anyone for whom that ground has more meaning. Land is something you crave or you don't; if you're born with a desire for it, you intrinsically understand why people like the Leins break their backs every day, at the ages of sixty-nine and seventy, to keep it. Doing so is less a question of vocation or aesthetics than a question of blood.

The farm is why Nathan came back to Oelwein after law school. During the three years he was away, Nathan grew his hair and used his college training in philosophy to try to undo the strict bounds of his religious training. Once loosed into the wider world, Nathan—in an effort to bury the discomfort of his narrow and isolated upbringing—did, by his estimate, every drug known to man, including methamphetamine. Even as he readied himself for a life built around the binding element of law, he worked his way step by step through the foundations of his life, attempting to destroy everything as he went. What he couldn't destroy was the need to return home or the connection to his family's land. In coming back, Nathan figures, he missed the last best opportunity he would ever have to get out of Iowa.

Nathan saw his home in a wholly new light on his return in 2001. He'd left as a sheltered, ultraconservative Lutheran and come back with a well-honed passion for environmental activism. Locally, that passion was aimed primarily at what he deemed irresponsible water-use laws that both unfairly favored farmers and ranchers and polluted rivers like his beloved Volga, a tributary of the Upper Iowa. Fiscally, Nathan remained conservative, though his social agenda was that of a classic grassroots liberal. In lieu of building more jails—one of Iowa's leading economies in the last ten years—Nathan advocated investment in state-mandated rehabilitation. He stopped attending church himself, but joined church-sponsored social change organizations. He read Aquinas and Kant, bought a VW bus, and organized trash cleanups on public lands. For a while he lived in Waterloo, an hour south of Oelwein, with the girlfriend he'd met in law school, and of whom his parents disapproved for, according to Nathan, her ample breasts, small stature, and short hair; her Jewish faith; and her roots in a city (Indianapolis), among other things on a long list. There was a falling-out, and Nathan, convinced he'd go the way of his estranged brother, who was living in San Francisco, gave up hope of ever taking over the farm. He consoled himself with the fact that his passion for environmental change was deeply out of whack with the prevailing sentiments of the old-guard farmers up around Oelwein, upon whose credos he'd only a few years before staked his claim to the family business. Still, he was lost and confused by his life, drawn to a place—home—in which he felt intellectually and spiritually confined. Nothing felt familiar. Moved to do something, Nathan did nothing.

That's when Larry Murphy called. Murph, as he's known around town, is a onetime meatpacking worker from a well-known Catholic Democratic family in Dubuque, Iowa. Of Larry's eight surviving siblings—there were initially ten—four are, or have been, involved in state politics. During his senior year in high school, Nathan had worked for Murph as a page during one of Murph's three terms as a state senator. In January 2002, one year after Nathan moved back to Iowa, Murph took office as the mayor of Oelwein, which was in dire straits financially. In addition to problems with the farms, Chicago Great Western had closed the roundhouse, and wages at the Tyson meatpacking plant in town were barely a third of what they'd been as recently as 1992. With a shrinking student body and falling tax support, Oelwein High School was in danger of being closed, which would have had the disastrous effect of leaving some four hundred students to be bussed, at great expense, to schools as many as fifty miles away.

Into this vacuum had moved the production and distribution of methamphetamine. Not only in Oelwein, but all across Iowa, meth had become one of the leading growth sectors of the economy. No legal industry could, like meth, claim 1,000 percent increases in production and sales in the four years between 1998 and 2002, a period in which corn prices remained flat and beef prices actually fell. Farmers, desperate to avoid foreclosure on their land, sold anhydrous ammonia (a common fertilizer) to meth cooks to make the drug. Others simply quit farming and went into the small-scale meth-manufacturing business. Meatpacking workers hoping to stay awake long enough to take on double shifts bought the drug in increasing quantities. As all manner of small legitimate businesses went bankrupt, meth labs opened in their stead. According to Nathan, farming and agriculture began vying with a drug to be Oelwein's lifeblood.

"Talk about a nightmare," said Nathan, reflecting back. "We'd lost all the bases of civilized culture around here. It was third-world. People began referring to Oelwein as 'Methlehem.'"

In March 2002, early in his first term as mayor, Larry Murphy called Nathan and offered him the job of assistant county attorney, along with a mandate to clean up meth in Oelwein. The new mayor appealed to Nathan's idealistic side and enlisted him to help make an example of how a tough town could succeed in difficult times. He also played on Nathan's innate desire to be closer to home. As he and his parents became more estranged, the problems between Nathan and his girlfriend increased; for the first time since returning to Iowa, he wanted to leave Waterloo and come back to Oelwein. Murph told him that a state job would give him plenty of time at night and on weekends to work at his parents' farm and to heal whatever wounds were festering between them. Nathan could be part of two solutions, Murph said—one personal, one civic. Nathan jumped at the chance.

"He's a very persuasive guy," said Nathan in 2005. "I went from totally apathetic to totally gung-ho in about a week. We were going to fix this place. I really believed that. In some ways, I almost still do."

Crank in Oelwein back in 2005 was largely considered a small-lab problem, as it was in most of the country. The year before (2004 statistics had just been released when I went to Oelwein), there were 1,370 methamphetamine labs seized in Iowa. In Illinois, the number was 1,098. Tennessee had 889, Nebraska had 65, and Georgia law enforcement officers seized 175. In Arizona, the number was 71, and in Oregon it was 322. Missouri beat them all with

2,087. Between 1998—Nathan's senior year in high school, when there were only 321 labs busted in Iowa—and 2004, there had been an increase of nearly 500 percent. And that's really only the tip of the iceberg. Oelwein chief of police Jeremy Logan, reflecting a reality nationwide, readily admits that law enforcement dismantles, at most, one in ten of the total number of labs in existence. Extrapolate that onto the number of children taken out of Iowa meth labs alone in 2003 and 2004 (700) and that means that at least 7,000 kids were living every day in homes that produce five pounds of toxic waste, which is often just thrown in the kitchen trash, for each pound of usable methamphetamine.

By the time I met Nathan, he estimated that 95 percent of all his cases were related to the drug in one manner or another: manufacture and distribution, possession, possession with intent to distribute, illegal sale of narcotics to a minor, driving under the influence of an illegal substance, etc. Of those, he had to offer a plea in about ninety-eight out of a hundred, he said. What bothered him most were the crimes, and these were numerous, in which children had been involved. Many of those included child rape. Others involved neglect to an order of magnitude—three-year-olds left alone for a week to take care of their younger sibling; children drinking their own urine to avoid dehydration—that had once been unheard of in Oelwein.

The population of Oelwein fell steadily through the 1980s and 1990s and continues to fall today, albeit at a slower pace. The result has been a long-term steady loss of tax revenue. In this environment, certain basic civic functions become indulgences. Keeping the streetlights on at night is no longer a given. Trials, which are expensive, are no longer economically feasible. Nor are lengthy incarcerations. As these problems extended throughout the county and state, there was simply no place to put meth addicts. The Fayette County jail was full. The local jail was full. The Iowa state penitentiary in Fort Madison was full. There were no rehab facilities to speak of in Fayette. The Department of Human Services

(DHS) was laying off workers each week; by October of 2005, Nathan's girlfriend, Jamie, would be out of a job.

Sitting with Murph one day that May watching the Oelwein Husky varsity baseball team lose a double-header to the Decorah Vikings, I asked Murph, who was now halfway through his second term as mayor, when he'd first noticed meth as a real factor in the life of Oelwein. Like Nathan, he said in 2003, and compared the number of labs to a plague. I asked him what he planned to do about meth, since it had been a problem for a couple of years. Murph, a warm and vibrant man of fifty who appeared, behind pilot's sunglasses and beneath a navy-issue baseball cap, to be in spectacularly good health, was uncharacteristically silent. "I honestly don't know," he said finally. "My fear is that there is no solution. That's how unclear the path has become at this point."

Murph understood, perhaps more than anyone, the manner in which Oelwein's financial difficulties of the last two decades reinforced its meth problem. His job was increasingly directed by the belief that in solving the town's economic dilemma, the drug problem, too, would abate. That was the hope, anyway. On another level, meth seemed to operate completely outside the bounds of any rational, calculated variables. If crank was supposed to appeal only to people with nothing to lose, why then, said Murph, did the "good families" suffer its consequences, too? Recently, the husband of the woman who owned a local beauty salon had been hallucinating so badly one night that he accused his wife of having sex with a stranger in the bed next to him (she was hiding with her daughter in an adjoining room at the time), and then he tried to kill her. It was as though, said Murph, a sense of nihilism had become endemic to Oelwein.

One example of the connection between financial loss and the increase in meth use was a feeling among the small-time cooks that they, like the moonshiners of the early twentieth century, were the last of a breed, not just of rebellious criminals, but of small-business people. In the wake of so many closed storefronts, it was the Beavis and

Butt-Head cooks, as the police called them, who touted their place as entrepeneurs in the increasingly weak economy of Oelwein. It was an added benefit of the vitality of their businesses that people, when they snorted or smoked local crank, felt good for days. Viewing themselves as modern-day Pied Pipers, the cooks by their very presence in town posed a question to which the answer was not obvious: What else was there to feel good about? It was a logic that had become pervasive. Across the street from Nathan Lein's house, ninety feet from his front door, a married couple who were batchers worked day and night until Nathan tried and convicted them in 2003.

Small-time cooks in Oelwein make a kind of methamphetamine called "Nazi cold," which relies on anhydrous ammonia, a chemical fertilizer rich in nitrate that farmers spray on their fields, and pseudoephedrine rendered from Sudafed and Contac. The name Nazi cold refers in part to the dependence on cold medicine and in part to the methamphetamine synthesis process used by the Germans in World War II, which depended on nitrate. Of the latter ingredient, the Germans had enormous supplies, for nitrate is also a key component in gunpowder. (With enough gunpowder and enough meth, one might conclude, anything seems possible.) German methamphetamine during the war, manufactured by the pharmaceutical companies Temmler and Knoll and sold under the name Pervitin, was in fact made in laboratories, and in huge quantities: millions of pills each month.

Nazi cold meth, on the other hand, can be manufactured wherever, and in quantities that rarely exceed a pound per cook, but which are more likely to produce only a few grams of what is locally called swag, shit, batch, and crank. Lab locations in Iowa in the past decade have included bait and tackle shops, river barges, networks of tunnels dug with backhoes, the cab of a combine, thousands of kitchen sinks, bathtubs, and motel rooms, a high school locker room, and a retirement home, in which the elderly residents were given excessive doses of opiates so that they would not wake up while the batchers worked. In one Iowa county, the school district banned bake sales after several children unwittingly brought to school meth-tainted chocolate chip cookies and Rice Krispies treats that sickened classmates.

Like dioxin, meth residue possesses a unique ability to bind to food, countertops, microwave walls, sink basins, and human lung tissue for days after being synthesized. Making the drug is a dangerous undertaking. The extreme "heat" of anhydrous ammonia, which is stored at negative two hundred degrees Fahrenheit, is such that it can burn through human tissue to the bone. By 2005, meth-making in Oelwein was a process more often completed in a twenty-ounce soda bottle than in an actual laboratory. At least one step in the process—adding lithium to anhydrous—can result in explosive boiling if not properly done. In another method of production, adding blue iodine to red phosphorus often produces phosphine gas, which is toxic enough to cauterize lung and throat tissue. The side effects of meth—bleeding skin-sores as your pores struggle to open and expel the drug, which often become infected; internal organs shrunken from dehydration; vast areas of the brain that according to CAT scans are completely depleted of neurotransmitters: a sense that a person is literally falling apart from the inside out—seem almost unnatural, something visited upon our waking lives from the unconscious. The cruel irony is that it is a horror completely of our own making.

"Lab," then, is largely a misnomer. All that is truly necessary to make Nazi dope, in addition to the anhydrous ammonia and the cold pills, is a lithium strip from inside a battery (accessible by unrolling the layers of zinc and aluminum that lie beneath the protective sheath), some Coleman lantern fluid, and a ninth-grade knowledge of chemistry. Using a soda bottle instead of a pair of buckets rigged with surgical tubing is called the single-batch system, and it became popular in Oelwein once the police had begun raiding so many homes in search of meth labs. Single-batching was devised as a way to cook while riding mountain bikes. If they strapped a soda bottle onto a rack over the rear wheel, single-batchers believed that the constant movement—unlike in a home lab—would diffuse the smell of the process. They further believed that the police wouldn't suspect people on bikes of cooking meth. (It didn't take long to catch on. In one story, a Fayette County sheriff's deputy pulls up to a kid sitting by the side of the road amid a wilderness of midsummer corn. His bike in pieces all around him, he has a soda bottle at his side, inside of which there is a small inferno of activity: he has decided, while he waits for his meth to cook, to take his bike completely apart and put it back together again. The boy asks the deputy why he stopped. "I got a call," says the deputy, in the bone-dry wit endemic to the Midwest, "that you needed to borrow a screwdriver.")

The first order of business for any Nazi cold cook is to amass quantities of cold pills. To do this, cooks generally hire people who will work in exchange for a portion of the product. These people stereotypically ride together in vans from one town to the next, pil-ing into gas stations, Wal-Marts, grocery stores, and pharmacies in order to steal or buy as much cold medicine as they can. They might do one county today, and another tomorrow. If they've been particularly active lately around Oelwein, they might run up to Caledonia, Minnesota, hit Decorah and Kendallville, Iowa, on the way, then rob their way home via Prairie du Chien, Wisconsin. Cops across the country, playing on the van element and the fact that the people riding in them are apt to be acting funny, call the process of amassing pills Smurfing.

Depending on how successful the cook is, he might have his own supply of anhydrous ammonia, which is generally to say that he gets it from a farmer who takes a cut of the profit. For small-timers, though, stealing is the order of the day. It's dangerous work, and a common source of injury. For use as a fertilizer, anhydrous is highly diluted; for use in making crank, it must be gotten in its concen-trated form, which is largely done at night and surreptitiously. One common and incredibly hazardous way of getting anhydrous from the heavy, thick-walled steel tanks in which it is stored is to prop the tank legs on bricks and then to drill holes just above the settling line of the anhydrous, easily identified, like studs in drywall, by rapping one's knuckles along the tank and listening to the pitch. Then, the thieves remove bricks one at a time from two of the legs of the tank, tilting the tank more and more. When the anhydrous pours out of the drilled holes, they attempt to catch it in buckets or small, reinforced kerosene containers. Dr. Clay Hallberg, the chief of staff at Mercy Hospital, tells one story among many of a boy who waited nearly two days to come to the emergency room following an accident while stealing anhydrous in which a small amount of the liquid had spilled on his jeans. He'd have come sooner, but he was still high, and he didn't want to go to jail. By the time he got to the ER, says Clay, one of the boy's testicles had melted off.

It's stories like this, told and retold every day among the farmers at Hub City Bakery or while shopping at VG's, that had begun to fray the sense of civility in Oelwein by summer 2005. Two years after a consolidated effort to rid the town of meth was begun, patience was waning. The police chief mandated—with Nathan's and Murph's full support—that his men pull over cars for almost any reason in hopes of finding meth. He had recently lobbied the city council to pass an ordinance outlawing bikes in town. The hope was that the cooks who brazenly cycled around making meth in their soda bottles would at least do so somewhere out in the country instead of right on Main Street. In reaction, there was talk in Oelwein that Murph and Nathan and the chief were infringing on people's civil liberties when they ought to be doing something about the meth labs, which regularly caught fire in residential neighborhoods, sending toxic plumes of smoke in whatever direction the wind happened to be blowing. Meantime, an Oelwein officer named David Bloem was being investigated for assaulting a meth addict named Jason Annis. According to the *West Branch* (IA)

Times, the accident began when Bloem arrested Annis with a meth-filled syringe "sticking out of his arm." Later, a video camera in the police station appeared to show Bloem shoving Annis to the floor, where he suffered a broken orbital bone at one eye and a compound fracture at his left cheek.

The effect was partly desperation, even panic, and partly a reversion to the overly simplistic version of events, which is that meth, and meth alone, was responsible for all that was bad in Oelwein. The addendum to the postulate is that whoever becomes hooked is weak. There's something wrong with them, and because of them, there's now something wrong with us. Even Nathan, whose own contradictions made him adept at looking at things evenhandedly, was quick to talk about the "shitbags" and the "scum": those whose addiction made everyone else pay the price. After three years as assistant county attorney, during which things had gone from bad to worse (in Oelwein), he found it harder and harder to see the nuances of life after meth.

Nathan's office is in a squat three-story brick building at the corner of Highway 150 and Route 3, across the street from the Oelwein Public Library. On the first floor of the building there is a small bank. The second and third floors, like so many commercial spaces in Oelwein, are empty. The basement is occupied by a two-man law firm, Sauer and Sauer LLC. The younger Sauer, Wayne, is, in addition to being a partner in the firm with his father, the county attorney. Nathan, every day that he's not in court, goes to his office there, which is ample, if not extravagant. There is a large desk and three chairs, two of them stacked with boxes of depositions and police reports. On the wall hangs the beard of a turkey that Nathan killed last spring, ten inches long and black and coarse, like the tail of a tiny horse. Next to that is a framed certificate of thanks to Nathan for one of the many cleanups he has organized on the nearby Volga River.

It's lunchtime, during which Nathan, who is proud of his frugality, would normally go home and eat last night's leftovers while watching TV. A second reason Nathan hardly goes out to eat is that he is constantly running into people he's prosecuted. Today, though, is Friday, the end of the workweek, and the May sun is finally out following five solid days of rain. Leo's Italian Restaurant, just three blocks away, has a special every Friday on the fried pork tenderloin sandwich with mayo and tomato and a side of broasted potatoes. It's still an expensive sandwich, if you ask Nathan: $5.95. But today it sounds too good to pass up. So Nathan reaches for his suit jacket, walks up the stairs, and heads out the glass door of the building into the warm sun.

Leo's is packed. Fronted by large windows that look onto Main Street and across at the movie house, Leo's feels as old as the building, built in 1907, that it has occupied for forty years. The tin ceiling is original, as are the wood walls. Business is good every lunch and dinner, twelve months of the year. At the tables sit farmers in their clean jeans, and technicians from the Tyson plant, along with some men in town to discuss the opening of an ethanol plant down the road.

Taking his place in a red Naugahyde booth against the wall, Nathan is feeling a little philosophical, perhaps because the waitress, Brigitte Hendershot, represents for him the difficulties faced by his town. Brigitte works five days a week. She is fifty-four, and what Nathan calls the salt of the earth. Her son-in-law is a sheriff's deputy; her daughter works for the state's Department of Human Services. It is people like Brigitte, says Nathan, whom the meth epidemic hurts the most. They work hard all their lives only to see their towns go to hell and to worry that their grandchildren will fall prey to a drug. In a sinking economy, he says, it's as though the harder they work, the farther behind they fall. It makes Nathan crazy.

"I think about the credos that I admire: Kant's call to action for the betterment of man; Aquinas's belief that every man's job is to help every other man achieve his ends. When I grew up," says Nathan, "everything in my parents' house had to be black and white. No interracial marriage, no booze, no sex, no voting for Democrats. I went to law school, and I thought: How does this narrow-minded horseshit aid in the callings of Kant and Aquinas? It can't, because it's too marginalizing.

"But now look where I am," he continues. "I've come full circle, because I see the people that I prosecute as case files, black ink on a white page. There's so fucking many meth-heads, I can't differentiate. I don't get a chance to see them in their homes. I don't really have time to see them even as people, because that's not how I'm trained. So how have I evolved?" he asks, rubbing quickly at his nose before answering his own question. "I haven't. I devolved."

Brigitte comes over to take Nathan's order. Her hair is dyed black to hide the gray, and she wears dark glasses that turn darker in the sun when she goes outside. When she leaves, Nathan leans forward onto the table and clasps his hands.

"Let's try to look at meth scientifically and economically," he begins. "First, there's the part of your brain that's evolved over thousands of years to reward you for doing the things that will regenerate the species. Have sex, feel good, in a nutshell. Then there's meth, which is twenty times better than sex. So, basically, meth becomes more powerful than biology.

"So you can put a tweaker in prison, and the whole time he's in there, he's thinking of only one thing: how he's going to get high the day he's out. He's not even thinking about it, actually. He's like, rewired to *know* that everything in life is about the drug. So you say, 'What good does prison do?'

"Meanwhile, whether he's in prison or out on the street tweaking, he's disengaged from the economy. There's a whole sector of the blue-collar workforce that's just gone around here. So what we have as an alternative is these state-mandated halfway-house things, where for two months you have to check in and check out each day; you have to hold a job; you have to take piss tests. Fine. But two months," says Nathan, "isn't shit. Two months clean on meth is nothing. Why not make it five years? Put money into building and staffing those places and try and keep people straight for years at a time while giving them something to lose—a job, a sense of security."

Nathan leans back. The pork tenderloin is here. Brigitte says warmly, "Enjoy, honey." Nathan has known both her and her children all his life.

"Thanks," Nathan says. As she walks away, Nathan looks at her. He says, "The problem is, no one who works an honest job wants to give the tweakers any more chances to fuck up."

He sits back and looks at his sandwich. Suddenly he's not hungry.

"Dealing with meth logically is a difficult.sell to the people of this town. I understand why. It's hard, knowing that the same dirtbag is going to be in court tomorrow for the third time this year. I mean, I'm sorry, but I leave work and go to the farm to work more. And sometimes I look at the guy who can't stop doing crank, and I just think, 'Fuck. It'd be easier to shoot the son of a bitch.'"

The thought makes him laugh. He laughs so hard that people turn to look. At the table next to us, an old farmer in blue jeans, his green John Deere windbreaker hung over the back of his chair, stares angrily at Nathan. Nathan coldly returns the favor. For a long moment, one of them might do something, if only he knew what.

CHAPTER 2

THE MOST AMERICAN DRUG

On a cold winter night in 2001, Roland Jarvis looked out the window of his mother's house and saw that the Oelwein police had hung live human heads in the trees of the yard. Jarvis knew the police did this when they meant to spy on people suspected of being meth cooks. The heads were informants, placed like demonic ornaments to look in the windows and through the walls. As Jarvis studied them, they mumbled and squinted hard to see what was inside the house. Then the heads, satisfied that Jarvis was in fact cooking meth in the basement, conveyed the message to a black helicopter hovering over the house. The whoosh of the blades was hushed and all but inaudible, so Jarvis didn't notice the helicopter till he saw the heads tilt back on their limbs and stare at the cold night sky. By then, Jarvis knew he had to hurry: Once the helicopter sent coordinates to the Cop Shop, it would be only moments before they raided the house.

Jarvis ran downstairs to the basement. He was wearing a Minnesota Vikings tank top, a pair of boxer shorts, and white tube socks. A divorced thirty-five-year-old father of four who'd been making meth since the mid-1990s and using the drug since he was sixteen, Jarvis had been in jail all but three of the last ten years. He did not want to go back. So bottle by bottle and container by container,

he poured down the flood drain in the floor of his mother's basement the chemicals he had stored there: anhydrous ammonia, Coleman lantern fluid, denatured alcohol, and kerosene. Finally he
poured two gallons of hydrochloric acid down the drain. Then he lit
a cigarette.

People around town like to say that Roland Jarvis blew himself
up. The sound Jarvis heard immediately following the click of his
lighter, though, was not anything like an explosion. It was a very
distinct and very quiet sucking sound. It took about a quarter of a
second for the ionized hydrogen in the hydrochloric acid to propa-
gate from the lighter's flame and into the drain. This made the entire basement into a vacuum. Jarvis heard a soft *Whoomp!* Then
came the blast, the force of which blew out the windows and singed
Jarvis's body wherever it wasn't covered by clothing. In the space
of several more tenths of a second, all his exposed body hair
burned off. When he looked down, he saw that his tube socks were
somehow no longer on his feet. When he looked up, he saw that the
wooden ceiling was consumed by animate, expanding rivulets of
blue flame. His mother, who was something of a packrat, had stored
her deceased husband's books, clothes, and fishing equipment in
boxes in the basement, alongside old furniture she couldn't bear to
sell, for it had been in her family since the days before her grandmother left Sicily. Now all of it was on fire. Oxygen poured into the
basement through the blown-out windows, feeding the flames. Jarvis's
tank top was burning, so he took it off and went running up the
stairs and out onto the porch. He stood there a while, thinking.
Then he decided to go back into the house.

For forty-five minutes, Jarvis made one trip after another into
his mother's home, even as the fire spread from room to room and
floor to floor. He filled a plastic mop bucket over and over, and fought
the fire relentlessly, stopping every now and again to bring a couch
or a table outside into the brutal Iowa night. At one point, dissatis-
fied with the water output of the kitchen sink, Jarvis claims that
he harnessed the superhuman strength afforded him by the dual

effects of his meth high and his panicked adrenaline rush to pull the sink from its housing in the counter and throw it against a wall in a blind rage.

Jarvis says he wanted to save the house. It's considered a foregone conclusion by the police that he was trying to retrieve the remnants of his meth lab, along with the formidable amount of dope that he had been making, for Jarvis, in a town full of meth cooks, was considered one of the finest and most prolific of their number. That, or he was attempting to spread the fire himself in order to burn as much evidence as possible. It's conceivable, too, that he was in such a state of psychotic disarray, emotional bankruptcy, and physical disembodiment that he was doing all three of those things. What stopped him, in any event, is that he began to melt.

Following one of his trips outside, Jarvis looked down and saw what he thought was egg white on his bare arms. It was not egg white; it was the viscous state of his skin now that the water had boiled out of it. Jarvis flung it off himself, and then he saw that where the egg white had been he could now see roasting muscle. He looked at his legs and his abdomen. His skin was dripping off his body in sheets. Panicked, standing there in the frigid night outside the inferno of his mother's home, naked but for his boxer shorts, which he'd inadvertently soaked in water while fighting the fire, Roland Jarvis began pushing sheets of skin from himself, using his hands like blunt tools, wiping and shoving the hide from as much of his body as he could reach. He'd have pulled the melting skeins of skin from himself in bigger, more efficient sections, but for the fact that his fingers had burned off of his hands. His nose was all but gone now, too, and he ran back and forth among the gathered neighbors, unable to scream, for his esophagus and his voice box had cooked inside his throat.

The police, says Jarvis, just watched. Jeremy Logan was still a sergeant, and a man with whom Jarvis had gone to high school. When Jarvis approached him, Logan moved away like a matador avoiding a bull, not because he took sadistic pleasure in Jarvis's plight, but because, as Logan later told me, no one knew what to do. Jarvis begged in vain for someone to shoot him. He was burning alive, and the pain was unbearable. Not even the paramedics knew how to respond, says Jarvis. He says everyone watching—the gathered neighbors, the police, the entire Oelwein Fire Department—wanted him to die. "And I don't blame them," he says. "What else could you do with a man like me?"

Methamphetamine is synonymous with the kind of deranged behavior exemplified by Roland Jarvis both that night and in the nineteen years leading up to it. The stories that Jarvis tells would hardly be believable, were it not for corroboration among his friends and within the pages of police reports that exist solely to catalog the known exploits of a single Oelwein, Iowa, meth cook. Jarvis is just one of many local legends around Fayette County famous for, among so many things, staying high on crank for twenty-eight days straight, an entire lunar cycle. Meth is also responsible for the physical destruction that Jarvis's body exhibits. By the time I met him, he'd had four heart attacks. He couldn't sleep and rarely had an appetite. Almost all his teeth were gone, and those that remained were black and decaying. He was in almost constant pain; his muscles ached, and his joints were stiff. Meth's destructiveness extended, said Jarvis, to his children, one of whom, born at the peak of his parents' intravenous meth use, was wearing a colostomy bag by the age of ten. Unable to shoot up with the finger nubs left him by the lab explosion, Jarvis had taught himself to hold a pipe and lighter so that he could resume his meth habit once again.

So, too, had there been by 2005 thousands of stories across the country blaming meth for delusional violence, morbid depravity, extreme sexual perversion, and an almost otherworldly, hallucinogenic dimension of evil. In 2004, an Ojibwa Indian named Travis

Holappa in Embarrass, Minnesota, had been tied to a chair in a rural swamp, tortured, shot eleven times, and then decapitated after running afoul of meth dealers. In a suburb north of Atlanta, in the space of one week that same year, thirteen bodies were found, bound and murdered execution-style in a single home used as a meth stash house. In Ottumwa, Iowa, a ten-year-old girl's stepfather was jailed for his habit of getting high on crank and then repeatedly forcing the girl, at gunpoint, to perform oral sex on him, an act that he justified, in his hallucinogenic, psychotic state, by saying to police that the girl was the devil and that she had begged him to do it. In Oelwein, in June of 2005, a man high on meth beat another with a glass vase, and thinking he was dead, rolled him in a blanket, then shoved his body behind the couch, where his teenage daughter found him the next afternoon. And yet, methamphetamine was once heralded as the drug that would end the need for all others.

Nagayoshi Nagai, a Japanese chemist, first synthesized desomethamphetamine in 1898. Almost from the beginning, the drug was celebrated for the simple fact that it made people feel good. It was not, however, until Akira Ogata, another Japanese chemist, first made meth in 1919 from red phosphorus and ephedrine, a naturally occurring plant that grows largely in China, that mass production of the drug became viable. Red phosphorus, the active ingredient on the striker plate of a matchbook, can be mined. Ephedrine, like coca or poppies, can be farmed. By 1933, meth was heralded in the United States as a drug on par with penicillin. In 1939, the pharmaceutical giant Smith, Kline, and French began marketing the drug under the name Benzedrine. In Japan, meth was sold as Hiropon; in Germany, it was marketed under the name Pervitin. In addition to narcolepsy and weight gain, methamphetamine in 1939 was prescribed as a treatment for thirty-three illnesses, including schizophrenia, depression, anxiety, the common cold, hyperactivity, impotence, fatigue, and alcoholism. In a world in which the winners were defined by the speed with which they could industrialize, meth suppressed the need for sleep, food, and hydration, all the while keeping workers "peppy," as the ads read. The miracle cure could even aid in the nightmare of war, once the industrializing nations of Germany, Britain, Japan, and the United States began fighting for world dominance.

According to a presentation given by former Harvard sociologist Patricia Case, reports authorized by the U.S. government in 1939 suggested that meth had "psychotic" and "antisocial" side effects, including increased libido, sexual aggression, violence, hallucinations, dementia, bodily shaking, hyperthermia, sadomasochism, inability to orgasm, Satanic thoughts, general immorality, and chronic insomnia. Nonetheless, Japanese, American, British, and German soldiers were all given methamphetamine pills to stay awake, to stay focused, and to perform under the extreme duress of war. Methedrine, according to Case, was a part of every American airman's preflight kit. Three enormous plants in Japan produced an estimated one billion Hiropon pills between 1938 and 1945. According to a 2005 article in the German online news source *Spiegel*, the German pharmaceutical companies Temmler and Knoll in only four months, between April and July 1940, manufactured thirty-five million methamphetamine tablets, all of which were shipped to the Nazi army and air corps. A January 1942 doctor's report from Germany's Eastern Front is illuminating. Five hundred German soldiers surrounded by the Red Army began trying to escape through waist-high snow, in temperatures of sixty degrees below zero. Soon, the doctor wrote, the men began lying on the snow, exhausted. The commanding officers then ordered their men to take their meth pills, at which point "the men began spontaneously reporting that they felt better. They began marching in an orderly fashion again, their spirits improved, and they became more alert." In an interview with the *Chicago Tribune* in 1985, one of Hitler's doctors, Ernst-Günther Schenck, revealed that the Führer "demanded interjections of invigorating and tranquilizing drugs," including methamphetamine. It's widely believed by many that Hitler's subsequent and progressive Parkinson's-like symptoms, if not his increasingly derelict mental state, were a direct result of his meth addiction.

Even into the 1980s, methamphetamine was widely prescribed in the United States. Ads for "Methedrine-brand Methamphetamine— For Those Who Eat Too Much and Those Who Are Depressed" appeared all during the 1960s, largely in women's magazines. Obedrin Long-Acting, according to another ad, was there to help a woman "calmly set her appestat," a particularly apt pun given that meth is well known to raise one's body temperature to dangerously hyperthermic levels. In 1967 alone, according to Dr. Case, thirty-one million legal meth prescriptions were written in the United States. In Dexamyl ads in *Life* magazine throughout the 1970s, a woman wearing an apron could be seen ecstatically vacuuming her living room carpet. How much legal pharmaceutical methamphetamine was being sold illegally, or without a prescription, during the period from 1945 to 1975 is hard to imagine. Headlines from the *New York Times* circa 1959 give some indication, however, citing multicity FBI stings in Los Angeles, San Francisco, Portland, Phoenix, Denver, Indianapolis, Chicago, Philadelphia, Brooklyn, and Manhattan.

Curiously, the fate of towns like Oelwein, which for one hundred years had been places of great prosperity, began to change at just about the time that meth's reputation began to disintegrate. Even as those towns started feeling the early effects of changes to the food-production industry, which would all but bankrupt them thirty years later, meth during the late 1970s and early '80s was being illegally produced by bike gangs like the Hells Angels in California and the Sons of Silence in the Midwest. The change, which can be characterized by the shift from pharmacy to "lab," is what would precipitate the modern American meth epidemic, itself only a large piece of the global meth pandemic. As Methedrine and Benzedrine became crank and speed, production moved from the controlled environment of corporate campuses to the underground production sites of bikers and outlaw chemists. The new form of meth, a drug that has always been popular among men and women doing hard labor, became both purer and vastly more available. It was no accident that just as rural economies were at the peak of their suffering in the mid-1980s, meth's place in the United States was becoming more entrenched than ever.

Part of meth's draw in U.S. small towns beginning in the 1980s is that it's both cheap and easy to make from items available, in bulk, at the farmers' co-op and the drugstore. The real basis of meth's attractiveness, though, is much simpler: meth makes people feel good. Even as it helps people work hard, whether that means driving a truck or vacuuming the floor, meth contributes to a feeling that all will be okay, if not exuberantly so. By the 1980s, thanks to increasingly cheap and powerful meth, no longer was the theory behind the American work ethic strictly theoretical: there was a basis in one's very biochemistry, a promise realized. And according to the magazine and newspaper ads, all of it came without any of the side effects which hardworking Americans loathe: sloth, fatigue, laziness.

In biochemical terms, methamphetamine is what is called an indirect catecholamine agonist, meaning that it blocks the reuptake of neurotransmitters. When you feel good, it's because dopamine or epinephrine has been released into the synaptic gaps between the neurons in your brain. Metaphorically, this microscopic emission is a simulacrum at the tiniest, most ethereal level for the release and subsequent satiation one feels for having performed some kind of biologically essential task, such as having sex. Later, the neurotransmitter is soaked up out of the synapses, like water into a sponge, by the inverse neuronal process, one designed to be as efficient as it is perpetual. Indeed, running out of neurotransmitters, the feel-good chemicals that reward you for remaining biologically viable, would be tantamount to the nihilistic meaninglessness that Oelwein mayor Larry Murphy feared had engulfed his town by 2005.

Methamphetamine, like crack (and therefore, like cocaine, of which crack is merely a smokable form), encourages the first part of this biochemical transaction and blocks the second. That's to say that because the reuptake of the neurotransmitter back into the "sponge" takes longer, you feel good for longer. Meth, though, appears to be unique among psychostimulants in one way, says Tom Freese, a doctor of clinical psychology at UCLA and a member of what is widely regarded as the foremost research team in the world studying the drug's human effects. Freese says that both meth and crack "lurk" in the space between the brain's neurons, where they stop the reuptake of dopamine, thereby "flooding" you with good feelings. But meth alone, says Freese, "goes inside the presynaptic cells to push dopamine out." That, he says, "makes for more of a flood, if you will." This ultimately might begin to account for why some neurological researchers see total depletion of neurotransmitters in sectors of the brains of chronic meth users. It's perhaps no wonder, then, that the 1950s-era Methedrine and Benzedrine addicts depicted in the David Lynch movie *Blue Velvet* are associated with anarchy. Moving through the world, and the movie, unable to feel anything but rage, they are the embodienent of late-stage meth addiction, the political expression of the existential scourge and the bane of the work-based American dream.

Meth works on the limbic system of the brain, which is the brain's reward center, as well as on the prefrontal cortex, where decision making takes place. A meth user's feelings are reflected in what are called his executive actions, or what Freese calls "his ability to choose between what we all know to be good and bad." Freese says that what feels good is tied directly to survival. The ability to make decisions, therefore, is in some ways controlled not by what people want, but by what they need. Meth, says Freese, "hijacks the relationship" between what is necessary and what is desired. "The result is that when you take away meth, nothing natural—sex, a glass of water, a good meal, anything for which we are *supposed* to be rewarded—feels good. The only thing that does feel good is more meth." Moreover, he continues, "there's a basic and lasting change in the brain's chemistry, which is a direct result of the drug's introduction." The ultimate effects are psychopathology such as intolerable depression, profound sleep and memory loss, debilitating anxiety, severe hallucinations, and acute, schizophrenic bouts of paranoia: the very things that meth, just eighty years ago, was supposed to cure.

Sleep loss alone, Freese posits, can cause enough emotional and biochemical stress to result in long-term functional deficits. Once the effects of days of sleeplessness are compounded by the panic of memory loss and one of the more common hallucinations from which meth addicts suffer (for instance, that insects are crawling out of their skin), it's no wonder that addicts do things non-addicts wouldn't dream of. As Dr. Clay Hallberg, the Oelwein general practitioner, says, "I'd much rather be in the emergency room with a paranoid schizophrenic—and I've been in the ER with plenty— than a meth-head. They're literally out of their minds."

Roland Jarvis used to have a good job at Iowa Ham in Oelwein. It was a hard job, "throwing" hundred-pound pans full of hog hocks into a scalding roaster and pulling them out again, a process he likens to playing hot potato with bags of sand. But he made eighteen dollars an hour, with full union membership and benefits. That would be a lot of money today in Fayette County. In 1990, it was the kind of money about which a high school dropout like Jarvis could only dream. Jarvis had a girlfriend he wanted to marry, so he took double eight-hour shifts at Iowa Ham, trying to put away as much money as possible. On days that he worked back-to-back shifts, Jarvis had a trick up his sleeve: high on crank, with his central nervous system on overdrive and major systems like his digestive tract all but shut down, Jarvis could easily go for sixteen hours without having to eat, drink, use the bathroom, or sleep.

According to Jarvis and Clay Hallberg, it was common in the 1970s and 1980s to get meth from Doc Maynard, a general practitioner in nearby Winthrop, Iowa. Into his seventies, Jarvis and Clay say, Maynard wrote thousands of illegal prescriptions for Methedrine, mostly for young girls who wanted to lose weight, but also for farmworkers and industrial laborers. A more powerful kind of dope occasionally came to northern Iowa from California in those days, too. A local from Oelwein, Jeffrey William Hayes, who insists on being called by his full name, had gone to Long Beach to look for work among the small community of northeast Iowans living there. Hayes had come back to Oelwein with the dope, which was called P2P, for the ingredient phenyl-2-propanone. Every now and again, Jeffrey William Hayes would load his wife and his young daughter, Hanna, into an eighteen-wheeler cab, drive to Long Beach, pack the wheel wells with P2P crank, and drive home to sell it.

For the most part, though, the methamphetamine market in Oelwein was hit and miss. When there was a lot, there was a lot, and when there was none, it was bone-dry. And though Jarvis was heterosexual, and gossip spreads fast in Oelwein, he says he didn't mind trading sex with men for meth. In fact, by the time he was working doubles at Iowa Ham, he'd do whatever he could to get the drug. Jarvis considered meth to be his job security. It made Jarvis into the ideal employee. He was like a gorilla throwing the ham trays around. Then he'd come home and he could have sex with his girlfriend for hours on end, drink without getting drunk, and be awake for work the next day without ever having slept.

By the early 1990s, more and more P2P dope was entering Oelwein via California, thanks in part to the connections that had been forged by Jeffrey William Hayes and his business partner, Steve Jelinek, whose parents owned Oelwein's flower shop. In 1992, Iowa Ham, a small, old canning and packaging company, was bought by Gillette. Overnight, the union was dismantled, and the wages, according to Jarvis and Clay Hallberg, fell from $18 an hour to $6.20. For Jarvis, who now had the first of his four children, it became more important than ever to work harder and longer in order to make ends meet. His meth habit increased along with the purity of the dope. And then one day he did the math. On the one hand, he was making $50 every eight hours to do a job in which there was a 36 percent rate of injury, thereby making meatpacking the most dangerous vocation in the country. For this, Jarvis, now that he worked for Gillette, got no medical coverage for himself or his children, no promise of workers' compensation should he be hurt, and no hope of advancement. (With Iowa Ham, every employee had not only gotten benefits; they'd owned stock in the company.) On the other hand, Jarvis was paying a hundred dollars at a time in order to buy enough meth to be able to work double shifts for five days straight. For Jarvis, the solution was clear: He would go into business for himself.

The high Jarvis has built his life (and at one point his livelihood) around has five parts: the rush, the high, the shoulder, the tweak, and the withdrawal. Snorting just a couple of lines of reasonably pure meth kept him involved in this continuum for at least twelve hours. Twelve hours is roughly the length of meth's half-life, and a measure of how long it takes one's body to completely metabolize the drug, as well as an indicator of how powerful the drug is. (The half-life of crack is only twenty minutes, or about thirty-six times less than meth.) The rush is just what the term suggests: an initial feeling of tremendous euphoria. Dr. Clay Hallberg describes it as "taking all of your neurotransmitters, putting them in a shot glass, and slamming them." The high is the hours-long period of an exceptionally vivid confidence and sense of well-being that Jarvis experiences while dopamine and epinephrine literally pool around his brain's neuronal synapses: a biochemical bacchanal. The physical effects include a litany of the body's most ecstatic and powerful reactions. Core temperature spikes and blood flow to the heart increases dramatically. For men, so, too, does blood flow increase enormously to the penis, and for men and women both, there is an increased need and desire to have sex, a fact that helps explain why meth abuse in gay communities is linked to huge increases in AIDS and hepatitis C. And none of it—not the "full body orgasm" so commonly referred to, or the ability to drink without getting drunk, or the ability to have sex for hours at a time without losing an erection—comes at an obvious, outward cost: no slurring, no falling down, no passing out.

The rest of the meth high, though, is not high at all. The shoulder period is when Jarvis's euphoria first plateaus and then decreases dramatically, on its way to falling completely to the floor. The fall itself is what's called the tweak, so named for the physical manifestations of what amounts to the brain's running on empty. The stores of neurotransmitters now depleted, and their synaptic effect no longer consistent with a sense of well-being, Jarvis becomes increasingly agitated. Tests on mice at the Scripps Research Institute by Dr. Kim Janda suggest an attribute unique to meth that would prove cause for increased agitation, to be sure: The body actually forms antibodies, effectively vaccinating itself against the drug and thereby making the "high" increasingly difficult to achieve. This, Dr. Janda's research indicates, results in a kind of self-perpetuating biochemical loop: the more meth Jarvis does, the more difficult it is to get high, leaving him no choice but to do more meth.

Unaware of how hard his body has been working, and the deficit at which he is operating, Jarvis begins to show physical depletion. Shaking hands, severe sweats, muscle cramps, and shortness of breath are all symptoms of the impending withdrawal. So, too, does the paranoid conviction set in that he's being followed—like the belief that a black helicopter was hovering above his house. (This hallucination is common; I heard the exact same story from dozens of addicts in Alabama, Illinois, Kentucky, Georgia, and California.) The desperation to make more meth, at whatever cost, and the hallucinations have been the defining features of Jarvis's life for nearly a decade. Every time he came home from jail, he was cash-stricken and eager to feel good, and he redoubled his lab's output.

Dr. Clay Hallberg was the company doctor at Iowa Ham when it was bought by Gillette in 1992. Within a year, he'd called the plant manager, an old friend who'd worked with Clay's cousin years before at a Hy-Vee grocery store in Cedar Rapids. Clay told the manager that he'd noticed an unsettling decline in the morale of the workers coming to see him since they'd lost their benefits. Clay was worried about the increase in drug use as well; more and more workers, suffering from depression now that they'd lost two thirds of their income overnight, were turning to meth. The plant manager said he'd look into it. A week later, Clay was fired.

That the surge in meth use in Oelwein was a direct result of wage cuts at the Gillette plant would be hard to argue convincingly. After all, Roland Jarvis had already been using the drug for several years at that point. But it would be naive not to see those wage cuts as yet another difficult turn in the financial fortunes of Oelwein, just as it would be foolish not to notice the 400 percent increase in local meth production that happened at the same time, as reflected in the number of labs busted in Oelwein. Or, moreover, not to see the link between a steady long-term rise in the abuse of a drug associated with hard work and a steady long-term decline in the amount of work available in rural America's defining industries. Not long after buying Iowa Ham, Gillette sold the plant to Iowa Beef Products (IBP); in 2001, Tyson bought the plant. With each sale, the number of workers was further cut and wages remained stationary despite rising inflation. In January 2006, Tyson closed the plant for good. By then, the initial workforce had been reduced from over eight hundred people to ninety-nine, a remarkable, devastating loss of revenue in a town of only six thousand.

The association between meth and work is part of why Dr. Stanley Koob, a neuropharmacologist at the Scripps Research Institute, and widely considered to be the world's leading expert on drug addiction, considers methamphetamine to be "way up there with the worst drugs on the planet." Hard work and meth conspire, says Koob, in formulating the drug's "social identity," which is essentially an attempt to analyze how acceptable a drug is. For eight decades, from the time Nagayoshi Nagai first synthesized meth in 1898 until the early 1980s, meth was a highly acceptable drug in America, one of the reasons being that it helped what Nathan Lein calls "the salt of the earth"—soldiers, truck drivers, slaughterhouse employees, farmers, auto and construction workers, and day laborers—work harder, longer, and more efficiently. It's one thing for a drug to be associated with sloth, like heroin. But it's wholly another when a formerly legal and accepted narcotic exists in a one-to-one ratio with the defining ideal of American culture. Meth's most disastrous physical and psychological effects develop more slowly than its rate of addiction; one's lucidity and ability to concentrate actually increases short-term. Add this to the fact that ours is a culture in which the vagaries of hard work are celebrated as indicators of social worth, and the reasons to do crank are in fact quite often—initially, at least—more numerous and compelling than the reasons not to do it. So much so that Patricia Case calls meth "the most American drug." In the metric that took hold of Oelwein at the beginning of the 1980s with the farm crisis—and extended through the next decade with the complicated demise of Iowa Ham—the ability to make something in your basement that promised work, success, wealth, thinness, and happiness was not necessarily too good to be true.

One day in May 2005, Roland Jarvis sat in the living room of his mother's tiny new two-bedroom house in a wobbly three-legged

La-Z-Boy covered in what looked like orange and brown carpeting. Outside, the world was fairly ecstatic with the first temperate, blue-skied day of spring following so much rain in northern Iowa. Nonetheless, Jarvis was watching TV with his back to the windows, the heavy curtains drawn tight against the warm sun. His face was thin beneath the baseball cap that he wore over his short blond hair. Visible in the semidarkness were fine bones and bright, shining blue eyes around which Jarvis's skin had liquified and reset in swirls. He rubbed at where his nose had been and coughed violently. Jarvis had just smoked a hit of meth by holding the glass pipe with his rotted teeth. Using what was left of his right hand, he jostled the lighter until it wedged between the featureless nub of his thumb and the tiny protrusion of what was once his pinkie, managing somehow to roll the striker of the red Bic against the flint. Suddenly, his eyes were as wildly dilated as a patient waiting in the low light of an ophthalmologist's office.

At thirty-eight, Jarvis had become a sort of poster boy around Oelwein for the horrific consequences of long-term meth addiction. Like Boo Radley, he hardly ever ventured out, though his was nonetheless a heavy presence in town. In two months, Jarvis was going back to jail, this time for possession of drug paraphernalia. (His sixty-year-old mother would be joining him in the lockup for the same offense.) He wore warm-up pants and wool socks. He was always cold, he said, and hadn't slept more than three hours at a time in years. His skin was still covered in open, pussing sores. He had no job and no hope of getting one. The last time he "went uptown," as he calls going to a Main Street bar, was eighteen months earlier. That night he was in his old hangout, the Do Drop Inn, when another customer hit Jarvis in the face because he wanted to know what it was like to slug a man with no nose.

"That," says Jarvis, "kind of put a damper on my Saturday night fever."

Nowadays, the one thing that could get him up and moving were the weekly visits he was allowed with his children, two girls and two boys, ages sixteen to nine. For the most part, he would accompany them to the town lake, out past the Country Corner Café, on the way south to Hazleton. There, weather permitting, Jarvis and his kids would fish for a few unsupervised hours, hoping to catch some bullheads and bluegills to fry for supper. Sometimes he would accompany the kids back to their mother's home for that purpose. He and his ex-wife were, he says, still on pretty good terms, given what he'd done to their lives.

Jarvis speaks in a metaphorical language of addiction, honed over decades of repeating the same scenes in his mind like tapes on interminable loops. Tweakers are rats, crank is cheese, cops are cats. At the end of each story, all three end up in the same house, the same motel, or the same barn, where invariably something either very bad or very funny, or both, has just occurred. The venues for these stories are small towns and middling cities, from Oelwein to Sioux Falls, South Dakota. Often the stories are compendiums of rural kitsch that, though they unfold over the course of many years, appear to stretch the year 1987 into several decades. In them, everyone drives a Corvette or a Trans Am and wears Porsche driving glasses. For Jarvis, it's the memory of the cars, more than that of the days at a time spent having sex with teenage girls, or of the houses he bought and sold, or of the thrill of outwitting the cats, that remains the enduring emblem of how once—a long time ago, and however briefly—he'd finally arrived.

Jarvis's mother has been listening from the kitchen as he speaks. Seen through a pall of cigarette smoke, backlit by the rays of sun pouring through the kitchen window, with her greasy black hair worn back off her steep, leather-brown face, she looks like a nineteenth-century Apache in a sepia-tone portrait. For the past few hours (if not the past few years), she and a neighbor have been playing gin rummy and drinking cans of Hamm's beer. Looking at her son now, she calls out, "Tell the man the truth, Roland."

Summing up his years as a batcher, Jarvis says dutifully, and loud enough that his mother can hear, "It was all a big mess. I lost everything of any value." His face, however, tells another story. For, as he remembers, it's the first time in hours that he has smiled.

CHAPTER 3

THE INLAND EMPIRE

As the weeks that I traveled around the Midwest, the Southeast, and California turned to months in the summer and fall of 2005, I was beginning to see meth in America as a function not just of farming and food industry trends in the 1980s and '90s but also of changes in the narcotics and pharmaceuticals industries in the same period. It would take a few more years of watching what happened in Oelwein, and in the United States at large, before I completely understood what I was seeing. That, for instance, as economies had dwindled throughout the Great Plains and the Midwest, they had aligned a certain way in Southern California, and that the electrical current sweeping between these two increasingly unrelated American places, the coast and the middle, would presage what came to be called the "meth epidemic" thirty years later. So, too, would it take a while to see that the changes that linked Long Beach and Los Angeles with Oelwein were in fact changes tied to the emergence of the global economy. And that meth, if it is a metaphor for anything, is a metaphor for the cataclysmic fault lines formed by globalization.

Back in 2005, these things were just coming into focus as I went to Ottumwa, a town in southeast Iowa. It was in Ottumwa that the Midwest's principal meth wiring had been installed, and to which the drug's early advancement into Oelwein could be traced. If Oelwein was shaping up to be the face of meth in modern America, and an indicator of life in modern, rural America in general, then in Ottumwa there was a picture of Oelwein's skeletal forebears. And eventually a picture of Oelwein's future, though that part of the story was yet to evolve.

Like Oelwein, Ottumwa had for most of its history been a very prosperous place. Also like Oelwein, Ottumwa was a kind of economic outpost, a wealthy waypoint on the trade routes running between St. Louis, Chicago, and Omaha. Thanks to the Des Moines River, which runs right through the middle of Ottumwa, industry and transportation came quickly to the area once it was settled by a land rush in 1843. In 1850, John Morrell and Co. opened a flagship, state-of-the-art meat-processing plant in the center of town. By 1888, there were 10,500 miles of railroad track in Wapello County. Fifty-seven passenger trains on seven lines, the Burlington Railroad being the most famous, crossed the county every day. By the turn of the twentieth century, factories in Ottumwa made everything from boxcar loaders to cigars, and corn huskers to violins. By 1950, Ottumwa was home not only to over fifty thousand people but also to the largest air force base in the Midwest. Almost half the working-age men in town were in the employ of Hormel (the modern incarnation of John Morrell's packing plant) or John Deere, the farm-equipment manufacturer, where workers could hope, at a minimum, to maintain a lower-middle-class existence.

By 1980, though, Ottumwa's fortunes had, like Oelwein's, begun to decline. The story was much the same. The railroad's demise was followed by the closing of the air force base and then, in 1987, by the sale of Hormel to Excel Meat Solutions, a subsidiary of Cargill. Along with layoffs, wages, as they did a few years later at Oelwein's Iowa Ham plant, fell by two thirds. Like the shrinking workforce, the population of Ottumwa itself dried up like a prairie pothole in a drought, falling by an astounding 50 percent in just twenty-five years. Soon the town, starved of tax revenue and disposable income, was verging on bankruptcy. And, as had happened in Oelwein, methamphetamine moved into the new economic gap. The difference was that Ottumwa, more than any other place, defined the development of the modern American meth business in the Midwest. Meth from Ottumwa first helped to create, and then to sustain, the market not just in Oelwein but also in towns all over Iowa, Missouri, Nebraska, Kansas, and the Dakotas.

How this happened depended in several trends and events that merged seamlessly into one another: emigration routes from the Midwest to California as working-class men and women headed to the coast in search of employment; immigration routes into the heartland as increasing numbers of Mexicans worked against the human tide in order to take low-wage jobs at meat-packing plants; the rise of industrial meth production; the increased lobbying power of pharmaceutical companies; and finally, government apathy, if not disregard, for the very drug war that at the time had been newly declared by First Lady Nancy Reagan.

At the center of it all, back in Ottumwa, stood a woman named Lori Arnold. It was she who was able to weave together these various political, sociological, and chemical threads into the Midwest's first and last bona fide crank empire, the official moniker for which was the Stockdall Organization, so named for Lori's second husband, Floyd Stockdall. Lori's contribution to what at the time was not yet referred to as a "drug epidemic" was that she essentially wrote meth's genetic code in the Midwest. With her, the very concept of industrialized meth in places like Iowa was born, and it flourished in relative anonymity for the next ten years. The irony is that, while Lori worked, the Drug Enforcement Administration fruitlessly lobbied for laws that, had they passed, would have prevented Lori from ever going into business.

Lori Kaye Arnold is Ottumwa, Iowa's most famous daughter. Ottumwa's most famous son is Lori's brother, the comedian Tom Arnold, who is perhaps better known as the ex-husband of Roseanne Barr. Lori is forty-five years old, with shoulder-length light-brown hair and a longish, blunt nose, like a skinning knife. With Tom, she shares a toothy, crocodilian smile and the low center of gravity and powerful legs of a middleweight wrestler. Since 2005, I have corresponded with Lori, who's in federal prison—coincidentally, at the medium-security women's work camp in Greenville, Illinois, just a few hundred yards from where I met Sean and James during November 2004.

One of seven step- and half-siblings, Lori was born and raised in Ottumwa in a family that she describes as studiously normal and benign. Despite this, Lori dropped out of high school as a freshman and began living in an Ottumwa rooming house where, in the evenings, there was a running poker game. The landlady was also a madame. In exchange for room and board, Lori and her young cohorts could either agree to sleep with the men who played cards or deliver illegally prescribed methedrine pills, an early form of pharmaceutical meth, to the landlady's clients. Lori chose the latter; thus her career (along with her legend) was born.

Lori kept herself housed by delivering and selling "brown and clears," as pharmaceutical meth was called during the 1970s, when it was prescribed by the millions as a weight-loss aid and antidepression drug. The landlady got most of Lori's profits, though, and to make ends meet, Lori still had to work six days a week at a local bar. (In Iowa minors can serve alcohol despite being legally unable to buy it.) By fifteen, Lori was married. By sixteen, she was divorced and was attending high school once again. By seventeen, she had dropped out for good; her peers, she says, seemed to her like children. By eighteen, she was married to Floyd Stockdall, who had come to Ottumwa from Des Moines in order to retire, at the ripe old age of thirty-seven, as the president of the Grim Reapers motorcycle gang.

Lori and Floyd moved into a cabin along the Des Moines River outside Ottumwa, where their only child, Josh, was born. Left alone to raise a son while Floyd pursued his retirement hobbies of drinking, playing pool, and selling cocaine, nineteen-year-old Lori became suicidally depressed. The bar, she now realized, had been her lifeline. In addition to the money she made, the people there were her people, the only family of which Lori ever felt a true part. Without the bikers and the factory workers with whom she had all but grown up, Lori felt horribly lost and alone; her life had become an interminable slog. Worse yet, Floyd was an alcoholic, and beat her whenever he drank.

Then one day Floyd's brother stopped by the cabin. He, too, was a Grim Reaper, and he had with him some methamphetamine, a.k.a. biker dope, which had been illegally synthesized at a lab in Southern California. This was 1984, and the Reapers were just beginning to sell meth whenever they could get it from Long Beach. There, according to DEA, former Hells Angels had gone into business with maverick pharmaceutical company chemists in order to produce saleable quantities of highly pure, powdered methamphetamine. Lori's brother-in-law cut her two lines on the kitchen table inside her run-down shack on the Des Moines River on a sunny, clear Saturday afternoon. Of the experience, Lori, who was no stranger to narcotics, says simply that she had never felt so good in all her life. The singularity of that feeling is what would soon connect Ottumwa to a nascent California drug empire. In doing so, a major piece of the meth-epidemic puzzle would fall into place.

The first day Lori got high, she went to the bar. She says she'd been given a little meth to sell because Floyd's brother wanted to see what kind of a market Ottumwa might prove to be. Lori gave away half the meth, knowing intuitively that this would help hook her customers. The other half quickly sold out. In the process, she made fifty dollars. What she found, though, was worth millions, for Lori Arnold knew almost immediately that dealing meth was what she'd been born to do. It was the answer not just to her prayers, but to Ottumwa's, which for three long years had been pummeled by the farm crisis into a barely recognizable version of its former proud self. Thanks to meth, says Lori, the workers worked and played harder, and she became rich. Within a month, Lori was selling so much Long Beach crank in Ottumwa that she went around her brother-in-law and dealt directly with the middleman in Des Moines. A month after that, she was buying quarter pounds of meth for $2,500 and selling them for $10,000. Unsatisfied with the profit margin, she began dealing directly with the supplier in Long Beach, dispatching Floyd to California once every ten days with instructions to return from the 3,700-mile round-trip with as much meth as he could fit in the trunk of the Corvette Lori had bought him. Lori, meantime, stashed money in the wall of her cabin. Only six months after she had met Floyd's brother, the wall held $50,000— nearly twice the median yearly income in Ottumwa today.

By the late 1980s, people like Jeffrey William Hayes and Steve Jelinek of Oelwein were buying massive amounts of dope from Lori and establishing their own meth franchises in Iowa, Illinois, Missouri, and Kansas by selling to the likes of Roland Jarvis, who, yet to start making his own meth, would take whatever he could get in order to work extra shifts at Iowa Ham. Lori, in turn, was dealing directly with what she calls the Mexican Mafia, a somewhat loose group of traffickers who manufactured large amounts of that era's most powerful dope: P2P. Made predominantly in Long Beach and Orange County, California, in large, clandestine laboratories, this stronger form of meth was more addictive, cheaper, and easier to produce than any other form of the drug available at the time. As such, it increased Lori's already burgeoning sales manifold.

The so-called Mexican Mafia with whom Lori dealt was built on the vision of two brothers, Jesús and Luís Amezcua, who'd been born in Mexico and lived in San Diego. For years, according to DEA, the Amezcuas had been nothing more than middling cocaine dealers. Until, that is, they perceived the convergence of two seemingly unrelated events. One was that, aided by former pharmaceutical engineers, the Amezcuas could access an enormous, completely legal, and unmonitored supply of the necessary ingredients to make P2P: ephedrine and phenyl-2-propanone. The Amezcuas' second insight was that they could move large quantities of the drug throughout California and the West, thanks to the increasing numbers of Mexican immigrants who picked fruit in the Central Valley, cleaned homes in Tucson, Arizona, or built roads in Idaho. Furthermore, the brothers could access the Midwest via the ballooning population of Midwesterners who had been chased off their farms, all the way to Southern California.

During the 1980s, large numbers of people from the corn belt left in what sociologists call out-migration. Within the space of just a few years, many Iowa towns, Ottumwa and Oelwein included, lost from 10 to 25 percent of their residents, many of whom headed for the booming labor markets of Los Angeles and San Diego. Family and social connections became business connections as Iowan, Kansan, Dakotan, and Nebraskan laborers in Orange County, eager to get rich, sent loads of the Amezcuas' meth back home. Or, like Jeffrey William Hayes in Oelwein and Lori Arnold in Ottumwa, either drove out to get it themselves or sent someone in their stead.

Throughout its hundred-year history, meth has been perhaps the only example of a widely consumed illegal narcotic that might be called vocational, as opposed to recreational. The market for meth in America is nearly as old as industrialization. Poor and working-class Americans had been consuming the drug since the 1930s, whether it was marketed as Benzedrine, Methedrine, or Obedrin, for the simple reason that meth makes you feel good and permits you to work hard. Thanks to the Amezcuas and Lori Arnold, these same people no longer needed to rely on expensive prescriptions and were able to get a stronger form of meth at a much better price—this at a time when the drug's effects were arguably more useful than ever. That's to say that as meth's purity rose, its price dropped. So too did meth become much more widely available at exactly the moment that rural economies collapsed and people

left. Under those circumstances, says Clay Hallberg, those who remained felt they needed the drug most.

By 1987, if you wanted meth and you lived in southern Iowa,
or northern Missouri, you went to the bar that Lori Arnold now
owned, the Wild Side. There, the increasingly beleaguered Ottumwa police, whose numbers were shrinking alongside county
and city tax revenues, had little chance of interrupting Lori's exorbitantly profitable crank business. At that point, says Lori, in addition to Floyd, she had a dozen runners going back and forth to
Long Beach to buy meth from multiple so-called superlabs, which
could produce up to twenty pounds of meth every thirty-six
hours—an astounding amount of crank in those days. Because the
cars that Lori's runners used were a drain on her profits (imagine
the mileage accrued by driving nearly four thousand miles every
ten days, month after month), Lori bought a car dealership. That
way, she could have access to as many vehicles as she needed; she
could also have her runners trade the cars and their tags with car
dealers in any state along the way, thereby making themselves
harder to follow. Then, to house her employees and further launder the money she was making, Lori bought fourteen houses in
Ottumwa.

This was just the beginning of the means by which Lori, who
had not made it past tenth grade, laundered her drug money at the
same time that she moved to fill new markets around the region. In
1989, she bought fifty-two racehorses—and hired the dozen or so
grooms, trainers, veterinarians, and jockeys it took to maintain
them—along with a 144-acre horse farm from which to run her
ever-multiplying, synergistic empires. People from Kentucky to the
Dakotas and from Indiana to Colorado race, breed, buy, trade, and
sell horses, making it the perfect cover for a narcotics distribution
business. Lori's runners, tooling along in their duallies, a couple of
geldings munching hay in the horse trailer, the wheel wells packed
tight with crank, became the down-home *Dukes of Hazzard* version

of coke-laden speedboats making the run from Eleuthera to Key Biscayne.

Lori's true stroke of genius, though, was to build under a series of military tents hidden in the wooded hills of her horse farm what for almost two decades would be the only meth superlab ever known to be in production outside the state of California. By then, she was in such good graces with the Amezcua brothers, the California "Kings of Crank," that they let her borrow a chemist, whom Lori flew to Iowa to teach her associates how to make meth in ten-pound batches every forty-eight hours: a state-of-the-art, up-to-the-minute operation. The effect was remarkable, for up until now, Lori had controlled sales of meth in Iowa and other parts of the Midwest while still having to rely on the Amezcuas for her product. Once Lori opened her own superlab, she was in control of the entire value chain: manufacture, distribution, and retail. And while she still bought meth from the Amezcuas, principally to maintain good relations, Lori had no real competition to speak of. In just the two years between 1987 and 1989, an unassuming high school dropout from little Ottumwa, Iowa, had succeeded in cornering part of what was becoming one of the world's most lucrative narcotics markets. What's more amazing is how close she came to never getting started.

According to several former agents, back in 1987, there was deep institutional ambivalence within the Drug Enforcement Administration (DEA) toward methamphetamine. Meth was seen as a biker drug, strictly falling under the purview of losers who didn't have enough financial sense to put together a large-scale operation. These were the Reagan eighties, and as tastes ran for big, deregulated corporate successes, so ran America's taste for drugs. Cocaine was king. As such, DEA, whose job is to curb the excesses of the period as they are embodied by America's choice in narcotics, wasn't interested in anything aside from the Cali and Medellín cartels, drug-trafficking organizations run like multinational corporations capable of exceeding their host nation's GDP. Who could have imagined the business being built by two lowly coke-dealer brothers in the part of L.A. called the Inland Empire, or that this business would be connected with a kind of narcotic principate in Ottumwa, Iowa?

Only one person, it turns out: Gene Haislip, the deputy assistant administrator in DEA's Office of Compliance and Regulatory Affairs. Haislip knew that large amounts of ephedrine, which was imported in bulk to make nasal decongestants, were being redirected to the Amezcua organization with no oversight. Ephedrine processing took place in only nine factories around the world, all of them in India, China, Germany, and Czech Republic. To Haislip, the narrow processing window posed a perfect opportunity to siphon off the meth trade; all that was required was the cooperation of those nine factories, along with the pharmaceutical companies that depended on the ephedrine made in them. What Haislip proposed in 1985, two years before Lori Arnold went into large-scale meth production, was a federal law allowing DEA to monitor all ephedrine imports into the United States.

According to a 2004 investigative article written by Steve Suo in Portland's *Oregonian* newspaper, Haislip got the idea based on his earlier work on the illicit U.S. trade in Quaaludes, a legal sleeping pill widely available on the black market. The manufacture of Quaaludes depended on the synthesis of another legal drug, methaqualone, which was predominately produced in Germany, Austria, and China. What Haislip noticed was that an enormous proportion of the methaqualone from these nations was being shipped to Colombia. There, the Cali and Medellín cartels were making it into an illegal form of Quaalude, which they sold in tandem with cocaine in the same market—one as an upper, one as a downer—in the same way that meth markets today are often saturated with Oxycontin, a prescription painkiller that smooths out the impending "tweak" of a meth high. In 1982, Haislip visited the nations whose factories made methaqualone and asked for their help in monitoring its sale.

Congress then banned the use of prescription Quaaludes, which were manufactured by only one American company. By 1984, according to DEA's annual narcotics threat assessment, Quaaludes no longer constituted a significant danger to the illicit U.S. drug market. With meth, Haislip simply hoped to keep organizations like the Amezcuas' (and to a lesser extent, people like Lori Arnold) from legally procuring ephedrine without hurting the production and sale of cold medicine of licit companies like Warner-Lambert, the makers of Sudafed. Haislip's idea took the form of language inserted into the Controlled Substances Act, which would be debated by Congress in the fall of 1986.

What's important to understand is that, despite the fact that Haislip's job was to write legislation, DEA is not a political entity. According to the cliché, one of which most DEA agents seem proud, the administration occupies a place that is all but outside the law. While FBI agents stereotypically tail potential bad guys in their sedans, and CIA agents listen to phone conversations, DEA agents are supposedly assassinating major narco-figures in the world's more inhospitable environments. Whether or not this is a fantasy is unclear. What it suggests is an institutional frustration regarding the governmental process: it's easier to shoot people in other places than to write legislation here, which must then be tailored to the concerns of members of Congress and the lobbyists who influence them.

DEA's proposals are subject to long, withering debates and years of compromise. And that is where the administration, if not actually a political entity, is a highly politicized one. Back in 1986, even as Nancy Reagan gave her famous "just say no" speech, Haislip had to bow to pressure from Democrats and Republicans alike not to raise the ire of pharmaceutical lobbyists, whose job, in part, is to comb through legislative bills looking for anything that could potentially upset their clients' sales. That's how Haislip's bill, according to the *Oregonian* article, came to the attention of Allan Rexinger, who was in the employ of a trade group called the Proprietary Association on behalf of Warner-Lambert. Rexinger didn't like what he saw.

For several weeks during 1986, according to Rexinger, he worked to change the language of Haislip's bill in a way that would exempt Warner-Lambert from the potential bane of federal importation oversight. When DEA and Haislip continued to resist his pleas, said Rexinger, he had no choice but to get the White House involved by making a phone call to, as he proudly told Suo in 2004, "the highest levels of the United States government."

By the time Attorney General Edwin Meese III presented Haislip's bill to Congress in April 1987, five years had passed since Haislip had initially imagined nipping meth production in the bud. Meantime, the Amezcua cartel had spread throughout California and the Desert West, and had linked up with Lori Arnold's Stockdall Organization in Iowa, which by now was well on its way to producing its own industrially manufactured P2P meth. The language in Haislip's bill proposing oversight of ephedrine had been drastically altered as well, allowing for the drug to be imported in pill form with no federal regulations whatsoever. All that meth manufacturers had to do in order to continue making the drug would be legally to buy pill-form ephedrine in bulk and crush it into powder—a small, added inconvenience. What Haislip had imagined as an early answer to a still-embryonic drug threat instead became both a mandate and a road map for meth's expansion.

In 1987, the year that Cargill cut wages at its Ottumwa meatpacking plant from $18 an hour to $5.60 with no benefits, Lori Arnold sold a pound of pure, uncut crank for $32,000. This meant that with the very first ten pounds produced at her superlab, she had paid off the $100,000 initial investment in equipment and chemicals and had cleared a profit of nearly a quarter of a million dollars, or over a century's worth of median wages for an Ottumwa adult that year. Meanwhile, she was still buying ten pure pounds at a time of Mexican Mafia dope from California, at $10,000 a pound, which she then sold for three times the price, again making nearly a quarter of a million dollars every time one of her runners returned from the West Coast.

Where crank's personality converges with its mathematics is this: No one with whom I spoke, and this includes varsity-level addicts like Roland Jarvis, can physically handle snorting, smoking, or shooting 98 percent pure methamphetamine. So while Lori only sold her product uncut, each pound, once it was distributed, equated to three or four pounds of ingestible crank, and probably more, given that each dealer along the line was likely to continue cutting it—with bleach, laundry detergent, or baking soda. Seen that way, Lori's lab wasn't producing ten pounds every forty-eight hours; it was producing the eventual equivalent of thirty to forty pounds. (By that stretch, the biggest labs in the Central Valley of California today would be producing the so-called street equivalent of up to five hundred pounds a day, while an Indonesian megalab would make five thousand pounds of saleable meth each week.) In one month alone during Lori's prime, that's somewhere on the order of a quarter ton of meth being distributed in the relatively underpopulated environs of the central Midwest. Add to that the dozen or so big loads she was getting from California each month, and it's easy to see how Lori was, by her own admission, involved in one manner or another with "thousands of people" and making "hundreds of thousands of dollars monthly." When pushed for an answer, Lori admits that she has no idea how much she made, in pounds or dollars.

When Lori first got into meth, a gram would last her an entire weekend. By 1991, Lori was snorting up to three grams a day. She remembers not sleeping for weeks at a time. She wore, she says, a lot of hats. Multiple-business owner, mother, drug baron: Without the meth, she could never have done it all. She was, she says, one of the main employers in Ottumwa, and a benevolent one, at that.

She donated plenty of money to the local police and to the county sheriff. She planned to open a day care center and video game arcade next to the Wild Side, so local kids would have somewhere to go while their parents were in the bar. Together, Lori and meth were an antidote to the small-town sense of isolation, the collective sense of depression and low morale that had settled on Ottumwa since most farms went belly-up, the railroad closed, and the boys at the meatpacking plant lost their jobs.

If you ask her, Lori Arnold will say she did more for the state of Iowa than all the politicians put together, who let the place go to hell overnight. People were proud of her, she says, and they should have been: she gave them back the life that the government and the corporations took away. If there was ever a problem with meth, says Lori, it wasn't with the clean dope she sold. Her dope wouldn't do anything freaky to you. It was the rot-gut the batchers cooked up that made people crazy. And it was always Lori's pleasure to put those people out of business—it was her civic duty to keep the likes of Roland Jarvis from selling too much crap-batch, getting people paranoid and blathering on about black helicopters and heads in trees. In Lori's reality, she was a businesswoman, not a drug dealer in what she calls "the classic sense." She's right, insofar as she had an unprecedented vertical monopoly, which she claims to have run at least in part to assuage the detrimental effects of the very monopolies like Cargill and Iowa Beef Packers that were born in that same era of deregulation. Add to this that Lori's rise required putting home cooks—the Iowa Hams of the meth world, if you will—out of business, and the self-styled Robin Hood of crank begins to look awfully corporate. At a deeper strata of irony, consider that Lori almost single-handedly ushered into the Midwest the next generation of the meth epidemic, which would be controlled by five Mexican drug-trafficking organizations that today enjoy the same kind of market control of meth that Cargill enjoys with respect to the food industry.

Perhaps inevitably, like Roland Jarvis, the kind of small-time tweaker for whom she had the utmost disdain, Lori did see a helicopter, though in her case it was real. It hovered over her house one day in 1990 while agents from the Bureau of Alcohol, Tobacco, and Firearms (ATF) took photos of her meth lab in the woods. Later that day, Lori was zooming around town in her green Jaguar Sovereign doing errands when she got the call from a stable boy that things were getting a little weird out at the farm. There were cars parked along the country roads, said the boy, and men with binoculars trained on the place. That night, Lori says, the feds sent in an army: ATF, FBI, DEA—you name it. By morning, she was in the local jail, telling jokes to the agents who stood guard. After all, says Lori, if you don't have a sense of humor, what do you have left?

Six months later, Lori Arnold's crank empire fell apart when she was convicted in federal court in the Southern District of Iowa of one count of continuing a criminal enterprise; two counts of money laundering; one count of carrying and using a firearm in conjunction with drug trafficking; and multiple counts of possession, distribution, and manufacture of methamphetamine. Floyd Stockdall was tried separately and sentenced to fifteen years in Leavenworth prison, where he died of a heart attack two months before he would have been paroled. Lori got ten years in the federal penitentiary in Alderson, West Virginia, and was released after serving eight, on July 2, 1999. Her son and only child, Josh, was fifteen years old; Lori had been gone for half his life. By then, the meth business in the Midwest had mutated into something Lori couldn't believe, though she was quick to comprehend that it was a new, much more fully developed phenomenon than that which she'd created along with the Amezcuas. And once Lori identified a spot for herself in the new order, she did the thing she'd been doing all her life: She went right back into business.

CHAPTER 4

FAMILY

In 2005, when I called Dr. Clay Hallberg, the Oelwein general practitioner, and asked him to characterize the meth epidemic in his hometown, Clay had told me that meth was "a sociocultural cancer." What he meant, he said, was that, as with the disease, meth's particular danger lay in its ability to metastasize throughout the body, in this case the body politic, and to weaken the social fabric of a place, be it a region, a town, a neighborhood, or a home. Just as brain cancer often spreads to the lungs, said Clay, meth often spreads between classes, families, and friends. Meth's associated rigors affect the school, the police, the mayor, the hospital, and the town businesses. As a result, said Clay, there is a kind of collective low self-esteem that sets in once a town's culture must react solely to a singular—and singularly negative—stimulus.

It was clear from the minute I got to Oelwein that Clay's position as a small-town doctor put him in the best possible place from which to observe the meth phenomenon. What would become clear to me over the next three years, though, is that the very thing he hoped to treat in others, the "collective low self-esteem," also took a brutal, withering toll on Clay himself. The first time we talked, he'd likened each day at work to running into a burning motel and having fifteen minutes to get everyone out. The motel was Oelwein, and Clay never had enough time before he had to retreat, fearful he too would burn alive. Indeed, three years later, Clay would need saving. It's partly in this way that his story parallels that of his hometown.

Clay and his twin brother, Charlie, were adopted when they were one year old from the orphanage in Waterloo, Iowa, by Doc Hallberg, Oelwein's general practitioner since 1953. Clay and Charlie are identical twins. They have opposite dominant eyes and hands, and part their hair on opposing sides—Clay on the right, Charlie on the left. Clay plays the bass and Charlie the drums. Clay earned degrees in biology and chemistry; Charlie, meanwhile, majored in philosophy and theology, with a minor in Egyptology.

From an early age, the boys had promiscuous interests, including chemistry; they used their chemical know-how to make pipe bombs and once blew up a neighbor child's sandbox. They had a shared active sense of humor as well, and delighted in giving guests glasses of water, only to announce minutes later they'd gotten the water from the toilet. For the first few years of their lives, their mother would turn their shared crib upside down and stack books on top of it to keep them from getting loose in the house and wreaking havoc. As teenagers in the 1970s, neither twin was, to put it politely, unfamiliar with narcotics. After graduating together from the University of Northern Iowa, in Cedar Rapids, Clay went to medical school at Southern Illinois University at Carbondale, and Charlie to law school at Creighton University. In 1987, Clay, recently married and finished with his residency, came back home to join his father's practice. Shortly thereafter, Charlie moved into a house down the street from Clay's and began work as the Fayette County public defender.

Clay is five feet eight and weighs 160 pounds. He has a welder's forearms and the hands not of a musician or a surgeon, but of a farmer: thick in the meat, with large fingers and deep creases in the palms. Clay's brown hair is going gray ("salt-and-turd," he calls it), and he wears it combed back. He has a short, manicured goatee and intense grayish-blue eyes behind fashionable frameless glasses. In contrast to his wife's deep northern Missouri drawl, Clay's accent is more Minnesotan, extending each opening syllable toward the innards of a word. His lexicon is unmistakable and specialized; he often says "how 'bout" and "okay," as when responding in the negative to a request: "How 'bout no way, okay?" Young men and women with multiple piercings "have gone face-first into a tackle box." Bars are "unsupervised outpatient stress-reduction clinics that serve cheap over-the-counter medications with lots of side effects."

Clay goes to work every day in a small brick building across the street from Mercy Hospital. Mercy, as it's called, is an imposing monolithic structure built sixty years ago by the Catholic church. Next door is the high school and a small residential neighborhood. Beyond that, the prairie starts in earnest, lonely and flat and constant. From the window in the waiting room of the Hallberg Family Practice, you can see a lot of sky, which makes the clutter of Clay's tiny office at the back of the building feel that much more profound. There's a desk and two chairs, one of which is inaccessible given the boxes of patient files that line the floor in stacks. On one wall are shelves covered with antique doctor's implements; many of them once belonged to Clay's father, who finally retired when his wife was killed in a car accident in 2003. Next to these are a hundred or so books attesting to the extent of Clay's duties: *Clinical Neuroanatomy*, *Pathophysiology of Renal Disease*, *General Ophthalmology*, *Patten's Foundations of Embryology*.

True to his roots, Clay not only sees patients in the exam room across the hall; he drives to their houses and farms, and also works two nights a week in the emergency room. He has delivered babies in the backs of cars, and once, in a barn. A few years ago, he served as assistant county coroner, which is to say, assistant to his father. He's also chief of staff at Mercy. In terms of what there is to see around Oelwein, Clay has seen it.

Contrary to what many people might think, the rural United States has for decades had higher rates of drug and alcohol abuse than the nation's urban areas. If addiction has a face, says Clay, it is the face of depression. Bad genes don't help, either, says Clay, but all genes, bad or good, are susceptible to a poor environment. He knows of what he speaks. Back in the mid-1970s, after getting his B.S., Clay was back in Oelwein, casting about for something to do with his life. His father, Doc Hallberg, was abusive—a disciplinarian who limped around the rural towns of Fayette County for forty years performing minor medical miracles, all the while suffering from debilitating arthritis in his right leg, which, thanks to polio, is eighteen inches shorter than his left and compensated by a substantial shoe lift. Clay was good at giving his father reasons to be stern. He played in a band, had long hair, and did a lot of cocaine. His love of homemade explosives had not abated. One time, when the high school was closed because of a snow day, Clay set off a pipe bomb on the campus lawn, just to see what would happen. The next morning, the Oelwein newspaper called it a terrorist attack and demanded that the culprit be hunted down and prosecuted federally. (Clay was never caught.) The more Clay bounced around intellectually beneath his father's brutal, withering glare without being able to land on something either of them found meaningful, the more Clay did drugs. Finally, he says, he realized he was either going to medical school or going to jail.

Things in Oelwein at that point were just starting to deteriorate economically. It would be a few more years before the sky fell, once the Chicago Great Western and Illinois Central closed operations in town and the farm crisis struck, but Clay attributes much of his anger and malaise to a simple socioeconomic postulate: "If you got no money, you can't go see the band. And if you can't see the band, you're fucked." What he means is that, without good jobs, little disposable income remains in the community to be spent at all manner of locally owned businesses, including at the bars. And during the last good days of the 1970s, Oelwein bars were known from Waterloo to Wenatchie for having the best local bands in the Upper Mississippi River watershed.

Once known as Little Chicago, says Clay, Oelwein boasted the best Italian food in the Midwest, every bar fielded a pool league in the winter and a softball team in the summer, and the Sportsmen's Lounge served the best prime rib in Iowa, thanks to the fact that Oelwein was the first overnight stop west from the Chicago stockyards. In the 1930s and 1940s, Count Basie and Glenn Miller regularly played Tuesday nights at the Oelwein Coliseum on their way from Minneapolis to St. Louis. According to Clay, the Coliseum's owner stipulated in the bands' contracts that they couldn't play any other venue within five hundred miles for at least one week following a show in Oelwein. Such was the clout of a town that employed two thousand people, or almost 60 percent of the working-age male population, in the lucrative rail business and could therefore be relied on for sold-out shows. In the 1950s, Buddy Holly played the Oelwein Armory four times. Once it was all gone, says Clay, the deep sense of disappointment that pervaded Oelwein only magnified the Hallberg twins' sense of loss.

Ever since then, the twins have fought to maintain a sense of balance through music, and in doing so, to share that feeling of wholeness with their community. Clay likes to say that he has been strumming and Charlie has been "banging on shit" since birth. When the boys were five or six, Clay, the aspiring bassist, would string fishing lines in the doorway to the kitchen; Charlie would hammer on pots and pans to bring the babysitter running, only to howl with delight when she tripped and fell over the strings. Clay, who still relishes a good bar fight, once reputedly pushed another band member out of a moving VW bus, then casually noted how the thud that resulted was in B minor. To this day, the brothers play venues all over northeastern Iowa in a variety of ensembles and make their own recordings in a studio that Clay bought, two blocks away from the IGA grocery store. For Clay, performing is an act of communal symbiosis; nowhere does he feel more at home and more complete than onstage with his twin, trying hard to make people dance and sing along to an ageless repertoire of good old-fashioned rock and roll.

Music visibly calms Clay, who smoked a pack and a half a day and drank heavily when I met him in 2005. Conversations could be measured not by minutes and hours, but in pots of coffee or cans of Bud Light. The breadth of his knowledge is staggering; keeping pace with the abrupt, multidimensional movements of his thoughts is like trying to keep track of a hummingbird. He is apt, say, while riffing on the history of Sioux medicine men, to be reminded of his favorite philosopher and to ask if you would like him to "distill Kant into three sentences, so that you're with me here"—all this as an addendum to a Chomskyan critique of the critical-care program at Mercy Hospital. Clay's is both an all-consuming and a consumptive energy; without music, he would be consumed for sure.

Eighty-five percent of what Clay does as a doctor is to minister to one form or another of the mental illness that he says ravages Oelwein. Mostly, he says, it's depression or anxiety, though there are plenty of bipolar people walking around town. In this way, says Clay, Oelwein is no exception; one in three Americans, by his estimate, suffer from some sort of psychological malady. It's just that, in places like this, where there is no money for proper help, the effects are magnified. Every year, Oelwein's population dwindles. The senior class at the high school shrinks, on average, by five students each fall. In 2004 alone, Oelwein lost $147,000 in tax revenues. It cannot absorb the social and financial cost of malady in the way that Waterloo (which lost $2 million in revenues in 2004) can. Nor is the problem aided, Clay says unapologetically, by the inbreeding and lack of education endemic to a place that is literally shriveling up: "How 'bout the first people to leave are of course the smart ones, and the people with enough money to get out. What you're left with—and I'm sorry, okay?—doesn't qualify Oelwein High as a feeder school for Harvard, okay?"

What Clay laments more than anything is that there is so little recognition of the complexities Oelwein faces. No one wants to talk about what's right in front of their eyes, a direct result, he says, of the tight-lipped, stolid stock that helped settle this area. A hundred years ago, it was socially advantageous for people not to speak of hardship, to act instead of to think. Now, says Clay, there's too little money to act. Talking, at a minimum, he says, would help alleviate the sense of helplessness. Looking for ways to cope, many people head to the church, where the best intentions of a wonderful man like Darwin Moore, the minister at Grace Methodist, cannot be mistaken for real job training in social and psychological programs. Or, unable to afford a visit to Clay, never mind the antidepressants he might prescribe, people self-medicate in one of Oelwein's eleven bars. That, he says, is where the meth dealers have easy pickings.

The methamphetamine problem, along with the sense of desperation that had developed in Oelwein, is what finally drove Clay's brother, Charlie, away. He got tired, he says, after seven years as public defender, of addicts showing up at his house at two o'clock in the morning, wondering why Charlie hadn't gotten their friends out of jail. He didn't feel that Oelwein was a safe place for his two middle-school-aged children to grow up. Charlie's wife, says Clay, was ready to leave him. So Charlie moved an hour and twenty minutes south, to the city of Cedar Rapids, where he went into private practice. As Clay tells the story, his jaw muscles flex, as though he could chew his way through the details in order to come to an understanding of how this had happened. They'd come home together, after all, to be part of a solution in Oelwein. Now Charlie was gone. The town's meth problem was the first thing that had separated the twins since medical and law school.

Charlie left in 2003, the same year that their mother was killed in a car accident. Clay was bereft. With his own children now out of the house and Charlie and his mother gone, he felt totally alone. He poured himself into his work, redoubling his efforts to help his increasingly beleaguered patients. But with his insurance rates rising each year, he hasn't found it easy. "Even if we get a hold of meth next month," Clay told me in our initial phone conversation, "we've already got three human stages of history to clean up. But seeing that we won't have it under control next month, we're going to have four, five, maybe six generations to deal with: the medical problems, the psychological ramifications—we don't even know what else. We've only settled into a long-term siege."

The toll it had taken on him was nowhere more evident than in the garage of his house when I went to visit him the first day; in one corner, there were three enormous trash bags full of beer cans. Most nights that he wasn't on call, Clay drank a twelve-pack by himself, pacing in the garage and smoking cigarettes, just to try to calm down. Then he tried to get some rest.

When you drive into Independence, Iowa, fourteen miles south of Oelwein, with the windows down on a warm late-June day, you feel the fullness of small-town America's pastoral charm. Despite its proximity to Oelwein and its comparable size, Independence feels both bigger and cleaner than its neighbor to the north. On Main Street, the antique buildings house no closed storefronts. People are everywhere, walking in the sun. There is a feeling of purposefulness, even in winter, when the warm lights of the restaurants shine invitingly in the dusk, and the snowplows patrol well in advance of impending storms, giving the impression that all is not only well, but also that things are accounted for and under control even before they happen.

I went to Independence in order to meet a recovering meth addict, his son, and his parents. I wanted to see the kind of generational effects about which Clay had spoken—the "multidimensional expansion of pathology," as he put it, that a drug epidemic engenders. In trying to understand the difficulties caused by meth addiction in just one family, I felt it appropriate to go to Independence, which is so much less rough around the edges than Oelwein. The lack of obvious corruption in Independence made that town feel decades behind its neighbor to the north in terms of economic or drug-related complications, as though one might get a peek at what Oelwein had been like when Clay and Charlie Hallberg first started playing the bars back in the 1970s.

That a large-scale social ill infects individual lives and relationships is certainly not news. Indeed, I had already begun to appreciate the effects of Oelwein's fate on Clay. Over more time, I'd see how the town's difficulties seemed to accord with Clay's growing abuse of alcohol. And while it's not fair to say that social divisions directly split individuals, testing marriages and relationships, it seems reasonable to consider the added stress of a larger difficulty when looking at the various human pieces. What came into view in Independence was the inverse of this: once a community has shattered, not only will families splinter, too, but members will feel compelled to look for succor in surprising places. Meth doesn't just drive people apart; it drives them together.

The recovering addict I'd come to speak with is known as Major to other members of the Sons of Silence motorcycle gang, or what he refers to as "the Family," of which he is a former member. The name seemed appropriate, given the comparatively astounding effect Major had had within his fairly limited realm. Then twenty-five years old, Major lived with his parents, Bonnie and Joseph, in a pretty redbrick home on a quiet tree-lined street five blocks off Main. At six feet two, 180 pounds, Major had wide shoulders, sinewy arms, strong calves, and a slim waist. His natural blond hair and blue eyes must have served him well in the Family, for the Sons of Silence are an Aryan Nation organization, and Major has *SS* tattooed onto his left deltoid. Fourteen months ago, at the peak of his meth addiction, he weighed 130 pounds.

The day I went to meet Major, we sat on the porch of his parents' house. Major had been clean for nine months by then, though he was still given to an addict's hyperbolic monologues punctuated with firecracker explosions of laughter. I found him to be personable, self-deprecating, and funny, a kiss-ass and an intimidator, someone who would say whatever it took to get out of trouble. He was obviously highly intelligent and low on self-esteem, which made for a kind of cartoonish charm. Everything about him seemed to be in a state of contagious turmoil, the result, I guessed, of his years of brainwashing by the Sons of Silence. To witness the fights that raged in him—between meth and staying clean; between remaining with his blood-parents or returning to the Family; between self-loathing and self-aggrandizement—made it almost impossible not to sympathize with Major.

In northern Iowa, the Sons of Silence, once the foremost bike and drug gang, are today essentially a mom-and-pop meth-production outfit, making a few pounds of Nazi dope here and there, with access to a built-in retail force in the form of their few remaining riders. Their leader, a man named Bob, is the father of Major's ex-girlfriend, Sarah. Sarah is the love of Major's life and the mother of Major's son, Buck. Bob, along with his wife and Sarah, lived on a farm in nearby Jesup, Iowa, where he continued to make meth. Bob's presence just twelve miles away, along with the memory of the life that Major lived with him, was a weight that Major couldn't seem to lift from the day-to-day drudgery of his sober existence.

At the time of my visit, Buck was two. He had white-blond hair, expressive dark blue eyes, and red lips that stood out against his rich, alabaster skin. His ruddy cheeks and already defined musculature seemed the marks of an older child. All around, in fact, Buck seemed developmentally ahead of the game for his age. He was personable and curious and talked a blue streak. He was anything but quiet, moody, and distant, often the marks of a so-called meth baby. And Buck is not just a meth baby, he is *the* meth baby of Iowa. When the Department of Human Services and local prosecutors, under the auspices of the Child in Need of Assistance (CHINA) statute, took him away from Major and Sarah, Buck's hair had the highest cell-follicle traces of methamphetamine ever recorded in state history. Number two on the list was Buck's half sister, Caroline, who was six at the time she was taken.

From where Major and I sat at a table on the porch, Major looked at his mother, who was inside the screen door, listening to our conversation. Buck was in the middle of yet another circumnavigation of the table via the four benches surrounding it. Major was clearly not going to say anything else while his mother was listening, and we all waited for several uncomfortable moments. I passed Buck over my lap so that he could go to the next bench, where, if his formula held true, he'd stop briefly to bang out a quick tune on the Tunnel Tuner—a plastic locomotive that whistles as it follows yellow tracks in a circle, one whistle per one push of a big blue button. Then he'd continue as before along his circular path.

"Mom," said Major, "can you just not stand there, please?"

Major watched Bonnie leave the doorway and retreat into the kitchen. Then he said that in 2003 he and Bob developed a way to increase their yield from batching meth by microwaving the coffee filters through which they strained the dope's impurities. Heating the filters yielded a good deal of powdered crank that had been absorbed by the paper. The problem was that the powdered crank also spread over the inside of the microwave, where Bob and Major cooked Buck and Caroline's food, thereby permitting the children to ingest untold amounts of the drug.

The long-term effects of infant methamphetamine ingestion were unclear in 2005 when I met Major and Buck, and remain hazy today. Only one researcher, Dr. Rizwan Shah, of the Blank Children's Hospital in Des Moines, has studied the problem for a significant period of time, twelve years, which is long enough to see trends but too short to track their continued effects. Buck did, said Major, exhibit some of the symptoms that Dr. Shah associates with children exposed to meth in the early years of their lives. Buck shook violently in the morning when he woke up, had trouble sleeping, and suffered from acute asthma. He was also quick to revert to violent anger as a form of communication and was maddeningly picky about his food, often refusing to eat. Whether these latter attributes were an indication that Buck was simply entering the terrible twos and beginning to exert his will or were related to his monumental exposure to meth was anyone's guess. So far Buck didn't seem affected by another common problem with meth exposure, which is an inability to interact with other human beings, a result, it is supposed, of long periods of frenetic, haphazard attention followed by days of lying helpless in a crib while parents sleep off their binges.

It's meth's long-term effects, though, that are potentially the most disturbing, in part because those effects are theoretical and based on observations made only among adults, many of whom suffer from liver and kidney failure, weakened hearts and lungs, high blood pressure, and severe anxiety. The worry is that whatever physical disabilities an adult suffers, a child, by definition weaker and smaller, will have these same deficiencies visited upon him manifold.

Meth's power, said Major, had never been more clear to him than the last time he was in jail. Major was panic-stricken without the drug. By turns he couldn't sleep or couldn't wake up. He couldn't eat. He had hallucinations. His body hurt as though he'd been in a car accident. And he, by a long stretch, had it pretty easy. According to an undercover narcotics agent in Ottumwa, Iowa, one addict became convinced in his jail cell that the impurities in the meth he'd been cooking and injecting—particularly the lithium battery strip used as a solvent in the drug's manufacture—were actually inside his body. Thinking that one of the veins in his arm was a strip of lithium, he sat on his bed and spent hours using his long fingernails to dig the vein out. Talking to Major made it clear that meth's physical withdrawals were only the beginning of his problems with quitting, for what was most striking about him was that he seemed to have no idea who he was now that he no longer used meth.

Buck was ready to cross my lap again in order to complete another turn around the table. "Hi!" he said. He picked up a lighter on the table and held it out to me. "For you," he said. He was wearing little red shorts that bulged with a fresh diaper. For Major, waiting to see what price his son would pay for his transgressions was a daily reminder of why he had to stay straight. But his anxiety and guilt were also an hourly motivation to get high. Major, when he allowed himself to think of what he might have done to his boy, wanted nothing more than to kill himself with a final, euphoric overdose of crank.

"Not for you," said Major, grabbing the lighter from Buck's hand.

Buck began crying. At first Major spoke soothingly to him. When Major picked him up, Buck hit Major in the face. Bonnie came to the doorway again, watching. Major looked at her, his face first registering the need for help, and then anger. Major looked back at Buck, who tried to bite his father's nose. Major shook him furiously as Buck howled. That's when Bonnie swooped in and took Buck away. Bonnie and her son stared at each other, Buck between them like a shield. Or like a threat, for Bonnie could at any time banish Major from her home, and Buck would have to stay with her.

"He's hungry," said Bonnie finally. "That's all."

A few days later, I met Joseph and Bonnie in the bar of a restaurant in Independence that looked like a T.G.I. Friday's done up with telltale small-town signs of color. Kitty-corner from a print of John Belushi and Dan Ackroyd in *The Blues Brothers* was a walleye mounted on an oak plaque bearing a gold plate engraved with the angler's name, the lake where the fish was caught, and the weight: seven pounds, three ounces.

It was July 5, and Joseph and Bonnie had come to talk to the owner about their youngest son's wedding rehearsal dinner, which they wanted to have in October in the restaurant's small reception room. But before reservations were made and the menu decided, they had a long talk about the owner's recent trip to a lake in Canada, where the owner had enjoyed the best walleye and northern pike fishing he'd ever imagined. Joseph and Bonnie had been to the same lake many times—they are both avid fishermen—and were clearly sorry they'd missed the action. They hadn't been fishing in over two years, which is about as long as they'd been taking care of Buck, who for all practical purposes had become Bonnie and Joseph's fifth child.

Technically, Bonnie, a social worker, and Joseph, a county magistrate, have custody of Buck. That they allow Major to live in their home is a circumstance that exists outside the bounds of custody litigation. It can be, to say the least, an awkward arrangement. Bonnie and Joseph were fifty-three years old when I met them in 2005. They had not planned to raise a two-year-old at this stage of their lives. Just a year earlier, Major and Sarah, still living at Bob's farm, would break into Bonnie and Joseph's house to steal whatever they could, then sell it to buy more cold medicine from which to make meth. One night Major stole his mother's panties and bras and hocked them at a bar. During another break-in, Major and Sarah decided to stash a large amount of meth in the air vents of Bonnie and Joseph's home. When Bonnie and Joseph turned the heat on, the meth-tainted air that blew through the vents made them ill, and they had to spend ten thousand dollars, or a quarter of Joseph's yearly income, to have the whole system replaced. That there was some resentment beneath the surface of their every interaction with Major was not surprising.

More surprising was how little resentment there was. Joseph, a heavy smoker with an ashen complexion, is an intensely quiet man given to wearing khakis, short-sleeve oxford shirts, and simple ties with no jacket. When he speaks, his words come out with the blunt force of body blows. Bonnie is soothing and kind, a tall, thin, pretty woman of Swedish descent with sharp features and a stately bearing. That day at the restaurant, Bonnie's articulateness was magnified as she sat next to her brooding husband. Since adopting Buck, Joseph and Bonnie have put their lives on hold. Retirement is no longer an option, never mind a goal. They cannot leave Major at home alone for more than a few hours at a time, so afraid are they that he will relapse, or that Bob will make good on the threat he has leveled in dozens of late-night phone calls: that he will kidnap Buck, murder Major, and burn down Bonnie and Joseph's home.

Bonnie lit one of Joseph's cigarettes, took a drag, and handed it to him. Referring to the day I'd spoken with Major on the porch, she said she didn't believe a lot of the things she'd heard him tell me about his time living with Bob and Sarah. Bonnie called her son by his given name, Thomas. Thomas had told me several stories about his and Bob's murdering rivals and making millions of dollars. "I think a lot of it is exaggerated," Bonnie said. "The things about how powerful and smart Bob is. Thomas likes to imagine he was so important and so marvelous. In truth, Bob is a putz."

"Jesus Christ," said Joseph, shaking his head. "By the time Thomas moved back in with us, he literally didn't know his name. He'd gotten so used to lying that he'd stumble over any simple fact."

"I think between the drugs and the games they played with him, they really got into his mind," said Bonnie. "That so-called family will stay at a farm for a while, never paying the rent, and then just leave and go to a new place. They've done that their whole lives. And if you talk to Bob, there's nothing at all scary about him. He's this little guy, and he's a total brownnose. He's like a weasel. Nothing Thomas says adds up."

It was the questions that were killing them, said Bonnie. Not just what had really happened while Major was with the Family but also how to help him recover. Even as a social worker, Bonnie knew comparatively little about how to aid in this process or what kind of outcome could reasonably be expected. In lieu of a blurry future, Bonnie and Joseph constantly replayed the past, looking for clues.

Bonnie said, "I mean, I keep thinking, 'What did we do wrong?' I breast-fed Thomas. I didn't smoke or drink when I was pregnant. After he got out of jail the second time, we rented him an apartment. He was back on meth overnight. So we moved him and Sarah into our house. In response, her father beat her up. Bob beat the absolute hell out of his own daughter for moving in with us and trying to quit meth. Once we got custody of Buck, Sarah tried to get DHS to take him away from us because we *smoke*. She said we were endangering her child. She told the police that we kidnapped him. She still calls thirty times a night, sometimes, and hangs up."

Bonnie paused to light another one of Joseph's cigarettes. This time she didn't give it back to him. The whole time she'd spoken, Joseph had silently rubbed his forearm with his blunt fingers, the way you might rub a favorite blanket or a piece of cloth. Bonnie said, "So that's what we get for trying to help."

Staying busy amid these circumstances, said Bonnie, was a blessing. What busied them more than anything else was overseeing a kind of in-house rehab for Major while they waited to see what, if any, problems Buck might develop. This was not Los Angeles, or Tampa, or even Poughkeepsie. There were no residential chemical abuse facilities around there. None that Bonnie and Joseph could afford anyway, despite making twice the median income for the area.

By law, Major had to attend Narcotics Anonymous meetings each week; meet with his parole officer twice a month; and hold down a job, which meant working construction. Had Buck still been in his custody, a DHS worker would have visited every week to assess the situation and to offer help, for an hour at a time, with the dizzying array of adjustments, however prosaic or monumental, that Major faced in his attempt to live a sober life. "That's as much as can be done for meth addicts and their children," said Bonnie in regard to comparatively well-off Independence, Iowa.

When Joseph finally broke his silence to offer his opinion on what should be done with meth addicts, it reflected this lack of available options. Brutally, dispassionately, quietly, he said that all addicts ought to be sterilized. While in jail, they ought to be put to work on behalf of the community they have sullied, milking cows and building roads. Then, echoing his wife, he said, "That's as good as can be done in Independence, Iowa."

Bonnie let him cool down. Then she reminded Joseph that while Major was last in jail, his third time, Joseph went to visit him every night. Furthermore, Joseph leveraged his position as a county magistrate in order to get Major out early. Had Major been sterilized during one of his incarcerations, Bonnie went on, they would never have had the profound pleasure of seeing Buck learn to walk. When she was done talking, she put her hand on his.

Joseph shook his head. Then he nodded in agreement. "Whatever happens," he said, "we've got the boy."

For a moment, it was unclear which generation of his progeny he meant: his son or his grandson. Then he said, "No matter how badly he screws up from here, Thomas can't change that."

CHAPTER 5

THE DO DROP INN

Before my second two-week stay in Oelwein during the summer of 2005, I'd spent ten days driving from town to town in southern Illinois, western Kentucky, and northern Missouri. In Benton, Illinois, a poor black-earth farm town in the sweltering hollows of Franklin County, I'd ridden around for a few days with J. R. Moore, who was not only the Benton police department's sole narcotics officer, he was also Benton's interim mayor and the owner of one of the town's three restaurants. All day, J. R. drove a black Mustang GT with tinted windows and an arsenal of shotguns in the bucket backseats, smoking Marlboro Lights and rolling down his window at stop signs to say hey to people he'd known all his life. In Chillicothe, Missouri, in the cattle- and prairie-rich heart of the state's northern river breaks, I'd spent the night in a motel and listened while, in the room above me, a man beat the woman he'd married that very evening, at that very motel. Like the hill country around Benton, the area around Chillicothe, 350 miles away, had a monumental meth problem, and the bride yelled loudly that her new husband would not have been doing this to her had he not been high on crank. When I called the police, a female officer talked to the groom outside the window of my ground-floor room. After he convinced the officer that nothing was wrong, she wound up her investigation by wondering what kind of out-of-towner had mistaken a good time for domestic abuse.

By then, it was no longer a question in my mind whether meth was a bigger problem in small-town America than in larger cities. San Francisco undoubtedly has many, many more meth addicts than the Central Valley town of Merced. There are thousands of meth addicts in Des Moines, while in Oelwein there are barely more than six thousand people total. Los Angeles is meth's ancestral home in the United States. Like New York, San Francisco, and Miami, Los Angeles has a large population of gay meth addicts. In the past five years, HIV and hepatitis C rates have increased among the gay population, and meth is widely blamed. The meth problem in those cities is significant, if not monumental. The difference is that Los Angeles can absorb the associated costs of those problems more easily than Oelwein or Merced or Benton. And the recourse of small towns in confronting meth seemed only to be growing bleaker.

The question was how to portray the meth problem in the rural United States without stereotyping—and ultimately trivializing— the places to which meth had called such attention by the summer of 2005. Beavis and Butt-Head, Smurfers, mom and pop—meth users had entered the lexicon as caricatures, which ultimately stemmed less from the drug and more from the environs with which that drug was associated. Oddly, nowhere were the prejudices against— and parodies of—small-town meth addicts more explicit than in Oelwein itself, the town that, according to Clay Hallberg, Jay Leno once referred to in a *Tonight Show* monologue as "possibly the worst place in the world." Even Nathan Lein struggled with the temptation to see the people he prosecuted as "shitbags." In some ways it seemed that the meth epidemic only added to a sense of isolation in Oelwein, as though the world was happening everywhere but there.

Viewing meth as a crime story vastly oversimplifies the problem. Similarly, Clay Hallberg had made it clear to me in our very first conversation that there was a lot more to this story than a drug and its effects. That drug stood for something. Now I was beginning to see what Clay had meant. Meth represented, in the words of Craig Reinarman, a sociologist at UC Santa Cruz and an expert on drug epidemics, "sociological fault lines." Back-to-back nights—one at the Do Drop Inn and the next at a party at Clay Hallberg's—painted these fault lines in stark distinction. What became particularly clear was that, despite one's best intentions, the divisions fostered by a drug epidemic seem to run along the lines of class—or at least along the perceptions of class. Major is not what's considered to be a "typical" meth addict, since he's from a successful family. And yet, because he was drug-addicted, he's considered to be less by his own father and by Nathan Lein, who grew up far poorer than Major.

Douglas Constance is a rural sociologist at Sam Houston State University in Huntsville, Texas. Constance puts Reinarman's point in a different context when he says that the United States is "psychological, not a sociological nation." What he means is that we will always hold the individual responsible over the group, blaming the drug addict instead of investigating the environment in which he grew up, and (conversely) celebrating the quarterback above the team following a win. In a small town, the distance between the winner and the loser is negligible, though the instinct to insulate is just as strong as it is in New York City. What connects people in New York and in Benton, Illinois, in fact, is that both resist believing that they have anything in common. Major's father seemed to associate himself automatically with his grandchild over his son. In a similar manner, what Nathan Lein must every day remind himself is that he does, in fact, share many things with Roland Jarvis.

The extension of Constance's analysis is that during a drug epidemic, instinct demands that we find something wrong with those who are addicted; the epidemic in effect tricks us into thinking that the relatively small number of addicts are anomalies, even as we acknowledge the drug's large-scale presence. In August 2005, *Newsweek* printed a now-famous series of photos of meth addicts, whose faces first seemed to age and then practically to disintegrate over time. I remember thinking the pictures looked like propaganda paintings from World War II of German soldiers, or "Huns," who had been deliberately dehumanized. Similarly, the addicts shown in *Newsweek* were so gaunt and lifeless that they seemed utterly disengaged from humanity. Those photos served in some way to distance not only the addicts themselves but also the rural United States, from which the addicts invariably came, from the nation at large. For me, a true chronicle of the height of the meth years from 2005 to 2008 must begin with a town and all its people. If meth alone were to define Oelwein—and through it, the entire small-town United States—the truth would be hopelessly obscured. And the truth is, Clay and Major, Nathan and Roland, Murphy and Lori and the people in the Do Drop Inn—these people are us.

Among the regulars at the Do Drop Inn are Josh and Ben, two obese, bike-riding nineteen-year-olds who more or less control the two seventy-five-cent pool tables. There is also Lisa, an unemployed, nearsighted epileptic known on the Oelwein karaoke circuit as Flipper; and Sophie, who by twenty-four was in a coma following a car accident, from which she emerged a year later having to once again learn to talk, walk, and eat, and whose social outlets are composed of walking her cat on a leash every night to McDonald's and then heading over to drink Diet Pepsi at the Do Drop Inn. Add to this a rotating gallery of white supremacist skinheads, tweakers, whiggers (the local moniker for white kids who wear the long, baggy clothing associated with urban blacks), bikers, and farm kids, and the Do Drop, in Clay Hallberg's formulation, can feel at times very much like an unsupervised outpatient clinic.

There is method to the mayhem, however. The Do Drop's owner, Mildred Binstock, is more den mother than boss, and knows pretty much everything about everyone who comes in. Mildred has pretty olive skin and dark brown eyes. She wears blouses in wild, colorful prints, has appliquéd eyebrows, and is not someone who shies away from lipstick. At five-feet-eleven Mildred is what might be described as well fed: not fat, exactly, but not without a predilection for chicken tenders either. She is sixty years old and has never married. She does not drink, and she's never smoked a cigarette, despite having worked from five P.M. to two A.M. nightly at the Do Drop Inn since she bought the place in 1984. That, says Mildred, was two years before what she describes as the "schnapps revolution," which accounts for the prodigious amount of flavored DeKuyper's behind the bar in peach, blackberry, and butterscotch, which she maintains nearly doubled her liquor sales.

Back in 2005, someone at the Do Drop Inn was getting busted— for assault, selling meth, fighting, or contributing to the delinquency of a minor—about once every two weeks on average. Most recently, the police went upstairs to one of the three floors where Mildred rents rooms weekly and monthly and kicked down the door to find a seventeen-year-old girl in flagrante delicto with a forty-year-old man. On the table next to them was the eight-ball of crank she'd just sold him. When Nathan Lein took me to the Cop Shop on my first day in Oelwein, I told him my plan to hang out at the Do Drop, in hopes of meeting any of the addicts and dealers as they appeared in mug shots on Chief Logan's computer screen, Nathan said, "Good luck. Even cops won't go in there alone."

Mildred watches the Fox News Channel whenever she is not asleep. She can tell you what shows are on at what times on a twenty-four-hour schedule. She refers to her decorating style as either High Amish Kitsch or Late Victorian Clutter. In front of an enormous television flanked by red lace curtains, Mildred's customers sit at formal dinner tables complete with high-backed dining room chairs decorated with Christmas lights. Behind the bar is a smoke-glass mirror in which, if you're observant, you can see the ever-frugal Mildred stealthily reuse the straw from one customer's finished whiskey and Coke in the fresh vodka tonic of another. The walls represent five decades of yard-sale finds: mounted fish, vintage pieces of bank china, calendars dating back to the Johnson administration. A sign stapled above the door to the kitchen reads "My office! No one allowed but ME!" Above the door is another television, which is often tuned to the man Mildred refers to as "my number-one honey": Geraldo Rivera.

In Mildred's estimation, Mayor Murphy and Chief Logan were crooks. They were what was wrong with Oelwein, pure and simple. The more ordinances they passed trying to rid the town of meth, the more Mildred considered them to be infringing on her civil rights. She was not alone. From an anecdotal perspective, Oelwein back in 2005 was deeply factioned regarding the police, the mayor, and Nathan Lein and his boss, county attorney Wayne Sauer. The upshot was that, in a poor town where half of all commercial space sat unoccupied, Mildred Binstock was not going to take kindly to police action in her bar. She was barely making it as it was, working seven days a week in an unending series of shifts that lasted deep into the night. Clay Hallberg, Nathan Lein, and Roland Jarvis all told me that more meth got sold at the Do Drop Inn than at any other bar in Oelwein. When I pressed Mildred about this, she insisted she was being set up. Then she added cryptically that, in her opinion, "The police are canoodling with the bad elements of this burg."

One early evening in particular brought home the complexity of the divisions in Oelwein, as expressed in its most notorious bar. It was a Sunday, and Mildred and I were the only two in the place. We were watching the news, which at the time was concentrated on the case of a young Mormon girl who'd been kidnapped from her Salt Lake City bedroom while her sister slept next to her; police suspected the handyman. Into the Do Drop Inn walked a man and a girl. The girl looked sixteen or seventeen, and the man over thirty. He was wearing denim Carhartts and a matching work jacket, each dirty enough to have been through a long day of building road in a dust storm. He had long, dirty, sharp fingernails, and he smelled like sour milk. The girl's hair was bobbed and greasy, and her body was lost inside an enormous gray sweatshirt that read "Duluth Is a Cool City" across the front, in homage to the brutality of Minnesota winters. It was immediately obvious to me from their dilated pupils and the man's aura of violently aggressive confidence that they were high on meth.

"You can't be twenty-one, honey," Mildred said to the girl as she studied her driver's license. Mildred then looked at the girl sternly with one appliquéd eyebrow raised, waiting for her to admit her true age. When the girl didn't respond, Mildred said brightly, "But if the state says you are, then you are." She looked at the man. "I know you're over," she said to him coldly. She gave them the drinks they'd ordered. Then, even though no one ordered any food, Mildred hurried into the kitchen, leaving the three of us alone in the empty bar.

The man was named Chad and the girl Ella. There was a computerized Keno machine at one end of the bar, and Ella went with her drink, sat down, and started tapping at the screen. She was four stools away from me, and seven away from Chad; I was between them. Chad and I talked about one thing and another, looking for some common ground. For instance, when I said I was born in Missouri, he allowed how he'd been in jail there once. His pupils completely obscured the blue of his irises.

Chad said, "Where's Ella?"

Ella was still four seats away, playing Keno. With her back arrow-straight and her feet dangling below her, she looked like she might actually be taking a computerized grammar test in a virtual high school. She wore no earrings, no jewelry at all, and she didn't blink as the light from the machine brightened and dimmed in the dark bar. Chad was looking right at her.

"Where's Ella?" he said again.

I started to say that Ella was sitting right there when I remembered what a woman in Cedar Rapids had told me about her ex-husband—that after he'd been using meth for a couple of years, he'd lie next to her in bed and ask where she was. Other times, he would mistake pillows and couches and dressers for his wife. If she would countermand his claims, she said, he would first panic and cry, sinking to the floor, begging her to reappear. When she did, he would accuse her of infidelity and beat her savagely with anything he could find: a lamp, an ashtray, and one time with a broken table leg.

Chad asked if Ella was with me. Then he scratched the wooden bar with his long fingernails, as though the bar had an itch that Chad could feel.

He asked me, in all seriousness, if I was having sex with Ella.

I said, "Right here?" When he picked up his empty beer bottle by the neck, I said, "She's playing Keno."

Chad said, "I can't believe Ella'd fuck you. I can't believe you'd do this right in front of me, Ella."

Ella, hearing her name and looking up from the Keno machine, said, "Coming." It was like a child's response when being called for dinner.

"He's a total fucking stranger!" said Chad. "How can you just fuck him like this?"

At that point, I got up and brought Ella to him. I asked her to hold his hand.

"See?" I said. "Here's Ella. This is Ella's hand."

Chad looked at her for several moments before he actually saw his girlfriend. When she let go of his hand and walked off a few seconds later, Chad looked at me and said, "What the fuck are you doing here?"

I told him I was just passing through.

"You're a liar," he said. He stood up to his full height, a good six feet two. He appeared to weigh two hundred pounds. I looked down the bar at the kitchen, into which Mildred had disappeared ten minutes before. There was no sign of her.

When Chad asked me if I worked for DEA, the window of diplomacy seemed to be closing once again. He said he'd be honest with me: he hated DEA. Nor, he said, would it be any skin off his teeth to make sure I never came back to town again. I was drinking whiskey; I wrapped my fingers around the tumbler so that if need be I could use it to break one of Chad's eye sockets.

That's when he sat back down. "Come on," he said. "Are you a narc or not?" He seemed genuinely interested. It was suddenly posed as a cordial question. He wanted to know, very sincerely, if I worked for DEA, for the reason that he had never actually met an agent, and had always kind of wanted to.

I told him I was sorry, but that he was out of luck. In general, meth dealers and the people trying to catch them often seem to dress in the same manner. Both constituencies are given to hair cut close to the scalp and a few days' growth of beard. I'd followed suit.

"Boy," said Chad confidentially, "you sure look like a fed."

"So much for fitting in," I told him.

Chad laughed, and so did I. He slapped me on the back. We shook hands. The agony he was in just a few minutes before was gone without a trace, replaced by a sense of euphoria that seemed to lift the heavy air of the bar. Both of us, I think, felt not just relieved, but elated. Chad was back up on the shoulder of his tweak, and he gathered Ella and rode the smooth wave out the back door of the Do Drop Inn into the alley across from the abandoned roundhouse. Right then, as though by magic, Mildred reappeared. She been watching all along through the space of the doorjamb. She said, "Isn't that terrible, the way people act?"

In some ways, it's true that, as people say around Oelwein, meth is confined to a few places. But it's just as important to see the places where meth is not in evidence, at least in its physical form. For even as the difficulties caused by the drug are an everyday part of life in Oelwein, so, too, are the rhythms of life there extant with or without meth. In this capacity, Clay and Tammy Hallberg excel.

Much of Oelwein comes through Clay's office on a weekly basis, or past him in the emergency room. Or, as happens on several holidays a year, into the Hallberg home to celebrate.

Clay and Tammy's house sits just across a narrow wooded gully from their neighbor's home, off a long gravel driveway half a mile west of town. Because Clay is not a farmer does not mean he doesn't grow corn on a couple of acres of his property, or raise a few chickens in the barn alongside his house. In front of the barn is the stable where Tammy keeps her horses, with which she has won riding competitions as far away as Kentucky. They can see most of their fifty-acre spread from the eat-in kitchen of the split-level ranch, with its big north- and south-facing windows.

It's July 4, 2005, and Clay and Tammy are having their annual hog roast. It's an occasion to be happy and to remember that life is indeed good, if only people would take the time to eat well and drink a little bit and enjoy one another's company. Gathered in small groups in the backyard beneath a looming eighty-year-old live oak, city employees from the water company mingle with bartenders and high school teachers, waiting for Tammy to give the word that a 250-pound pig provided by the local UPS driver is, after six hours, finally done roasting. Clay's twin brother, Charlie, is here, along with his wife. They've brought with them another friend, a Chilean expatriate who works as a translator at a windowpane plant down in Cedar Rapids.

While the UPS man stands beside his custom-made hog oven, a submarine-shaped barbecue so large it had to be towed behind a pickup, the Hallberg twins hold forth on their latest gig, which took place last night in a bar in Wadena, Iowa, where the hundred or so listeners twice asked them to reprise Lynyrd Skynyrd's "Free Bird," a crowd favorite for a quarter century. Meanwhile, Tammy advises a group of women on the finer points of her famed beer-can chicken recipe, the gist of which is to insert an open, full Bud Light into the gutted cavity of a homegrown broiler, then to stand the chicken, legs down, on the grate of a charcoal grill. For the best results, says

Tammy, use a medium-hot fire. And if your M.D. husband isn't looking, brush that sucker every fifteen minutes with a warm bath of salt, melted butter, and—as ever—more beer. After an hour of that, she concludes in her thick drawl, you'll never eat so good.

What unites the partygoers beyond the obvious bond of community is that Clay, all the while with Tammy working as his receptionist, delivered most of the guests' children. As the children grew (many of them were now adults themselves), he was their pediatrician, even as he treated their parents for problems ranging from skin cancer to gout. During his tenure as assistant county medical examiner, Dr. Clay made official the pronouncements of their parents' deaths. Oelwein itself is a crossroads in northeast Iowa, and Clay's and Tammy's lives together serve as a point of intersection of Oelwein's socioeconomic and cultural axes, the coordinates of which remain unchanged, even as Oelwein's demographics have shifted further and further toward a baseline of poverty. Oelwein, with its familiar and often complex social circuitry, is much like a family, and Clay and Tammy are in many ways at the center of it. Regardless of the trends in community health in the last thirty years, and in the corresponding changes in the chief medical complaint (it had once been sore muscles and broken bones; now it is depression and meth), if you have a problem or a reason to celebrate, you go to see the Hallbergs.

The Chilean translator, whose name is Jorge and who goes by George, is at once the party's most curious guest and its most affable curiosity. He left Santiago de Chile when General Augusto Pinochet took over the country from Dr. Salvador Allende, the socialist pediatrician who'd been elected president in 1970; had given over the vast holdings of Chile's elite to the underclasses; and had been killed three years later (while barricaded in his office at the Chilean White House) at the hand of Pinochet's coup. In a sea of Levi's, Dockers, and short-sleeved polo shirts, George stands out in his Wranglers, denim shirt, and shiny black cowboy boots. His wire-rim glasses and instinctive command of Marxist economics brand him a left-wing, idealist intellectual of a certain era in Latin American history, one heretofore unknown in Fayette County. The nephew of Salvador Allende's secretary of education, George (by far) defines the furthest edge of the gathering's largely centrist political agenda, which hinges on keeping taxes moderate and crop prices high; putting more money in the public education system; and keeping God in your life, but out of the government. By his mere presence, George also embodies the party's, and the town's, intuitively inclusionist sensibility.

Nonetheless, most people think George is Mexican. In a place where everyone has a grandfather whose native language was Norwegian or German or Italian, George represents the latest in the history of American immigration, complete with its unexpected quirks and hard-to-understand accents.

George, once he'd been exiled by Pinochet under the threat of death, had somehow ended up in Minneapolis, Minnesota. From there, a marriage took him to Cedar Rapids, Iowa, by way of Memphis, Tennessee. Divorced now, he spends his weekends playing music in local jazz ensembles. By day, he registers workers' injuries to management at the windowpane factory on behalf of the mostly Mexican and mostly illegal labor force, a job he likens to selling Bibles in Kabul. Tammy Hallberg allows how all of that is "pretty darned interesting." What she wants to know, though, is why more Mexicans can't learn English. Even the Amish, she says, can do that.

Clay, seeing an opening, offers his explanation in terms of Hegelian dialectic and Whorfian hypothesis. Basically it amounts to this: If you're not allowed to integrate into society (i.e., if you move from abusive job to abusive job, with no standardized manner of tracking your movements), then your choice of language will reflect this. It is a response with which George agrees so vehemently that only his native language can provide the right word to express his enthusiasm.

"Claro," says George, nodding. "Claro."

Tammy, too, relies on her native skills of communication, which are hammer-blunt. "Clay," she says, "stop talking—right now." And Dr. Clay does.

The food, excluding the hog, is potluck. When the UPS man is done carving the pork and heaping it on platters, he takes the platters to the kitchen. Tammy goes to the deck above the yard and rings a brass dinner bell. Surrounding the platters of pork are every manner of dish and container—Tupperware and Ziploc and microwaveable glass. What the containers lack in continuity, the foods make up for in their consistent use of corn as an ingredient and an equally consistent use of the loosest definition regarding the word "salad." There is corn on the cob and corn that has been boiled and then shaved from the cob and mixed with butter and salt; corn bread with jalapeños; and roasted corn tossed with onions and chives. There is Idaho Red potato salad, and next to that, an enormous bowl of the same dish, this one made with baby Yukon Golds. There's Jell-O salad, and bean salad, and a pot of boiled collard greens. For dessert, there is more Jell-O, this time molded like a wheel and resting on a seashell-shaped dish, and slices of warm, thick-crusted rhubarb pie with homemade vanilla ice cream.

When it's all gone, except for the unending mounds of pork, the women stay inside, smoking in the kitchen or helping with dishes while Tammy divvies up twenty or so pounds of leftover hog meat into large bags, to be handed out to the guests when they leave, like door prizes. Meanwhile, the men retire to the yard. There, the drinking, in the finest Lutheran tradition, becomes steady and workmanlike as they sit in their chairs and smoke cigarettes and tell jokes, their voices hushed in the still night.

George the Chilean sits next to Charlie and listens while Clay tells the one about Earl and Maynard down at the VFW.

"Maynard," begins Clay in his smoke-scarred voice, "is drunk as usual, sitting on his stool at the bar with Earl. And the next thing you know, Maynard pukes on himself."

"I love this one," says Charlie, leaning back in his camp chair. "This is a good one."

"So Maynard says to Earl, 'My wife just bought me this shirt. She'll kill me.'

"Earl says, 'Don't worry. Just tell her I did it.'

"Earl reaches in his wallet, takes out a twenty, and puts it in Maynard's chest pocket. 'Tell her,' he says, 'that I gave you twenty dollars for a new shirt.'"

Clay reaches out his hand and acts out the exchange by pretending to put something in the breast pocket of George's cowboy shirt.

"So," Clay continues, "Maynard goes home, and his wife gives him hell. 'But, honey, Earl did it!' says Maynard. 'And he gave me twenty dollars for a new shirt.'

"Maynard reaches in the pocket, pulls out the money, and hands it to his wife.

"She says, 'There's forty dollars here.'

"'Right,' says Maynard. 'That's because Earl pooped in my pants, too.'"

PART 2

2006

CHAPTER 6

MIRROR IMAGING

During 2006, meth, combined with America's complicated reaction to it, began to accomplish what sociologist Craig Reinarman had said is the central function of drug epidemic: to "trace a culture's sociological fault lines." This happened in several ways. First, the American media made meth a cause célèbre. Second, state legislatures, tired of being ignored, began passing their own meth laws. This, in turn, drove the federal government to react to a drug it had ignored since Gene Haislip's first failed campaign against meth at DEA, back when the Amezcua brothers were turning the drug into a blockbuster industry. Between the newspapers—mostly the *Oregonian*, in Portland—and the anger directed against Congress by state legislatures, a history of the federal government's complicity in the meth trade was unearthed. What came into view is that pharmaceutical industry lobbyists had blocked every single anti-meth bill in the last thirty years with the help of key senators and members of Congress. Moved by so much bad press to do something immediately, Congress passed its first ever blockbuster meth law, the Combat Methamphetamine Act, in September 2006.

In some ways it was as though the United States was looking in a mirror, seeing itself in the rural towns to which methamphetamine had drawn the nation's and the government's gaze. Ironically, meth made Olwein's connection with the rest of the country stronger and more visible than it had been for a long time. Nowhere was this more apparent than in Washington, D.C., where the drug's effect on small-town America was now a salient political issue. The effect, as it registered in the public pages of national newspapers, was the kind of broad-scale unity that had never before existed, given that the drug had for ten years been regarded as a regional, not a national, phenomenon. Suddenly people in New York City knew what—if not exactly where—I was talking about when I mentioned meth in Oelwein, Iowa. The *New York Times*, the *Boston Globe*, the *Washington Post*, and the *Atlanta Journal-Constitution* joined the *St. Louis Post-Dispatch*, the *Des Moines Register*, the *Fort Worth Star-Telegram*, and the *Los Angeles Times* in running stories about crank almost daily. The nation seemed to feel a shared and equal sense of outrage, whether over meth-induced increases in HIV among San Francisco's and New York's gay populations, or the apocalyptic violence that resulted from shifts in the meth market along the Texas-Mexican border. The message was that civilized society was falling apart, that people were going crazy, and that the proof was no longer just in the hinterlands; it was everywhere.

When Congress began debating the Combat Meth Act, it was without a trace of bipartisan rancor. Indiana Republican congressmen Mark Souder stood next to California Democratic senator Dianne Feinstein as they declared their moral obligation to take on meth and win. This seemed to be a macrocosm of what was happening in Oelwein, where Mayor Larry Murphy and the heretofore divided townspeople began to put aside their differences and rebuild. The message was that what was bad for the towns was bad for Washington, D.C., too; when it came to meth, everyone was working for the same thing. On a clear day, flying from New York to Los Angeles, or from Chicago to San Francisco, you might have looked at the small communities beneath the airplane in a different way, understanding better what they were up against, and in that way, you might have understood something of their vanishing place in the nation.

And then, just as suddenly as it started, the meth epidemic—along with the chance to understand what that epidemic really meant—was over. President George W. Bush's National Drug Control Policy director, or so-called drug czar, John Walters, announced in August 2006 that "the war on meth," for all intents and purposes, had been won. Shortly thereafter, the same newspapers that had briefly made the drug a cause célèbre began questioning whether meth had ever been an epidemic or just the creation of an overzealous media hungry for a good story. The popular media's brief but intense exploration of meth in rural America, highlighted by several documentaries on both cable and network television, also ended. As the drug went back to being a regional bogeyman, the rural United States went with it, taking its place once again in anonymity.

What remained, however, was a town (and a nation) with a drug problem. The need to keep looking remained as well. In meth's meteoric rise into the national consciousness and its subsequent fall, there were many clues to its deeper meaning in American culture. The fault lines, whether or not they made headlines, still overlaid the national topography just as completely as before. And maybe more so. What continued to take shape for me was the portrait of a town that stood as a metaphor for all of rural America and its problems. That's to say that the evolution of the meth epidemic had occurred in lockstep with the three separate economic trends that had contributed to the dissolution of small-town United States. By looking closely at the events of 2006, one can see the parallel trajectories of meth and small-town economics—the one rising, the other falling—dating back to the days of the Amezcuas. And the things that spurred this simultaneous rise and fall: the development of Big Pharmaceuticals, Big Agriculture, and the modern Mexican drug-trafficking business. To look closely at the history of meth from 1990 to 2006 is to see more clearly than ever what Nathan, Clay,

Murphy, Jarvis, and Lori Arnold have always been, and continue to be, confronted by.

It's important to understand how a government that had for upward of a decade completely ignored meth's spread from the West Coast into the Midwest and the Gulf States suddenly became alarmed. And how, just as suddenly, newspapers with only sporadic interest in reporting on the drug became obsessed with it. In some ways, the driving force behind each was the same: Steve Suo's work at the *Oregonian*. Suo had written his first crank story back in 2003 when, in researching Oregon's foster care system, he came upon a statistic that startled him: Eight in ten children under the state's care admitted that their parents used meth. It's in that way that Suo's interest in the story changed. At first his question was, "Why is there so much meth in Oregon?" Eventually Suo turned his attention to how the drug had gotten to Oregon. Answering that question led him to Washington, D.C., where he uncovered the causal connection between meth, the pharmaceutical industry, and the U.S. government. By the time Suo left the meth beat at the end of 2006, he'd written, along with other reporters, a combined 261 articles for the *Oregonian* in less than two years.

What Suo's reporting revealed was a timeline of failure, most of it at the crushing and unfair expense of Gene Haislip, DEA's deputy assistant administrator in the Office of Compliance and Regulatory Affairs from 1982 to 1996. Up until 1987, Haislip had worked against the lobbyist Allan Rexinger, who represented the pharmaceutical company Warner-Lambert, to pass a bill that would monitor shipments of ephedrine powder entering the United States. Companies like Warner-Lambert, which used the ephedrine to make nasal decongestants, resisted the idea, fearing that it would lead to more stringent oversight. Rexinger, by appealing directly to the Reagan White House, had won the battle with DEA, forcing Haislip into a compromise that allowed bulk loads of ephedrine to enter the U.S.

unmonitored, so long as the ephedrine was in pill—not powder—form.

The production of methamphetamine at the time was just industrializing, largely at the hands of the Amezcua brothers, who'd understood the lucrative, illegal application of the lax laws governing ephedrine imports. Once Haislip's watered-down law passed, the Amezcuas simply bought ephedrine pills from legitimate sources, crushed them into powder, and used the powder to make meth. In addition, they began importing ephedrine powder into the port at Mazatlán, on Mexico's Pacific coast, then driving the powder north across the border. As trade increased between Mexico and the United States, culminating in 1993 with the ratification of the North American Free Trade Agreement (NAFTA), truck traffic at ports of entry like San Ysidro, California, increased 278 percent, according to a study by UC-San Diego economics professor Joan Anderson. As a result, border security became more difficult to enforce, making it easier than ever to drive loads of ephedrine right into Los Angeles and the Inland Empire. Months after Haislip's weakened bill passed, according to Suo, meth purity was at an all-time high throughout the West, indicating a glut in product. The spread of large amounts of the Amezcuas' meth into Iowa and several other Midwestern states—thanks in great part to Lori Arnold of Ottumwa and to lesser extent to Jeffrey William Hayes of Oelwein—is one of what is sure to be many unreported side effects of this first, defining breakdown.

Haislip, though, was not done trying. By 1993, he was moving to close the loophole that his earlier bill had created, writing new legislation to limit imports not only of ephedrine powder but of pills, too. The law passed and seemed to produce immediate dividends: DEA, according to Suo, intercepted 170 metric tons of illegal ephedrine pills in eighteen months, reducing by a large chunk the available methamphetamine in the United States. In addition, Haislip took the unprecedented step of approaching the International Narcotics Control Board in Vienna, asking it to help DEA broker a deal with the nine factories in Germany, India, China, and the

Czech Republic that produced the ephedrine. All the companies agreed. Using bills of lading to trace bulk loads of both raw ephedrine powder and finished pills that had been sent from their plants through third-party nations to Mexico, DEA was able to limit the number of countries through which ephedrine would travel to only those nations willing to keep serious records—all without significantly cutting into the profit margins of pharmaceutical companies. In just twelve months, according to Haislip, DEA blocked or seized 200 tons of ephedrine, or one sixth of the world's annual production at that point, all of it earmarked for meth labs. Haislip's sixteen-year-old plan of crippling the drug's production by implementing multinational precursor controls seemed to be bearing fruit: across California, meth purity was down to an average of only 40 percent, an indication that production was slowing to a crawl.

The problem was that Haislip repeated his earlier mistake and left a loophole in the ephedrine legislation that allowed pills containing pseudoephedrine to remain unregulated, this despite the fact that DEA chemists had warned him that meth could be made from pseudoephedrine just as easily as from ephedrine. The loophole, according to Suo, was the direct result of intense lobbying, eight years after he'd derailed Haislip's original anti-precursor bill, by Allan Rexinger, who proudly characterized his involvement to Suo by saying that he simply "pulled the plugs" on DEA. In fact, pointing traffickers to pseudoephedrine was the biggest favor that anyone could have done for the makers of meth; it set the stage for fifteen years (and counting) of arguably the worst period in American narcotic history.

From a drug chemist's standpoint, ephedrine and pseudoephedrine, or pseudo, are identical; good crank can be made from both. But from a drug trafficker's standpoint, pseudo is far superior. Ephedrine, as a licit pharmaceutical, has a strictly limited number of uses: first, as a stimulant used to bring surgery patients out from under anesthesia, and second, as a nasal decongestant. Pseudo, on the other hand, has for three decades been the dominant ingredient in cold medicine, 80 percent of which was (and remains) controlled by American companies. As such, the availability of pseudo in the world, along with its importance as a revenue source, is many orders of magnitude greater than that of ephedrine. And because pseudo is deemed the most reliable precursor for megadrugs like Sudafed, Actifed, and NyQuil, the drug lobby protecting pseudo is many times more powerful than that protecting ephedrine, which had already shown a proven ability to cripple DEA.

By 1996, the Amezcuas were in jail. In their absence, other Mexican drug-trafficking organizations, only too aware of the lucrative potential of meth, had begun to fill the Amezcuas' shoes. Slowly, those loosely defined organizations were melding into what DEA would come to call the five major DTOs, each of which was destined to quickly become many times more powerful than the Amezcuas had ever been. The DTOs were aided by the wider opening of the border and the expanding immigrant presence in the United States engendered by NAFTA. Within the population of illegals streaming across the border to work in meatpacking plants throughout the Great Plains, in the fields of California's Central Valley, and in the orchards and orange groves of the Southeast, there was unlimited potential for a narcotic retail and distribution force. One that, because it was nationwide, mobile, undocumented, and protean, was almost impossible to track by law enforcement. In addition, the DTOs controlled the manufacture of meth by following Amezcua's practice of importing precursors into Mexico, thereby achieving business's holy trinity: dominance of the entire value chain. In one fell swoop, the Mexican drug traffickers directed every aspect of what was now a major international narcotics phenomenon—in the same way that Cargill, Tyson, and ADM were taking control of the food business "from plow to plate," as the marketing slogan went.

Within months of Haislip's newest legislation, the nascent DTOs made the switch to pseudoephedrine combined with red phosphorus. This new Red-P, or Mexican dope, was considered to be more powerful still than the old P2P meth of Lori Arnold's day, especially when the traffickers soaked the powdered Red-P in refrigerated trays of denatured alcohol, a process that turns the drug into the pretty, icelike shards that would come to be known throughout the world as crystal meth. This more powerful form of the drug again increased the DTOs' range and effectiveness, for the simple reason that it was more addictive, allowing them to saturate old markets even as they opened new ones.

The move to pseudo was really the blockbuster moment in the modern history of the meth epidemic. That's because the DTOs were able firmly to tie the fate of their illicit product to perhaps the world's most lucrative legal drug. This, really, is the genius of the meth business. Cocaine and heroin are linked to illegal crops—coca and poppies, respectively. Meth on the other hand is linked in a one-to-one ratio with fighting the common cold. Not only was the phar-maceutical industry likely to fight harder against pseudoephedrine monitoring than it had regarding ephedrine, but the shear bulk of pseudoephedrine being produced also made it difficult to track compared with the relatively small amount of ephedrine being manufactured. Add to that that 50 percent of the world's pseu-doephedrine was (and is) manufactured in China—a nation that has been increasingly unwilling to negotiate with the United States—and Haislip's dream of international cooperation in moni-toring meth's precursors had, after a short and unprecedented vic-tory, fallen completely apart.

Still, Haislip wasn't done. In 1995, he proposed a bill stipulating that any company wishing to sell more than four hundred tablets of pseudoephedrine at a time would have to get a license from DEA and would have to keep records of its sales—hardly, notes Suo, a rigorous law. But it would have at least given the DEA's Office of Diversion Control a place to start in the inevitable task of identifying companies that diverted large amounts of pseudoephedrine to the meth trade. This time, it was not Allan Rexinger who came to the aid of the big drug companies; it was Senator Orrin Hatch, Republican of Utah, then chairman of the Senate Judiciary Committee.

Senator Hatch had a history of aiding the pharmaceutical industry, and had, among other things, supported legislation curbing federal regulation of dietary supplements, namely Methedrine, a form of methamphetamine illegally prescribed by the billions of pills during the 1970s and '80s. What the Hatch camp wanted in 1995 was proof that pseudoephedrine was being used to make meth. DEA had what it thought to be incontrovertible verification: nearly a quarter of all the meth superlabs it had dismantled in the last year had already made the switch from ephedrine to pseudoephedrine. Even in labs that were still using the old method, agents had founds bills of lading for bulk orders of pseudo, a further indication that the market was in the midst of a dynamic shift. Hatch, though, didn't consider this compelling enough, and he tabled the proposal by calling for more investigation.

Haislip was distraught. Despite help from Senator Dianne Feinstein of California, the bill languished with Hatch's committee for over a year—while the DTOs' production of crystal meth went unhampered. It wasn't until the spring of 1996 that Hatch and Haislip finally agreed on language that was acceptable to both the government and the pharmaceutical companies: vendors of pill-form pseudoephedrine would be subject to DEA licensing and bookkeeping unless those pills were sold in the now-ubiquitous clear-plastic containers with aluminum backing. Hatch's logic, it seems, was that the narco-empire built around methamphetamine would crumble in the face of the tamper-proof blister pack.

The connection that Steve Suo doesn't make explicit in the *Oregonian* is that the aggregation of the Mexican drug traffickers during the 1990s into five enormous DTOs mirrors the consolidation of the pharmaceutical industry in that same period. As both types of organizations grew, they increased their market share, their wealth, and their power. Warner-Lambert was subsumed by Burroughs Wellcome, which was ultimately added, along with Pharmacia, to the pharma-titan Pfizer. That's to say, over a short period in the 1990s, fewer companies shared increasing profits. In 2003, Fortune 500 rated the U.S. pharmaceutical business the third most profitable in the nation and valued the industry at $593 billion. (That was the first year since 1995 that the industry had not been rated the number-one most profitable American industry.)

A similar consolidation was occurring in the illegal drug business during the late 1990s. Throughout the 1970s and '80s, the American narcotics market was split between the competing interests of the Colombians, the Mexicans, the Nigerians, the Vietnamese, and the Filipinos, among others. By 2003, 85 percent of all the illegal drugs sold in the United States—whether meth, cocaine, heroin, or marijuana—were controlled by the five DTOs, each of which controls at least one major port of entry with the United States.

The simultaneous growth of these two businesses had remarkable and tragic consequences for the modern meth trade between 1987 and 2003. Had DEA forced more oversight of the rapidly deregulating pharmaceutical industry—one that is hallmarked by its production of cold medicine—the DTOs would never have had access to the drug they needed in order to make meth. Had the DTOs not been able to make meth, it's less likely that they would have so thoroughly monopolized the U.S. drug market.

One might ask if the drug companies should really have been made to monitor their imports simply because cold medicine happens to be made from the same drug as methamphetamine. It's a question that lobbyists like Allan Rexinger made a career of asking. It's also one that needn't ever have been posed. For, beginning over a decade ago, American pharmaceutical companies could have chosen to make cold medicine from something other than pseudoephedrine.

According to Suo, in 1997 a research team at the University of North Texas began testing a new nasal decongestant in dogs and rats. The team was in the employ of Warner-Lambert, which the year before had taken over the manufacture of Sudafed and Actifed from Burroughs Wellcome and added those lines to Warner-Lambert's highly profitable antihistamine, Benadryl. By then, Sudafed's brand recognition was so widespread that the product, like Xerox to both photocopies and the machines that produce them, had become synonymous with the industry of cold remedies. All three nonprescription medicines—Sudafed, Actifed, and Benadryl—relied on pseudoephedrine for their manufacture. Fearful that pseudoephedrine would come under federal control, or worse, that it would be outlawed completely by legislation being pushed by Gene Haislip and DEA, Warner-Lambert had developed a new product based on a biochemical technology called mirror imaging. By Christmas of 1997, according to interviews published in the *Oregonian*, trials on dogs and rats at the University of North Texas showed great promise for the drug.

Mirror imaging is a process whereby a chemical's molecular structure is reversed, moving, for example, electrons from the bottom of a certain ring to the top, and vice versa. Pseudoephedrine, ephedrine, and methamphetamine are already near mirror images of one another. To make meth from ephedrine, it is necessary to remove a single oxygen atom from the outer electron ring. Thus ephedrine and methamphetamine not only look the same under a mass spectrometer, but both dilate the alveoli in the lungs and shrink blood vessels in the nose—hence ephedrine's use as a decongestant—while raising blood pressure and releasing adrenaline. The key difference is that meth, unlike ephedrine, prompts wide-scale releases of the neurotransmitters dopamine and epinephrine.

What the 1997 tests at the University of North Texas showed was that, at least in lab animals, mirror-image pseudoephedrine was equally as effective as regular pseudoephedrine as a decongestant. Unlike regular pseudo, however, the mirror-image version didn't cause any side effects to the central nervous system, such as high blood pressure and a racing heart: the common "buzz" that one associates with cold medicine. Better yet for Warner-Lambert, mirror-image pseudoephedrine could only be synthesized into mirror-image methamphetamine, which, according to the *Oregonian*, had no stimulant effects and could not then be made into regular meth.

Had Warner-Lambert been unable in the end to develop mirror-image pseudo—or to bring it to the market—it had yet another option that would have significantly helped Haislip and DEA. Also in 1997, chemists at Warner-Lambert had begun experimenting with additives that would make it impossible to extract pseudoephedrine from Sudafed. This combination would undermine the basic building block of Nazi cold meth production, which is to pour anhydrous ammonia onto crushed-up cold pills in order to extract the pills' pseudo. On this project, researchers at Warner-Lambert had, according to the *Oregonian*, been working closely with DEA. Moreover, the additives were already FDA-approved. Therefore, any drug containing them would not be considered new and would avoid the costly testing period mandated by the FDA. At the very least, manufacturing cold pills with these additives might have reduced the ever-increasing legions of small-time cooks like Roland Jarvis in states like Iowa, which at the time was seeing small-meth-lab increases of 300 percent a year.

If the cold pills with additives or, particularly, the mirror-image pseudoephedrine had come to market, the effect may well have been enormous. Were the U.S. cold medicine market, the largest in the world, suddenly dependent on any new form of pseudoephedrine, it stands to reason that the nine factories that provide all the planet's pseudo would have begun producing large amounts of the new meth-resistant drug. This in turn would have drastically reduced the amount of meth-ready chemicals available to the DTOs. Either drug could have effectively accomplished what Gene Haislip and DEA had five times been unable to achieve between 1984 and 1996.

Instead, by the time Pfizer bought Warner-Lambert in 2000, all research into a cold-medicine alternative ceased. Why should Pfizer worry about DEA when its predecessor had had such an easy time lobbying Congress? In 2002, meth lab numbers in Iowa topped one thousand for the first time, and were nearing two thousand in Missouri.

CHAPTER 7

THE COP SHOP

Oelwein's difficult and unsure rebirth in 2006 began in the same place in which the town had been born 134 years earlier: in a cornfield. In 1872, Oelwein was founded on land belonging to Gustav Oelwein, a poor Bavarian farmer, as a place for what was then called the Rock Island Railroad to take on water and coal between Chicago and Minneapolis. The center point of town was plotted at the intersection of Charles and Frederick streets, so named for Gustav's two sons. (Oelwein's principal thoroughfare has three names—Charles, Frederick, and Old 150. Around town, all three are often referred to in the aggregate as "Main.") By 1905, the population had soared to 5,134 people, and Charles and Frederick were among the wealthiest men in the Midwest. Driving south on Frederick Street today, you can still see the cabin where the Oelwein brothers were born. Heading farther south after a dogleg at the Country Cottage Café, what is now South Frederick dead-ends at Highway 150. To the left is an open parcel of land; to the right is a campground. Across Highway 150 is what might be the most important of all Oelwein's undeveloped properties—the 250-acre Industrial Park. By the spring of 2006, the IP, as Mayor Larry Murphy calls it, was ready to be shopped to prospective customers and had unceremoniously been denuded of the corn that had grown there. Murphy foresaw the IP as the bright, shining future of his beleaguered town.

Unlike Gustav Oelwein, though, who'd already contracted with the three separate arms of the Rock Island Railroad (the Burlington, the Illinois Central, and the Minnesota), Larry Murphy did not know for whom he was preparing the IP's land, which is bookended on one side by the two baseball diamonds of the grandiosely named Oelwein Sports Complex, and on the other by the once-famed Sportsmen's Lounge. The idea was that, to reference one of Murphy's favorite movies, *Field of Dreams*, if Oelwein cleared the land, somebody would come. The fact was that Oelwein had nothing to lose. And nowhere was this sentiment more clear than in the decrepit presence of the Sportsmen's, whose mixed history underscores both the hope and the danger of a down-and-out place literally dying to grow bigger and stronger. It's said around town that the Mob fronted the Pirillo brothers the money to open the Sportsmen's, thereby adding to an already long and storied connection between the Cosa Nostra and the town that, in the 1950s, became known as Little Chicago.

Mafia history in Oelwein is taken today as a foregone conclusion. It's a piece of the town's cultural tapestry that's at once as obvious as the cornfields and the railroad tracks and as illusory as the fading memories of the rail workers who once rubbed elbows with such American luminaries as Bugsy Malone and Jimmy Hoffa. Whether Little Chicago was really ever a cooling-out place for mobsters who needed a few days away from the heat in the Windy City is arguable, though the stories seem too well known, too oft-repeated, and too finely detailed to be false. These include how, for instance, the homes of three particular Italian families were not only immediately rebuilt but were rebuilt in grander style shortly after the tornado of 1968 nearly wiped Oelwein from the map. According to Clay and Nathan, those families—the Leos, the Pirillos, and the Vanattas—owned the bars and the clubs on Main Street beneath which the gaming dens were located, replete with revolving doors and hidden rooms dating back to Prohibition. The Sportsmen's Lounge was founded by Dominic and Pete Pirillo shortly after they returned from World War II; they'd served only after an Oelwein judge gave them a choice between the army and jail. The Sportsmen's was famed as much for the Pirillos' twenty-four-hour slow-cooked prime rib as for the poker game that reportedly went on for five decades in the back room, which regularly had an audience of what were politely referred to as "dancing girls." Mafiosi, people swear around Oelwein, would circulate between the Pirillos' bar, the Leos' Highway 150 South Club, and the Vanattas' Pink Pussycat, all the while unafraid that any of Oelwein's three cops (one of whom was part-time) would give them up to federal agents sent from Chicago.

The only undeniable truth in all the stories is that the more sinister side of the "good old days" has either been forgotten completely or has come to be shrouded in the golden glow of longing. Today, the Sportsmen's Lounge is little more than a hulking afterthought. In place of the prime rib—which Larry Murphy remembers as being so tender you could cut it with a fork—there is something called a Blooming Onion, which involves a Vidalia that's been crosscut, battered, and deep-fried. And that's only when the Sportsmen's is open, which doesn't seem to be that often. The meaning of the place is palpable, if not quite tangible, and is less about that particular structure than the era in Oelwein's history it evokes. Clay Hallberg laments the loss of the raucous Saturday nights of yore at the Pink Pussycat strip club, after which he claims Mrs. Vanatta would make her girls sit in the front pew down the street at Sacred Heart Catholic Church. Nathan Lein wishes that there was a strip club somewhere—anywhere—closer than Waterloo. Seventy-five-year-old Herman "Gus" Gaddow, a former railman turned farrier, thinks back fondly on the 1950s and 1960s. Back then, says Gus, people had good manners, and three cops were enough to keep crime nonexistent. The implication is that no one stepped out of line for fear of having to answer to the boys from Chicago. It's in this way that the melding of Oelwein's history and present circumstance provides a case study of the complexity of trying to regain a throne that was perhaps epically tarnished in its heyday.

And so it seemed only fitting that the key to Murphy's economic stimulus plan was the Industrial Park, kitty-corner from the Sportsmen's, where in March 2006 a gridded road system already cut the acreage into blocks. Among the weeds sprouting up now that the farmer who once leased those 250 acres was no longer spraying herbicide, a sign read "Oelwein Industrial Park—Come Grow with Us!" Murphy said the city had been courting a call center to lease the space, but it had two competitors: a similar-sized town in Nebraska and a town near Mumbai, India. If the call center prospect fell through, there were bound to be other options, said Murphy. It just wasn't entirely clear what they might be, or when they'd make themselves available. Meanwhile, things in Oelwein were growing more desperate every month. On March 17, 2006, Tyson had closed the doors of what had, a long time ago, been the old Iowa Ham plant, costing the town another hundred jobs. Upon getting the news, Murphy chose to look at things with his characteristic optimism. Rock bottom, he observed, provides a firm foundation. From there, Oelwein could do nothing but push itself up.

Larry Murphy is fifty-five years old. A compactly built five feet eight, he has the sun-bleached blond hair of a road worker; dry, ruddy cheeks; and an open, friendly face dominated by a wide nose and alert, mischievous blue eyes. He keeps his hair short and wears aviator-style Ray-Ban sunglasses. Murphy put himself through school—first at tiny Loras College, in Dubuque, Iowa, and then at Drake University, from which he graduated in 1975 with a degree in journalism—by working the graveyard shift on the kill-floor of a slaughterhouse in Davenport, Iowa. Before the night's work began, he says, he'd head across the street to the bar with the axmen and the sledge-heads who'd worked at the plant for decades. They drank boilermakers—shots of whiskey dropped into pints of beer— to help deal with a job that was by turns brutally boring and just plain brutal.

Murphy is a lifelong Democrat who makes his political home on a tightrope stretched between a staunch support of unions and a solid rejection of abortion. He works at home, in the den of his house, in order to save Oelwein the money it would cost for him to have a proper office. Political activism predicated on liberal fiscal beliefs seems less a calling for Murphy and more a part of his genetic coding. He was in his twenty-fourth straight year of elective office in Iowa, including stints as county supervisor, state senator, and now, mayor. One of his seven surviving siblings, Pat, had just become Speaker of the Iowa House of Representatives after seventeen years in office. Murphy's father worked at the telephone company in Dubuque for thirty years and was a lifelong member of the Communications Workers of America. Murphy's sister Margaret left a convent in order to organize migrant laborers in California and Arizona on behalf of César Chavez. His brother David is a former welder turned nurse, and his brother Bob is a negotiator for the United Food and Commercial Workers. Murphy himself organized his first labor union, at a grocery store in Dubuque, in 1959, when he was fourteen years old.

Murphy said he had little trouble understanding why people with difficult, low-income jobs would do methamphetamine, and why, once they'd lost those jobs or had their wages slashed, they'd turn to making the drug themselves. Murphy knew well the utility of a little pick-me-up before beginning the graveyard shift at a slaughterhouse, even back in the day when you could make a decent wage, get health insurance, buy a car, and put yourself through college doing that kind of work. It angered Murphy that trends in the industries that had once buoyed towns like Oelwein now contributed to the numbers of people digging in the trash behind the Conoco station. To scenes like this, Murphy still reacted with disbelief. Every time he saw a destitute person in his town, it got his dander up. A proud, action-oriented Midwesterner, Murphy just couldn't square what he saw now with the little town he'd moved to in 1977. The rundown homes and the trash piling up on the lawns broke his heart. What bothered him most were the kids who, abandoned by their parents and set adrift in the foster care system, flunked out of Oelwein High. At that point, those same kids were summarily condemned to the Alternative School, which, for an astonishingly bleak 60 percent of the students, was nothing more than a stepping-stone to jail. It killed Murphy, he said, that there was no money to help the kids of addicts or their parents, beyond visits by underpaid and overworked DHS in-home caseworkers. That, or the Northeast Iowa Behavioral Health Clinic, which had but one addiction specialist to minister to the needs of a town of over six thousand people.

If Oelwein could just kick-start itself, said Murphy—if it could just get some decent business into the IP—there'd be time to consider more sides of the equation. Maybe Murphy, given his extensive connections in state government, could create some momentum for Nathan Lein's idea that meth addicts serve five-year probationary periods, during which they have to hold jobs and attend mandatory meetings with a counselor. Maybe, once there was more revenue in town, they could bring in an actual treatment facility, as Clay Hallberg had begged him to do. Some real treatment alternatives might help Oelwein nip drug abuse in the bud, rather than simply treating its symptoms—even as those symptoms gained ineluctable momentum.

For now, though, that was all a pipe dream. There was no excess revenue for anything, never mind treatment. Murphy's task was to raise the town from the ashes. He had to build a foundation of decent economic growth, and he had to do it ASAP. Businesses like the call center could afford to be choosy—every hard-luck town in the United States was courting them. In fact, Murphy believed that most companies were looking for a certain modicum of poverty as a fail-safe against union organizing. If people were desperate, they'd concede this essential ground to the company. Murphy understood the game. As he once put it to me in an e-mail, he was "enough of a student of economic trends in the last two decades to understand [he had to] play on the edges for wage and benefit rates." The trick was to look like something in between a union town and a town that was downright criminally dangerous. Oelwein had to appear complacently impoverished but nonetheless like a nice place to raise a family.

That meant that social order needed to take precedence, even if it involved taking a few un-civil liberties, and Murphy's sympathy regarding meth addicts was trumped by a certain mercilessness. No business was going to invest in a town with a bunch of tweakers riding around cooking dope on their bicycles, blowing up their own homes, and shaking inside their overcoats as they picked through the Dumpster behind the gas station. The trick, if Murphy could succeed in getting a handle on Oelwein's meth problem, would be to lure businesses that wouldn't automatically reinvigorate the meth industry by offering substandard jobs. Oelwein needed work, but it didn't need the kind of work that had inundated Greenville, Illinois: half-time jobs with no benefits at Wal-Mart or Super 8, which injected little revenue into the local economy. Oelwein didn't need any more meatpacking plants, either, which offered high worker-injury rates and minimal compensation. Bad jobs, Murphy knew, had gotten Oelwein in trouble in the first place. Being treated poorly by employers, he said, had sucked the hope out of people's lives. It made meth seem like the only alternative. Nowadays, bad jobs came with the added burden of immigrant workers who couldn't afford their hospital bills and whose children had to be taught English by the already overextended schools. And yet towns across the nation were clamoring for whatever jobs they could get. It was an almost impossible situation in which Murphy found himself.

Compared with this, his past battles as a liberal pro-lifer had been a cakewalk.

During 2004 and 2005, Murphy had done everything possible to run the small-lab meth business out of town as a means of preparing Oelwein to rebuild. This was not just to compete with the towns in India or Nebraska that might lure the likes of the call center. It was to compete with Oelwein's more immediate neighbors. Nathan had told me, along with several other people, that DHS workers in nearby Buchanan County—home of pretty, prosperous little Independence—had for years been recommending that their worst cases move to Fayette County, and particularly to Oelwein, where taxes were low and the rental market was burgeoning. A kind of economic cannibalism had set in following the farm crisis, the ravages of population loss, and the onset of the meth epidemic. Towns, unsure of their own futures, hedged their bets, often to the detriment of their neighbors. According to a local real estate broker, Independence had effectively made Oelwein its ghetto. "Low rent," the broker went on, was synonymous with "meth lab." It's in this way that ridding Oelwein of its small labs became a kind of shoving match between two city-states, with the de facto goal of running the people from Buchanan County out of Fayette.

To this end, Murphy had given wide authority to police chief Jeremy Logan. Logan in turn had instilled a culture of aggressiveness in his men. He'd built a new canine unit around a twelve-thousand-dollar drug-sniffing German shepherd. And he'd put himself in charge of enforcing new ordinances, passed by the city council, ordering the cleanup or destruction of run-down properties—just the kind of grimy, falling-apart rentals, said the real estate agent, that the castoffs from Buchanan County favored.

Every morning, Jeremy Logan leaves his house and drives five blocks to work in a blue Ford Expedition emblazoned with the words

Oelwein Police in the town's green and yellow colors. Logan is of middle height and weight. His short brown hair is in a crew cut, which, along with the sharp features of his face and the acne scars along his cheeks and jawbones, gives him a decidedly military air. It takes only minutes, though, for Logan to reveal a deeply ingrained streak of friendly sarcasm and a sharp appreciation for the irony that surrounds him. According to Clay Hallberg, for decades, if not since the police department's founding, the men saddled with protecting the citizens of Oelwein have been a violent bunch, and disdainful of the rights of the citizens in this notoriously tough railroad town. (When asked to confirm this, Nathan Lein smiled and said, "I wouldn't want to be arrested, put it that way.") Of the ten-man force, Logan is the only one with a college degree. Many of his officers are built more like offensive linemen; almost all of them shave their heads. Knowing this and taking into account once again Logan's physical characteristics—the army crew; the soft middle signaling a distaste for the gym—is to understand that Logan is a reflection of his job, which exists in the delicate middle ground between the brute strength of the department and the slick, erudite bonhomie of Larry Murphy. Sarcasm, says Logan, is more than a coping mechanism. It's like a second language.

Being the chief of police is perhaps the only job in town more visible than being mayor. Murphy, when he's not running Oelwein, has a political consulting business that sends him regularly to Des Moines, a three-hour drive south. Murphy's kids are grown, and he works from home, meaning that he can choose to hole up for a couple of days should things get tough—as they did when he lobbied to make riding a bike on Main Street illegal. Logan cannot. He is constantly on display, whether picking up his three young children from school or heading to the scene of an accident in his truck. When he does things that people don't like—agreeing to arrest students at Oelwein High, for instance—it's not just he who hears about it. It's his wife, too, who has to smile and nod while she waits for her latte at the Morning Perk. Still, says Logan, this is a walk in the park compared with the year before Murphy made him chief of police. That year nearly drove Logan out of the town where he'd lived his whole life.

Details vary, but the consensus around town is that the former police chief, under whom Logan had achieved the rank of sergeant, ran a loose ship. All Logan will say on the record is that there was a certain "laxness around the department," and that he thought it appropriate to one day approach the chief and tell him how unhappy he was with the situation. The chief, according to Logan, thanked him for his input and said he'd think about what to do. Two days later, according to Logan, his wife called him at work to say he was being accused of peeping in the bedroom of a local teenage girl. Further, said Logan's wife, the rumor around town was that the chief was suspending Logan indefinitely without pay. Criminal charges were expected shortly, followed by the high likelihood of a civil suit. This was the first Logan, who was on duty when his wife called, had heard of the charges.

According to the story that Logan tells, the charges filed against him accused Logan of routinely setting up surveillance near the girl's house, only to use binoculars to ogle her in her bedroom. Several times, it was alleged, he sneaked up to the girl's window at night as she undressed and masturbated in the bushes. Logan denies the charges vehemently, and maintains that they were payback for questioning the former chief's authority. It wasn't long before Logan's home life was a shambles. His wife threatened to leave him. Unable to find another job, Logan was going broke. The legal bills alone were ruining him, he says. So he violated the unwritten code that is often referred to as the Blue Wall, by which police officers refuse to publicly discuss departmental conflict. Logan told Larry Murphy everything he knew about the department and its officers, and how he was being set up. Thus began the first few months of Larry

Murphy's first term as mayor, in 2002. By the end of that year, Logan—so recently fearful of jail time—had been made chief of police.

The Logan case still lingers around town these days, much like the specter of the Mob. A lot of people, Mildred Binstock included, think Logan did it. And a lot of other people think he didn't, and that the whole case was another example in a long line of shady insider dealings in town. According to Nathan Lein, former mayor Gene Vine, who sat on the city council until his death in 2008 from cancer, told Larry Murphy to get rid of Logan. Whether guilty or innocent, Logan was too much of a liability, said Vine. The county attorney, Wayne Sauer, said the same thing. The only thing that everyone can agree on, as Nathan put it, is that "making Jeremy Logan the Oelwein chief of police took major nuts." That, and Logan has been hell on meth cooks.

According to Logan, the Oelwein Police Department, which has jurisdiction only within the four-square-mile incorporated area of town, was dismantling two meth labs per month back in 2002, his first year as chief. Labs could be anything from a house with a fairly complex setup in the basement to a guy and his wife single-batching in a Johnny on the Spot behind the dugout at the Sports Complex. No matter where the labs were, though, the Oelwein police were exposed to the toxic waste and the harmful fumes while wearing nothing more than their regular uniforms. As recently as the late 1990s, Logan told me, the police, unsure of what to do, let labs burn. Other times, knowing how much it would cost to clean them up, the police burned the labs themselves.

Anecdotally across the nation, cancer rates among first-responders to meth disasters have been climbing since the 1980s. Bill Ruzzamenti, a former DEA agent and the current director of the Central Valley High Intensity Drug Trafficking Area (HIDTA) in California, likes to tell the story of how he smelled so bad after dismantling superlabs in San Diego during the 1990s that his wife would have to hose him down in the garage and burn his clothes. Still, said Ruzzamenti, the stench of ether and what smelled like cat urine would be so thoroughly soaked into his hands that they'd have to throw their phone away each month: the receiver and keypad stunk too bad to keep using.

As a result, DEA, in conjunction with the Environmental Protection Agency, passed a law in 2003 providing a standardized protocol for anyone given the task of dismantling a meth lab. The training necessary is available only at the Federal Bureau of Investigation headquarters in Quantico, Virginia. Finding money to send someone for training is not easy, says Logan, although the alternative seemed to him far worse: years of lawsuits when one of his men got cancer. Upon becoming chief, Logan immediately demanded that an Oelwein officer be sent for training. By the time that officer had completed the course, in 2003, the town's so-called Beavis and Butt-Head meth problem had increased to an almost incomprehensible order of magnitude: Logan and his officers were being called, on average, to one meth lab every four days. And every lab that got cleaned up cost the town an average of six thousand dollars.

Logan has a long list of disaster and near-disaster stories when it comes to meth. He also has enough cynicism to see the humor in places where, for many people, the joke would be obscured. One story is of an ex-Marine sharpshooter who was also a prolific meth cook and lived alone with his teenage daughter, whom Logan describes as an academic star at Oelwein High School. In 2003, increasingly paranoid that he would get caught making meth, the ex-Marine knocked out all the windows from his home and replaced them with black plastic garbage bags taped to the frames, thereby keeping people from looking in. They also provided a good way to defend the house, for he'd cut holes in the center of the bags from which he planned to shoot whoever came to shut down his lab. Near the windows, he had placed nineteen firearms of various kinds, along with seven thousand rounds of ammunition. What Logan thinks is funniest about the story is not that the ex-Marine aroused his neighbors' suspicions by going outside in his underwear to dance in the street in the middle of the day; or that his daughter was home at the time, studying; or that the man, when the police came, tried to hide by lying still in the concrete gutter of the street, thinking he was camouflaged. What gives Logan a laugh is that the man had the most firepower stacked around the house's highest windows, those in his daughter's room, which provided the best vantage points for shooting. There he had two AR-15 fully automatic assault rifles, a Remington 12-gauge shotgun, and seven hundred rounds of ammunition. "Had he not decided to lay down and hide in the gutter," said Logan, laughing, "there's no question he would have killed every single one of us."

Starting in 2004, Logan, with the blessing of Nathan Lein, demanded that his men pull over cars for what Nathan describes as "every little ticky-tack violation that gets us to the vehicle": a cracked taillight; going five miles per hour over the speed limit; a dirty license plate; or a broken headlight. In addition, Logan schooled his men to use their familiarity with people they questioned to their advantage, and to use history and common knowledge to garner information and to catch people in lies. No more niceties and letting people off for having had a little too much to drink. Search every vehicle. Assume everyone is guilty and put the screws to them. Make them nervous. Logan instigated the practice of leveraging jail time in order to develop confidential informants, in hopes of getting those informants to give up their friends who were batching with them. Never mind if you went to high school with a guy or grew up on the farm next to him. This was like a war.

For some people, these tactics, while legal, defied the very foundations of life in a small town, where people's familiarity with one another means everything. Logan's attitude smacked of the sleight of hand and outright trickery associated with an urban existence. Mildred Binstock called Logan a Nazi. It was Logan who was the criminal, she said. Mildred was not the only one who felt this way. One morning at the Hub City Bakery, I overheard an octogenarian farmer declare to his coffee mates that, in an earlier time, a man like Logan could have easily been made to disappear.

To other people, though, Logan was a godsend. They felt the tweakers deserved no better. Even as the debate raged and people divided over their feelings, Logan's tactics worked. Lab busts fell steadily until, during the last four months of 2005, the Oelwein police didn't dismantle a single meth lab in town. By then, the city council had passed the ordinance calling for the demolition of derelict houses, which in many cases had been turned into meth labs. The town offered sales tax incentives to allow neighbors to purchase run-down homes that didn't—or couldn't be made to— comply with the new codes. That, or the council sold the concept of bulldozing under the more politic auspices of "adding green space." Some people said Murphy and Logan were running people out of town and picking on those who could least afford to fight back. Roland Jarvis accused Murphy of trying to salve Oelwein's economic woes by sacrificing the poor at the time when they were most vulnerable.

I told Nathan of Jarvis's opinion. He was silent before saying that, every day, he saw the pain that the turnaround caused some of the people in his town. His girlfriend, Jamie, labored as a social worker in order "to clean up the pieces." In the end, though, people had to understand that, as Nathan put it, "you have to plow some dirt in order to raise a crop."

By late spring of 2006, Oelwein was entering Phase II of Larry Murphy's town revitalization plan. Murphy liked to say that most men, when they turn fiftysomething, build a new house, buy a new car, or chase after a new woman. He, on the other hand, preferred to spend his time rebuilding a town. And Phase II involved literally tearing down parts of Oelwein in order to start over.

This would not be easy. Even Oelwein's demographics were against it. The median age was forty-one, making it one of the oldest communities in Iowa, and one with a poor employment base. There were lots of other things to spend money on in Oelwein, where 20 percent of the children lived in poverty, and 80 percent of the kindergartners were eligible for free or reduced-price school lunches. The town's median income, according to a 2005 EPA report, was half the state average. As Murphy saw it, Oelwein had an empty dance card. If it didn't doll itself up quick and find a partner, he said, the dance was going to be over.

Phase II would begin by improving a seven-block area of downtown. The plan was to pull up the streets and build new sewers, water mains, and gutters to aid with the withering and destructive effects that an average winter had on Oelwein's century-old streets. In addition, Murphy wanted all new streetlamps. He wanted shrubberies and trees, which he hoped would boost morale around town. He wanted new sidewalks, too; the old ones were buckling and breaking in places. All this, Murphy reckoned, would cost a shade below four million dollars.

Second, Murphy wanted to encourage businesses to relocate to Oelwein by building a new septic system. The old one, installed a hundred years ago and augmented in the 1950s, was already in violation of sanitation codes. It couldn't even keep up with the use of a shrinking population, not to mention the hoped-for industrial and population growth that something like a call center would engender. What the city council wanted was an overflow septic system of twelve million gallons. It would be both environmentally sound and highly cost-efficient, with sewage beds of common reeds that could naturally compost waste initially treated by the old system. That compost could then be used as fertilizer on farmers' fields. Building the new system would cost nine million dollars.

For an entire two-year mayoral term, Murphy and the city council labored to come up with the money. As Murphy said to the council one night, either they push full steam ahead or else they slide inextricably backward. Those were the two choices faced by Oelwein in a global economy. Murphy essentially leveraged the next election on how much he could raise, selling people on the theoretical hope that business would eventually come to Oelwein, if only the improvements were made. He applied for Vision Iowa grants, which netted Oelwein $3.4 million. He and the council members, including former mayor Gene Vine, whom Murphy had unseated, lobbied for real estate tax assessments for the sixty-five commercial business owners in Oelwein. Murphy spent three weeks talking to each owner individually, going again and again to their homes and to their stores, asking them to agree to the passage of an ordinance that would essentially increase taxes with no guarantee of increased profits. He begged the townspeople to pass a referendum calling for a higher sales tax, which passed in late 2005, and a school bond referendum worth $2.5 million. Murphy and the five council members secured another $3.4 million in private donations from some of Oelwein's wealthy old families.

What's remarkable is that Murphy and the city council got the money they needed for the planned improvements and more—enough to build a new library with Internet access. Raising the money was in some ways the easy part. The hard part would come next, when Oelwein would either be buoyed by an economic resurgence or sink further. Once ground was broken for the street revival project in May 2006, it was anyone's guess what would happen. Maybe in twelve months the shops would fill up, the call center deal would go through, and the long-empty Donaldson plant, with 160,000 square feet of prime industrial space behind the roundhouse, would find a new tenant. Maybe Logan would continue to keep the meth users under control and would prevent a new crop of batchers from moving in. Maybe Independence wouldn't use Oelwein as its ghetto. Echoing the Kantian philosophical tradition that pervades that part of the Midwest, and through which Murphy, like Clay Hallberg and Nathan Lein, understands the world, Murphy said that his only wish was to provide the genesis that Oelwein so sorely needed. Oelwein in the spring of 2006 was in the midst, as Kant describes it, of acting to the limits of its knowledge and its environment. From there, only a leap of faith would carry the town forward, no matter what actual advances it made. If Oelwein failed, then a subsequent generation would have to address the same issues. At the very least, said Murphy, Oelwein, just for trying, would regain the very thing that had been missing these many years: its dignity.

CHAPTER 8

WATERLOO

Ever since Nathan had moved back to Iowa in 2001, he'd wrestled with what he referred to as the Girl Problem. The Girl Problem was formed when he'd fallen in love with Jenny, the woman from Indianapolis whom he'd met in law school and who moved with him to Waterloo, Iowa, where he worked as a judge's clerk, she as a public defender. There, they lived together while Nathan's parents smoldered with indignation, for to them, cohabitation before marriage is a sin. Because Nathan's parents would not be damned by God, they would be damned if they spoke to their son. In a roundabout way, it was the Girl Problem that brought Nathan back to Oelwein, putting him in a position to help his hometown rebuild itself. In another way, the Girl Problem represented a once-intractable dilemma, like meth in Oelwein, that seemed suddenly to be solvable.

Nathan might have been mad as hell about his parents' treatment of Jenny, but his anger didn't change the fact that he had been raised to respect their judgment. Add to that the idea that any hope of ever being involved in the central feature of their collected lives—the farm—would vanish if his relationship with his parents disintegrated, and Nathan was caught between two very powerful gravitational forces: anger and honor. He assaulted the problem with all the intellectual tools of his training in philosophy, to no avail; it was like a fortress whose walls would not be breached. He appealed to instinct, and this proved murkier still, for he did not see himself as the marrying type. And yet the idea that he and Jenny might never legalize their love did not minimize the obligation he felt toward the woman who had moved to Iowa to be with him. As the problem churned in his gut, he grew more and more withdrawn, more inward. For a year, it went on like this, with no answer. The war between his instinct and his desire settled into the trenches, where it threatened to destroy his life, not via entropy, but by attrition.

Then, in 2002, Larry Murphy had called and offered Nathan the job of assistant Fayette County prosecutor. He moved to Oelwein, and Jenny stayed behind in Waterloo. He still loved Jenny, he said, and she him. But the one-hour drive between the two towns felt longer all the time. Slowly, wordlessly, Nathan began spending more time at the farm. His parents never talked to him about the fight they'd had, and the familiarity of the silent understanding they'd reached reinforced the pull of his family. The very fact that nothing needed to be said made him feel the weight of his place back in the fold. With Jenny, he said, everything had been about discussion, about argument. When he and Jenny talked, it was like two lawyers debating. Though he understood the emotional liabilities of silence, Nathan found he preferred not talking to arguing. Nathan saw other women, including a DHS caseworker, though he couldn't commit to anyone. He bought a tiny, two-bedroom house on in Oelwein's Ninth Ward. And then, in June of 2005, Nathan's half brother, David, died of heart failure in San Francisco at the age of thirty-eight.

David was Nathan's closest confidant; being raised together in that house on the prairie gave them a shared understanding. It was thanks to David, who'd had the courage to get out of Iowa for good, that Nathan could see that leaving wasn't an ideal solution. And it was thanks to Nathan for having the courage to return home that David still had an advocate for him with his difficult mother and his stepfather, not to mention a connection to the place where he'd grown up. When David died, Nathan was crushed.

Nathan's parents had no money to go to California for a funeral. So it was he who went to get David's cremated remains and bring them back to Iowa. Burying his brother was the hardest thing Nathan Lein ever did. He said a few days afterward that it would be a long time before he was "right again." Three years later, he still, he said, wasn't right.

But David's death had also offered Nathan a solution to the Girl Problem. He didn't ask Jenny to accompany him to the funeral—he asked the DHS caseworker, whose name is Jamie Porter. Why he did so was unclear. Perhaps, he said, David's death put his own life in perspective. After the funeral, Nathan unburdened himself to Jamie of all the secrets he'd kept pent up for twenty-eight years. And so, as the town of Oelwein began rebuilding itself from the ashes of the meth epidemic, so began a new era in Nathan's life, born out of the ashes of his brother's death.

Jamie Porter is a year younger than Nathan. Standing next to him, she looks small, even at five feet seven. She has blond, shoulder-length hair and blue eyes bordered by long, delicate lashes. With her red cheeks and porcelain skin, she has the flushed, healthy look of someone just coming in from the cold. She attended Wartburg College in her nearby hometown of Waverly, Iowa, where she was an All-American softball player as a second baseman. She is still built in a way that suggests a home-run threat: strong, powerful legs and wide shoulders. She knows her way around a pheasant stew and is perfectly at home in a tent pitched somewhere on the Volga River. In the evenings during December's late bow-and-arrow deer-hunting season, Jamie is known to climb into the tiny hayloft above Nathan's woodstove-heated garage and sit next to the swing-door. There she can look down on a small field bordered on one side by an unincorporated spit of timber and on the other by the neighboring houses; Nathan's street defines the point at which Oelwein ends and the country begins. Dressed in heavily insulated camo coveralls, with a book in one hand and a cup of tea in the other, Jamie waits in the ambient heat of the woodstove for the whitetails to pass through the field. Next to her is the bow Nathan bought her for their first Christmas together. To date, she has killed three deer from the garage window—two bucks and a doe.

Jamie has an undergraduate degree in psychology. She has worked since mid-2006 as a contractor for the Iowa Department of Human Services. DHS contractors are assigned cases by the courts; much of their work is in-home visits. On a typical day, Jamie might have three appointments: one with a child who has complained of physical abuse; one with a child whose mother or father is in jail for manufacturing meth; and a third with a recent parolee in the halfway house in West Union. Aside from the Northeast Iowa Behavioral Health Clinic, which has only six employees, there isn't much in the way of other job opportunities for social workers in Oelwein.

Working with DHS, where she's essentially a freelancer, gives Jamie the feeling that she is doing all she can in order to help people who would otherwise not be given any help. The job's frustrations, she says, stem in part from the fact that Jamie sees a lot of the same people over and over again. Trouble often seems to wrap itself around certain families—the Jarvis clan is one—whose members show up constantly in jail, in halfway houses, and on Jamie's list of appointments. The rest of her frustrations Jamie characterizes in stark economic terms. Rural Iowa grows older and smaller each year, while the number of cases Jamie is assigned seems to stay stable. The region's poverty means there are more problem behaviors, and also less money to minister to those behaviors—especially under the kind of long-term treatment that Jamie says would be needed in order to turn a family like the Jarvises around.

What Larry Murphy says is that there is always greater pressure amid a fiscal crisis to cut spending altogether on non-revenue-generating programs like human services. Fayette County and the town of Oelwein are businesses like any other, and presently both of them are losing money. Sociologist Douglas Constance's observation that ours is a psychological rather than a sociological culture is once again apt. Much of what Jamie has to deal with are the ravages of meth; when one is forced to choose between blaming the addict and blaming the system that created the addict, it can be difficult to blame the former. During the late summer of 2005, three of the five members of the Jarvis family—Roland, his mother, and his brother—were in jail on drug-related charges. The brother was in federal prison and would not be paroled for another half decade. Instances like this make Jamie wonder if some people can ever be helped.

The instinct to assume that the Jarvises will not change no matter how much the state intervenes might begin to explain how Jamie was out of work for over a year, between mid-2005 and mid-2006. The theory of one of Jamie's co-workers was that, with money tight all over Iowa and public sympathy at ebb tide regarding drug addicts, it had become more convenient than ever for state government to look at a man like Roland Jarvis and throw in the towel. In that same year, says the co-worker, nine out of ten social workers in northeastern Iowa lost their jobs. As a result, Jamie had taken the only job she could find, as a bartender in a little town called Strawberry Point, twenty miles northeast of Oelwein. During this difficult time, Jamie moved in with Nathan. She could get only a few shifts a week, mostly during the daytime; the woman who worked nights had no intention of handing Jamie the only lucrative shifts in a small-town bar. Money was short, given Nathan's modest state salary, and Jamie spent a lot of time around the tiny house, trying to keep busy. The arguments she had with Nathan were a case study in relationships being tested by hard financial times. For his part, Nathan couldn't understand why Jamie didn't get up and go do more—though exactly what more she should be doing wasn't clear. From her perspective, she'd gone and gotten the work that was available, even if it embarrassed her: she was too well educated to work in a bar, never mind a bar that was forty miles away, round-trip, in a time of rising gas prices. What did he want her to do beyond swallow her pride and work as best she could? She said to Nathan over and over that she was the only one who hated all the time she had on her hands more than he did.

Meantime, Nathan kept up his usual schedule of working at the office during the day and going to the farm at night. His parents loved Jamie; they'd met her at David's funeral and taken an immediate liking to her. Unaware that they were living together, Nathan's father asked him all the time if he'd heard from Jamie or seen her. He wanted to know why Nathan didn't bring her to the farm at night to help, or why Nathan didn't bring her by for Thanksgiving supper or on Christmas eve. It's an interesting question, and one that Jamie herself was anxious to know the answer to. After all, she and Nathan were living together in a small, tight-knit, gossipy community just twelve miles away from Nathan's parents. It couldn't long remain a secret that they were in love and were living in sin. Nathan's parents might be Luddites, but they weren't living on Mars. And if Nathan was so adamant that Jamie do more than work in a bar while she waited for another social worker position, then why didn't he bring her to help at the farm? That was the good, honest kind of work that Nathan could respect, and it would help his family, to boot. What was with all the secretiveness?

Nathan's response was that, no matter how interested and nice his parents seemed now, they would eventually turn on Jamie. That's what they'd done his whole life, he said: lured women in, only to then become so critical that it ended up ruining Nathan's relationship. Because he cared about his relationship with Jamie more than any other, he wouldn't let that happen this time. He'd finally learned his lesson, he said, and had no interest in subjecting Jamie to his parents' scrutiny. And so until something happened—what that something would be Nathan couldn't say—he and Jamie would have to keep their living arrangements a secret from his parents, and Jamie would not accompany him to the farm.

As far as Nathan was concerned, this represented a genuine coup in his love life. He *was* in love, even if he couldn't say it to Jamie. He was living with her and happy with her and his parents were not angrily shunning him. Eventually, the situation began to feel pretty natural to Jamie. Her training in psychology made her more sympathetic than most people might have been to Nathan's plight, and she was genuinely able to help him. That in turn made Jamie feel needed in a time when she had to work in a bar in Strawberry Point. Her family loved Nathan, and they weren't any the wiser when, on holidays, Nathan went alone to his parents', then came home in the afternoon or the evening to have a second Thanksgiving or Christmas meal with Jamie and her parents. For Nathan, it was as good as it was likely to get, for things with the girl were splendid. Problem solved.

Around the time that Nathan's brother died, Clay Hallberg entered a rocky period in his life. One night, Clay played a gig at a bar called the Eagle's Roost, in Hazleton, Iowa, just five miles south of Oelwein. As usual, much of Clay's compensation had come in the form of beer. After a couple of rowdy encores, Clay had sat around with the bar's owner, an old friend from the better times of the 1970s, and drank until closing time, before loading his equipment into his Toyota Highlander and heading home. Knowing he was drunk, Clay skirted town, instead taking South Frederick north, past the Country Cottage Café and Lake Oelwein, before hanging a left on Tenth Street SW. When he got to his street, Q Avenue, he knew he was safe, for Q Avenue is nothing more than a farm road that was graded back when the prairie was divvied up into quarter sections. But after driving a few hundred yards, Clay fell asleep. He missed the right-hand turn into his long gravel driveway, jumped the irrigation ditch, and T-boned the fence. His truck, with significant damage, came to a clattering stop in his cornfield.

The real wake-up call for Clay, though, came at the end of 2005, just a week before the two-year anniversary of his mother's death. Again, he'd been down in Hazleton, playing a gig. And again he had stayed too late and driven home drunk. Only this time, an Oelwein cop pulled him over just north of the Fayette County line. Clay had been smoldering for two years about what he saw as the complicity of the Oelwein police in the death of his elderly mother. She'd been complaining to the Cop Shop for months about an Amishman whose Clydesdale was always wandering onto Highway 150 in the evenings, thanks to a hole in the Amishman's fence. But the police had ignored her pleas. That was the very horse that, startled by her headlights as she drove home late one cold winter night, bolted onto the road. The collision killed her, totaling her car and throwing it into the ditch out of which the horse darted.

Clay was also boiling mad over police treatment of a young meth addict in town, Alan Coffman. Clay and Tammy had all but adopted Alan, who was best friends with their son back when he was a kid because Alan's parents were never around. Now twenty, Alan had landed a good job as a welder in town. He'd started doing meth, and after an arrest had been compelled to become a confidential informant by the Oelwein police. Alan had to wear a wire each night and make the rounds of the Oelwein bars, trying to make deals with people on the police list of most wanted meth manufacturers while the cops listened. Many of these dealers and batchers were Alan's friends, and would kill him, he said, should they find out about the wire. If Alan could help the cops get convictions, the charges against him would be dropped. If not, he'd go to jail. It was all part of Oelwein's new hard-line stance on meth. Clay thought this was a gross infringement of civil rights, though he reserved his disdain for the police rather than aim it at his friends Murphy and Nathan.

So when Clay was pulled over while driving drunk on his way

home from Hazleton, he unleashed a year's worth of frustration at once in the form of an expletive-laced tirade. The incident didn't end well for Clay, who claims that the officer assaulted him verbally and threatened him physically. In retrospect, Clay says, getting pulled over amounted to a kind of breakdown for him, unleashing aggression and animosity that had been building for several years. Things in Oelwein weren't good. Things at the hospital weren't good. His twin brother had moved to Cedar Rapids, his mother was dead, and his kids were grown and out of the house. Insurance rates were making it harder to practice medicine, and the budget cuts the hospital was facing made it harder to get the most basic supplies Clay needed to do his job. In order to make money, he couldn't be the old-fashioned doctor that he'd once been, and that his father had been for fifty years. That's to say, Clay couldn't take his time with people; he had about fifteen minutes to listen to and diagnose each patient. Dr. Clay couldn't solve everyone's problems in fifteen minutes. And it was killing him.

As a result of the drunk-driving incident, Clay was charged and pleaded no contest to operating a vehicle while intoxicated. The county installed an Intoxilock on his truck, which consists of a long tube attached to a breath-analysis machine on the steering column. Clay had to breath into the Intoxilock, registering less than an illegal amount of alcohol on his breath, in order to start his truck. He also had to attend substance-abuse meetings. For these, he chose an Alcoholics Anonymous group in Iowa City, a two-hour drive southwest of Oelwein. It was these meetings, which he went to once a week in the relative anonymity afforded by Iowa's largest city, which had begun to mold Clay into a new man by May of 2006.

I went to Oelwein for two weeks in the spring of 2006 to spend time with Clay, Nathan, Jarvis, and Murphy, and also to Independence to visit Major and his son Buck. Phase II of Oelwein's refurbishment was under way. The streets had been torn up, and the new sewer lines had been marked in the dirt with wooden stakes topped with bright pieces of orange ribbon. The mood around town was expectant, though there was a good deal of crankiness and doubt, if not outright cynicism, concerning the notion that so much money had been spent in order, it was hoped, for Oelwein to lure businesses. After all, when was the next time Oelwein would be able to come up with money for anything, never mind the ten million dollars Murphy and the city council had raised in order to complete the refurbishments? Slowed by excessive spring rains, these improvements were nowhere visible. Indeed, much of Main Street appeared to have been razed by an invading army. The questions were obvious: What if Murphy was wrong? What if he'd gotten people on board, via tax hikes and referendums and bond issuances, only to invest that money poorly? What the hell was Oelwein going to do then?

One night, just as I'd done the year before, I joined Clay at a party. Only this time, it wasn't a Fourth of July shindig at Clay's house; it was a Saturday-night hoedown at a neighbor's farm. A few dozen people had decided to get together in a barn and eat from an enormous table covered in the usual potluck delicacies, which, for all their varying applications, traced their origins to two sources: pig and potato. Soon people would start dancing in the dust and the dirt and the hay chaff, once they finished their smokes and beers. Clay was set to go onstage—this time without Charlie. That in itself was a development, a sign of progress, as though Clay were growing more independent, not just of his twin but also of his old self. For now, he sat at a picnic table drinking Diet Coke. Not surprisingly, he was talking about the reformulation of his life in terms of the Whorfian hypothesis, one of his favorite theories, which he sketched by drawing a number of concentric circles on the back of a paper plate.

The upshot of the exercise was essentially that Clay, unanesthetized by booze, was freer to hear the disparate rhythms of his life's burdens, and that this clarity was helping him to minister to his needs. Clay was finding out who he was. As a side benefit, he was turning into one hell of a musician; he'd stopped standing onstage in his own selfish, alcohol-fumed cloud and had started to learn how to be a part of something bigger than himself.

"I've been reduced to a precognitive state now that my booze-hole no longer needs constant filling," Clay said. "I'm learning all over how to communicate. This Whorfian shit really works, okay?"

As Clay and I sat there talking in the barn, I was reminded of something that had happened almost exactly a year before, when Nathan had seen Jenny for the last time. It, too, was a moment of clarity—a clear line between the beginning of one thing and the end of another. Nathan and I had gone to Waterloo to see the exhumation of a murder victim. Afterward, Nathan had gone briefly to Jenny's place in a three-story apartment complex next to a park on the East Side. The murder involved two identical twin brothers in their late twenties named Tonie and Zonie Barrett, from Waterloo. Zonie had just gotten out of jail for attempted murder; according to the confession that Tonie had given the Oelwein police the previous evening, Zonie had instructed Tonie on how to kill his girlfriend, Marie Ferrell. Marie was a recent arrival in Oelwein and had lived downtown on the second floor of an old building just across the street from the movie house, kitty-corner from Leo's Italian Restaurant. Nathan said that Marie had been encouraged by a DHS caseworker in Waterloo to move to Oelwein, for the reason that so many people—Nathan and Jamie and Murphy among them—resent: lower taxes and a lower cost of living. Apparently, Marie had been cheating on Tonie.

Tonie had let himself into Marie's small apartment on Main Street in Oelwein and bludgeoned her to death. Then, as his twin Zonie had instructed, Tonie rolled Marie's body in a blanket and drove her to Waterloo. There he stashed her beneath one of a long line of disassembled tractor trailers that had been sitting in disuse for a decade or more outside the abandoned Rath meatpacking plant. He'd dug a shallow grave, put the blanket-wrapped body in it, and covered the whole thing with an old wooden shipping pallet. That was four days before the rains started.

By the time Nathan and I got to Waterloo to see Marie's body exhumed, it had been lying there in the 105-degree heat for the better part of a week. It had also rained five inches the night before. According to Tonie's videotaped confession, he'd "missed" his girlfriend, as he put it, and wanted to "check on her," which he did twice, apparently just crawling beneath the eighteen-wheeler and squatting there for an hour or two at a time. On one of those visits, he took advantage of the privacy offered by the line of flatbeds in the dead of a sultry June night and moved his bowels next to the grave. The smell of human feces—compounded by the rain and the heat and the raw, visceral stench of the woman's decomposing corpse—was indeed remarkable. So much so that nine vultures had gathered on the ledge of the packing plant's roof as Buchanan County detectives readied themselves to remove the body by rubbing Vicks vapor rub beneath their noses.

Maybe being that close to a body had solidified something for Nathan. After all, it was only a week since he'd buried his brother and unburdened his heart to Jamie Porter. It's hard to say exactly why Nathan got in his white Diesel Jetta and drove from the disinterring of Marie Ferrell—whose case he would eventually try and win—straight to Jenny's apartment. But that's what he did, and when we arrived, Nathan walked familiarly through the glass security door at the side of the building and up the stuffy back stairs to the second floor. Jenny's door at the end of the hall was open. As it happened, she was moving to another apartment in town now that her roommate had decided to move in with her boyfriend.

Jenny's place smelled like fabric softener, for she'd been washing her clothes. Jenny sat on the floor with her legs tucked under her and her back against the foot of the couch, surrounded by boxes of varying sizes. When Nathan walked in, she rose and they stood a moment, facing each other. The pause was awkward. Then Jenny, who is five three, hugged Nathan—or, rather, disappeared against his nearly seven-foot frame. Neither of them said anything for a while. Then Jenny said, "I'm almost done."

Nathan looked around and nodded. There were small nails in the walls at even intervals where Jenny had hung her photographs; next to them were the roommate's pictures, which had yet to be removed. In the little eat-in kitchen, an open cabinet revealed four shelves, two of them cleared of plates and glasses, and two of them still fully stocked. It was as though the whole place had been cleaved in two, and the half emptiness filled the place with a heavy sadness.

Then Jenny looked high on the wall adjacent to the kitchen entry-way, where a series of three plates had been hung decoratively down the middle of the wall. Two of them were packed; but the third, the highest, was still hanging. Jenny would have needed a stepladder to get it off the wall, though even then she might not have reached it. In a flash, Nathan had noticed her gaze resting there, and without a word, he had unfurled his full height, stretching out his hand and gently lifting the plate from the two small wall-hooks.

Nathan handed the plate to her. He said, "Well then, I guess I'll just get out of your hair while you get the rest of this done." He bent down and kissed her on the cheek. Then he ducked as he went back out the door. Without saying much, he'd said all there was to say. Then he headed home to Oelwein.

CHAPTER 9

THE INLAND EMPIRE, PART TWO

While Lori Arnold was in prison in Alderson, West Virginia, from 1991 to 1999, Cargill consolidated more and more of the meatpacking industry—and the food industry in general, along with Tyson, Archer Daniels Midland (ADM), Swift, and ConAgra. Like the big pharmaceutical companies, the food industry grew both its lobbying power and its political leverage alongside its profits. Meatpacking companies began openly courting immigrant workers from Mexico—many of whom were illegal, had no identification, and whose movements were nearly impossible to monitor. (According to a *New York Times* article from 2001, a government study found that 40 percent of agricultural workers in the United States are here illegally, while Immigration and Naturalization Services estimated that one in four meatpacking workers in the Midwest is illegal.) As meatpacking plants employed illegals at abysmally low wages, the economies of places like Ottumwa suffered still more. Meantime, DEA had a continued lack of success fighting the meth industry, thanks to the powerful pharmaceutical lobby.

With each Mexican drug-trafficking organization controlling one segment of the U.S. and Mexico border, essentially splitting the 2,500 miles into 500-mile increments, these organizations could tap into the expanding immigration routes throughout the United

States—routes blazed by the very illegals who were coming to work in the packing plants. In those illegals, the five major DTOs had a built-in retail and distribution system that, because it is so hard to track, is all but impenetrable by law enforcement. In 2001 a CBS news report on *60 Minutes Wednesday* made the point clear when it found that 80 percent of the workers at a Cargill plant in Schuyler, Nebraska, were Hispanic and 40 percent were there illegally. For thirteen hundred dollars, two CBS correspondents were able to purchase stolen social security cards and birth certificates.

This was the environment in which Lori Arnold says she found herself when she got out of prison in 1999. Her husband, Floyd, was in Leavenworth, where he would soon die of a heart attack. Her son, Josh, was eighteen, had graduated from high school, and was working at a Foot Locker shoe store. In eight years, Ottumwa's Mexican population had grown from zero to the highest per capita in the United States, thanks mostly to the Cargill-Excel plant, where, according to Lori, wages were pegged at five dollars an hour. She was living with her parents, and she took a job at the plant trimming hams. Wearing fifty pounds of protective steel mesh, Lori had ten seconds to sever the cone, or bottom, of a twenty-five-pound hog hind; remove the fat; heave the ham onto a conveyor belt above her head; and resharpen the knife before the next one reached her. The room temperature was maintained at just above freezing, and her feet would freeze inside steel boots. Lori was continually dumping hot water over her boots to try to regain feeling in her toes. Each eight-hour shift, she got two breaks: fifteen minutes in the morning, thirty minutes at lunch. The union had long been dissolved as a condition for keeping the plant open, and she had no insurance, and no access to worker's compensation should she be hurt. To Lori, who'd been just spent seven years in prison, and had once hidden in her car with her newborn son while Floyd shot at them with a .44 Magnum, life had never felt so hard.

It wasn't long after Lori took the job at Cargill-Excel that she also began taking stock of the schism in the local crank market.

After Lori had gone to jail, the good crank stopped coming to Ottumwa from California—and from her superlab. In Lori's absence, many of the blue-collar white addicts had come to rely on the local batchers who made their own Nazi dope, of which there was never enough to go around, as the cooks could only make a few grams or ounces at a time. Meantime, Mexican dealers out of Des Moines, Iowa, and Sioux Falls, South Dakota—in an attempt to take over relatively lawless Ottumwa as a lucrative distribution point—had begun flooding the market with Red-P methamphetamine. Red-P dope, or crystal meth, was made at Mexican-run labs in California's Central Valley and in the state of Michoacán, in west central Mexico, and then driven through ports of entry like Nogales, Arizona, before being distributed throughout the West, the Great Plains, and increasingly, the Southeast.

Back in Lori's drug-empire heyday, in the late 1980s, Mexican-run superlabs had produced anywhere from ten to twenty-five pounds of meth every two days. By 1999, thanks to the failed DEA legislation monitoring red phosphorus and pseudoephedrine, superlabs were capable of producing up to a hundred pounds a day of crystal meth, which is up to 95 percent pure and therefore offers a much cleaner, more powerful high than the P2P crank of Lori's early days. Given its purity, the "tweak" associated with coming down off a crystal binge—the paranoia, the Parkinson's-like shaking, and the schizophrenic hallucinations—was popularly considered to be far easier to handle than it had been with P2P. So, too, did crystal's translucent quartz-like appearance help diminish meth's reputation as a "dirty" drug and, as many people at DEA suppose, make meth attractive to a broader range of people. (Eventually "chrissy" would become the drug of choice among urban gays in New York and Los Angeles.) As Lori said, "Crystal was both a crank addict's and a crank dealer's dream."

Still, it was difficult for the Mexican traffickers to take control of the retail meth market. Many whites in Ottumwa, meth habit or no meth habit, resented Mexicans for working at the packing plant for so little money; it was their fault, it was said, that the wages at Excel—and along with them, the hopes of Ottumwa— had plummeted. Mexicans were framed as interlopers, and mistrust or even outright racism was common. Then there was the language barrier. Mexican dealers had a hard time finding customers, despite the fact they employed a strategy of giving away small amounts of highly pure meth in order to create a base of addicts: the same strategy Lori had used on her first night selling crank back in 1984.

By 1999, according to both Lori and a former Mexican employee, Ottumwa's Excel plant had become a clearinghouse for illegal immigrants. That same year, Cargill-Excel placed newspaper advertisements in the poor, industrial border towns of Juárez and Tijuana offering two free months' rent to workers who could make it to Ottumwa from Mexico. For Cargill and the rest of the packing conglomerates, employing illegals would appear to have been the best of all possible situations, for the simple reason that these employees, lacking legal identification, didn't technically exist, and therefore had no rights. Nor were they apt to argue with the harsh conditions of an industry that continues today to have the highest rate of employee injury in the United States. A failed 2001 federal criminal case brought against a Tyson plant in Shelbyville, Tennessee, made clear that corporations would essentially not be held liable for employing or recruiting illegal immigrants to work in the plants. Despite the fact that two Shelbyville managers were caught on tape by federal investigators asking human traffickers for five hundred undocumented workers over four months, Tyson's defense team successfully maintained that it's too difficult for Tyson employees to determine who's who among legal and illegal employees. The ruling institutionalized the notion that employers of immigrants are not beholden to offering the same rights to workers that other companies must, for the simple reason that they don't know— and don't need to know—who works for them. Alternatively, how can there be any hope of enforcing laws on people who are not who they say they are? According to two former employees of the Cargill-Excel plant in Ottumwa with whom I spoke (both of whom were in the United States illegally), the going rate on stolen social security cards at the plant in 2005 was one thousand dollars, though the most prolific vendor offered the equivalent of a package deal if you wanted more than one.

On the one hand, what Lori saw back in 1999 made her angry. Who did these Mexicans think they were, she thought, taking jobs from Americans and then selling them dope? On the other hand, Lori could plainly see that the middle of the value chain, the most dynamic part of any economy, was totally undefined: it was wide open because the white addicts simply didn't like the Mexican dealers. All that was needed was someone with the guts and the connections to approach the Mexican Mafia, as Lori calls them, and start helping them move all their good, cheap dope.

That someone, though, wouldn't be Lori Kaye Arnold. Lori was on probation for what seemed to her the rest of her life. She had to urinate in a cup every couple of weeks so her parole officer could send the sample to the state lab in Iowa City for drug tests. She had a son to get to know after serving eight years in prison. Lori had amends to make, and Narcotics Anonymous meetings to attend, and a lot of sober time to get under her belt before anyone would start trusting her again. She had new friends to find, too—the people she used to hang around with were either in jail or still using meth, and she knew damn well she couldn't be near them. She would need to work hard if ever she wanted to pay off her back taxes or move out of her parents' home. If she could just get her own apartment, Lori thought, she might finally start making up for lost time—maybe her son could even move in with her. And so for a year and a half, Lori left Cargill-Excel most evenings and worked the night shift at Wendy's, trying not to think about the business that had made her the most famous woman in Ottumwa ten years before.

And then one night, Lori went to a bar. It was a Friday, and Lori, fresh off her shift trimming hams, was damn square sure she deserved a cold one. In fact, she deserved about eight cold ones, which would be one for every year since she'd had the last beer. Then an old friend offered Lori a bit of crystal meth nicely arranged in the middle of a piece of aluminum foil. Lori lit a match, held it beneath the foil to liquefy and then vaporize the dope, and smoked it through a glass tube. For a woman like Lori, who eight years before used to snort an eighth of an ounce of meth a day, smoking one measly foil somehow didn't seem like that big of a deal.

Nor did she think it was anything to worry about when, a few days later, she decided to make a quick fifty bucks selling a small amount of crystal that a friend needed to get rid of in the worst way. Lori had just that week started renting her own apartment; now she wanted, as a means of making things up to her son, to help him pay off some old debts. So Lori quit the night-shift job at Wendy's and began selling small amounts of meth. Then, because she just couldn't pass up such a peach of an opportunity, she approached a Mexican trafficker in Des Moines and made a deal with him. By 2001, two years after she got out of prison, Lori was moving so much Mexican-made crystal from so many different traffickers that she bought a nightclub—just as she'd done back in 1989—to help launder the money.

At the time, Lori was hitting the meth pretty hard herself. She does not, she says, remember sleeping more than one night a week, at most. Because she was still on parole and had to submit to urinary analyses every couple of weeks, she paid the four-year-old daughter of one of her employees five dollars apiece for cups of urine to sneak into her tests. She bought a house and paid her son's debts. She bought another Jaguar. She got reacquainted with an old boyfriend and planned to marry him soon. Then, on October 25, 2001, she sold a quarter pound of meth to an undercover narcotics officer in the Ottumwa Police Department. Shortly thereafter, Lori was arrested, tried, convicted, and once again sentenced, this time to seven and a half years in the medium-security federal work camp for women in Greenville, Illinois.

The woman who founded the Midwest meth trade fifteen years before had now helped usher in the drug's new era by teaming up with the DTOs, which had grown in part out of Lori's original link to the Amezcua brothers. Once again, the tenth-grade dropout from Ottumwa was at the head of a trend sweeping across the nation. By 2001, all the pieces were in place. The newest era of the meth epidemic was in full swing.

The United States is broken into seven regions by the Drug Enforcement Administration. Operations in each region, all of which are secret, are coordinated by a special agent in charge (SAC), whose DEA experiences run the gamut from U.S. street assignments to operational tours of duty in foreign countries. SACs are invaluable in understanding the recent history of narcotics in the United States and in the world—for instance, the broad context in which Lori Arnold's Stockdall Organization fit in with the DTOs. In 2006, the piece of the puzzle that was still missing for me was exactly how the DTOs had become so powerful so quickly. While the discovery of the industrial meth market had been an instrumental part of the process, that alone didn't account for how five mega-organizations had evolved from the business put into place by the Amezcua brothers before their capture in 1996. Ironically, I was told by two former DEA SACs that it was a blow to the Colombian cocaine cartels in Cali and Medellín that provided the final, triumphant piece for the formation of the five Mexican DTOs.

Operation Snowcap was the code name for DEA's 1987 multinational cocaine-control effort in Central and South America. The approach was twofold: to seize large amounts of cocaine and to cripple Colombian distribution routes that passed through Guatemala. By almost any measure, Snowcap—coupled with operations to limit distribution via the so-called Caribbean Corridor feeding the Miami port of entry—was a huge success, resulting in a dramatic decrease in the amount of Colombian cocaine entering the United States. But Snowcap also had an unforeseen consequence: it redirected the distribution of cocaine from the Colombian cartels to what were then small-time Mexican narco-operations.

Back in the 1980s, Guatemala was what was called a "trampoline" state. Planes coming from Colombia laden with cocaine would stop there to refuel before "bouncing" to locations in Texas, Arizona, and California. In that way, Guatemala played the same role the Dominican Republic, Jamaica, and the Bahamas did with marine delivery of cocaine via the Caribbean. As soon as Operation Snowcap limited the Cali and Medellín cartels' two principal options for delivery into the United States, the Colombians approached the Mexican organizations that controlled access to the twenty-five hundred miles of essentially unprotected U.S. border. The Colombian cocaine and heroin empire, which had for years depended on cooperation with Guatemala and the Bahamas, was now dependent on Mexico. According to Tony Loya, the ex-SAC who ran Operation Snowcap from Guatemala City, "What happened was not the lesser of two evils; it was the greater. Our success with Medellín and Cali essentially set the Mexicans up in business, at a time when they were already cash-rich thanks to the budding meth trade in Southern California."

In essence, the Mexican organizations based along the border— in Tijuana, Juárez, Nogales, Nuevo Laredo, and Matamoros, each of which would become the base of operations for the five DTOs— were able to heavily influence the price of cocaine by controlling its entry into the United States. DEA's success with Snowcap essentially awarded the Mexican organizations gate-keeping rights in the most valuable narcotic market on earth, at the same time as those organizations were building a separate but related business in the meth trade. What the Mexican organizations did subsequently, however, was far more significant. For the favor of allowing the Colombians to ship their cocaine into the U.S. marketplace, the DTOs demanded payment not in cash, but in product. For every kilo of cocaine the Mexicans let cross their border, they kept a kilo for themselves.

A senior American official assigned to the U.S. embassy in Mexico City who also worked on Operation Snowcap explained the result this way: "By controlling the entry point for all of the cocaine into the U.S., the Mexicans controlled the price. How else will Colombia get its product to its customers? It depends on the DTOs. By taking payment in cocaine and distributing it themselves, the DTOs created fifty percent market share overnight. If you control the price, along with half the retail and distribution, you basically own the business."

The shift in power from the Colombian cartels to the Mexican traffickers had two major consequences. First, the DTOs grew rich enough to buy larger amounts of precursors to make meth. Second, DEA was unable to adjust to the new paradigm. The Medellín and Cali cartels had relied on Bahamians, Dominicans, and Americans to distribute and sell their cocaine. Those businesses were, according to the embassy official in Mexico City, highly centralized. Their movements were predictable, and decisions came from the top—most famously from Pablo Escobar. In contrast, the DTOs, said the official, are decentralized and protean. They rely only on Mexican nationals to distribute and sell their products, making it harder for DEA to infiltrate the organizations. Because individual distributors have more decision-making power, the movements of the organization as a whole are much less predictable.

Seen in one respect, the DTOs are an expression of the immigrant labor force as it was successfully portrayed by defense lawyers in the 2001 Tyson case—virtually invisible and nearly impossible to follow. Lori Arnold's description of the reality of many illegal immigrants at the Excel plant—using fake identification, moving from town to town and packing plant to packing plant—sounded a lot like meth's trajectory around the country as I tried to trace it back in 1999: there, but never quite visible.

According to a Pew Hispanic Center report in 2005, there are twelve million illegal immigrants in the United States. Eight hundred and fifty thousand more arrive every year, the report found, along with the fact that 25 percent of all agricultural jobs in the United States are done by illegal immigrants. The link between the agricultural business, meatpacking, and illegal immigration would appear to be self-evident. As University of Missouri sociologist William Heffernan says, "Cracking down on illegal immigration would cripple the [food production] system." What also appears to be true is that the DTOs employ a miniscule percentage of the illegal immigrants in this country. Ironically, that fractional number is harder still to police within an ever-expanding multitude of people that is overwhelmingly law-abiding.

But there's also a more subtle connection between meth, immigration, and the food industry. That relationship is driven by the conceit that drugs, like viruses, attack weak hosts. Or, to put it another way, narcotics and poverty—along with the loss of hope and place that Clay Hallberg has described—mutually reinforce one another.

Consider what used to happen in Oelwein, Iowa, before the large-scale consolidation in the 1980s and '90s of almost every niche of the food-production chain. Corn farmers, such as James and Donna Lein, would have bought seed from the local seed company. Once harvested, that corn would go to a grain elevator, also locally owned. It would be shipped to a small feedlot in order to fatten cattle raised in Nebraska, Wyoming, Florida, or Arizona; or perhaps it would go to a dairy in northern Missouri, a chicken farm in Indiana, or a pork outfit in Kansas. The variables were infinite, and the market was dynamic. The barge, truck, or railroad car that carried the grain was likely independently owned, too, as would have been the pigs, cows, and chickens it fed. At each stage, the price would have to be "discovered" as multiple potential customers vied to handle the product, with competition keeping the price "true," or fair, in the context of the marketplace.

Eventually, the Oelwein corn used to feed sows in Topeka might return to Oelwein in the form of hocks to be disassembled, packaged, and shipped at the Iowa Ham plant by people like Roland Jarvis. From there, a whole new market, just as complex and multifaceted, would take over in order to distribute the food and sell it at a retail level, perhaps at the grocery once owned by the Leo family (which today is an IGA). James and Donna Lein would have been the essential building blocks in a vibrant system in which the variables contributed at all stages to what's called the "social capital" of rural communities. In circulatory terms, there was blood flow even in the capillaries.

Beginning with the precedent set in 1987 with the IBP takeover of Hormel in Ottumwa—and the subsequent takeover of Iowa Ham by Gillette—a few companies would come to control most of the U.S. food business. Today, according to sociologists like Heffernan, the dynamism essential to the marketplace has been lost because there is no longer a multifaceted context. Price discovery no longer happens; the value chain is controlled by a limited number of entities. Seed is not sold; it's biogenetically engineered by companies like Monsanto, which entered a joint venture with Cargill in 1998. Cargill—not the farmer—owns the corn that is grown, too, because it's more than likely that the farmer, who would once have chosen a buyer for his crop, has been contracted to sell only to Cargill. In the Illinois and Ohio river valleys, Cargill owns 50 percent of the grain elevators and other storage facilities. Along with Tyson, Swift and Co., and the National Beef Packing Company, Cargill owns 83.5 percent of the beef packing industry. Cargill, Hormel, ConAgra, and Carolina Turkey own 51 percent of turkey production and packing. Cargill is number one in flour milling; number two in ethanol production and in animal feed plants, producing nine million tons a year; and number three in soybean crushing. If you are a corn farmer almost anywhere from Pennsylvania to Iowa, you are likely to work for Cargill in at least one of several ways. Even in places like Fayette County, Iowa, where Cargill's presence is implicit rather than explicit, family farms must grow to an enormous size in order to compete. This squeezes out all but the heartiest souls, like the Leins, who care enough about their way of life to essentially take a vow of poverty.

Douglas Constance characterizes the changes in rural America in terms of Karl Marx's critique of the theory of political economy posited by Adam Smith. With many buyers and many sellers, says Constance, there is perfect competition and no need for government intervention. Smith's "invisible hand of capitalism" works, in theory, to effect the highest amount of economic blood flow at all levels. In reality, says Constance, Marx's countertheory has unfortunately proved more insightful. Strapped with the mandate to "grow or die," businesses are encouraged to cannibalize competition until there are no longer many buyers and many sellers, but rather, many buyers and an increasingly limited number of sellers. The flow of capital is dammed up. Once competition has been annihilated, Constance says, the surviving companies, like Cargill, begin to effect political decisions through their enormous lobbying capabilities. The government no longer governs unimpeded: it does so in tandem with the major companies, just as Marx predicted. It was less than a century ago that Teddy Roosevelt made his reputation by "busting up the trusts" that had become too powerful. Those "trusts," not coincidentally, were in large part the industrial meat-packers of the early twentieth century.

The ability to influence the governmental decision-making process is something the U.S. food and pharmaceutical industries share with the five Mexican DTOs. The two catchphrases repeated by John McCain and Barack Obama in the lead-up to the 2008 presidential election were "earmarks" and "pork barrel spending." Both expressions are, like the "trusts" of Roosevelt's time, meant to imply the depth and unhealthiness of the relationship between the federal government and major corporations, be they in the food, the oil, or the defense industry.

One former DEA official who spent eight years in Mexico told me that the DTOs—because of their wealth, their propensity for violence, and the sheer numbers of people they employ both directly and indirectly—have potentially more lobbying power than any legal business in that nation. Fortunately, the comparison between the traffickers' and the food industry's ability to sway government ends with the ungovernable violence that accompanies attempts by Mexico City to curtail the drug trade. Unfortunately, the same American immigration policy that provides a low-wage workforce ideal for the food industry is what keeps the DTOs in business. That's to say that the DTOs do not directly influence the U.S. government. There is no earmarking for the Arellano Felix Organization (AFO) or the Gulf Cartel. But by directly influencing the Mexican government, the AFO and the Gulf Cartel, along with the other three DTOs, do in fact play a role in U.S. politics, for the interests of the DTOs are aligned with those of the likes of Cargill and ADM. So, too, are the interests of the DTOs served by unrestricted free trade, which has been a common priority of both governments at least since NAFTA. A key component of George W. Bush's first victory, in 2000, was his appeal to Mexican Americans, which he engineered in part by appearing with then-president Vicente Fox of Mexico to appeal for a more open border. In the five trafficking capitals, from Tijuana to Matamoros, there must have been dancing in the streets.

By 2006, it was clear that the Combat Meth Act would require two things in order for it to work. First, the Mexican government would have to stand up to the DTOs by making it more difficult for them to import bulk pseudoephedrine. Second, the U.S. government would have to stand up to Big Ag and Big Pharma by forcing the former to curtail its employment of illegals and the latter to make cold medicine from something other than pseudoephedrine.

What's interesting is that the man who stood at the nexus of the immigration debate raging throughout the U.S. government in 2005 and 2006 is the very congressman who all but single-handedly pushed the Combat Meth Act through: Representative Mark Souder, Republican of Indiana. At the same time Souder was working on the meth legislation, he was an outspoken proponent of President Bush's plan to solve the "border issue" by heavily reinvesting in technological strategies like eye scans and drone planes. In Souder's politics, it's possible to see almost all of the ironies and complexities of the meth epidemic in stark relief.

Back in October 2005, I went to visit Representative Souder in Washington, D.C. Souder's district, which includes Fort Wayne, in northeastern Indiana, is home to several poultry plants run by Tyson. The area is much like that around Ottumwa and Oelwein: overwhelmingly agricultural, with one dominant type of employment and many smaller places that have been struggling economically since the mid-1980s. The Third District is also, as Souder put it, "defined by its meth problem."

At the time, a year before the passage of the Combat Meth Act, Souder was the chairman of the Congressional Subcommittee on Criminal Justice, Drug Policy, and Human Resources as well as a member of the Homeland Security Committee. As such, he had three principal obsessions: meth, immigration, and terrorism. The immigration debate had reached a boiling point within the Republican Party, even as President Bush was putting together a policy that would be put forth in his January 2006 State of the Union address. Bush would recommend the use of technology and National Guard troops—along with fence construction—to secure the largely uninhabited and invisible "line" between Mexico and the United States. Souder, like many representatives of both parties, insisted the president was right: technology would stop illegals from entering the country.

Souder took for granted American's dependence on immigrant labor—that is, the idea that large companies must be able to pay as little as possible in order to remain relevant in a global economy. Souder also worried deeply about immigration as a contentious divide that threatened to tear the Republican Party in half. That day in his office, Souder described the party's growing schism this way: some Republicans saw immigrants as a necessary evil, and others were on what Souder called the "We Don't Want Them Here" side. The former camp included businesses like the meatpacking plants. On the other side, said Souder, were the people who think the illegal Mexicans and other immigrants take jobs from Americans. "Not necessarily racist," said Souder, "but they don't want them around."

It was difficult to get Souder to give his own take on immigration. At one point, he said, "I'm on the side that says that immigrants in this country have always had the crappiest jobs." Later, he told a story about his great-aunt Elly, who come to Indiana from Germany, the point of which was that two people can look at one thing and see great differences. When pressed, though, Souder framed the debate first by blaming U.S. workers for their unwillingness to do hard jobs—a contention for which he offered no evidence—and then by highlighting the power of the large corporations that import foreign labor. As he put it, "Maybe Americans will do these jobs. Or maybe they won't, and we have to have Mexicans and OTMs [other than Mexicans] to do them. Either way, it doesn't matter, because if we make the companies pay higher wages, they'll go offshore. It's as simple as that. And when that happens, we're not only going to lose the six-dollar jobs; we'll lose the twelve-dollar and the quarter-million-dollar jobs, too. That's just reality."

When I suggested the often-repeated potential solution of fining companies that employ illegal immigrants while heavily taxing the products of those that move offshore, Souder ignored my suggestion. He instead recited from memory the statistics that had become the pivot points of 2005's national debate on immigration: three hundred thousand illegal immigrants crossing the Mexican border each year; at least one million undocumented people living in the United States (according to the Pew study, the number is twelve million); rampant identity theft; overburdened hospitals going bankrupt by treating people who can't pay their medical bills. Souder said that he—along with the Republican Party and the support of many Democrats—was advocating heavy new investments in eye scans and computerized fingerprint images to keep track of people who enter the country. He said this would ensure that companies employing guest workers would be better equipped to keep track of their employees. He reiterated the need for infrared sensors and unmanned planes—the very things advocated by Tom Vilsack, then the Democratic governor of Iowa, and Republican senator Jim Talent of Missouri, both of whom I'd also recently interviewed.

My visit in 2005 to the Nogales, Arizona, border crossing underscored the ridiculousness regarding the idea that illegal aliens desperate enough to risk their lives crossing the desert will stop at checkpoints for eye scans. Given the distance between the checkpoints as well as the harshness of the terrain, one could understand how the term *border checkpoint* is oxymoronic. The idea that someone in this environment would go out of his way to be checked—or would be stopped by a fence—is beyond reason. Further, my private conversations with Immigration and Customs Enforcement agents served to reiterate doubts about the usefulness of drone planes sending immigrants' geographic coordinates to ICE agents, when in fact the agency is hopelessly understaffed. Really, though, spending time with illegal immigrants in Iowa is all it took to convince me that, as long as there are jobs, there is no reason to think people will not cross the border to get them. In that way, talk of increased border technology seems only to work in tandem with—and as a cynical addendum to—an utter lack of interest in removing the real impetus to walk across the desert: Cargill-Excel in Ottumwa is always hiring.

Representative Souder, who admits he has never been to Nogales, Arizona, is a strong supporter of DEA and law enforcement. The day we spoke, he said he knew all about the DTOs. He'd been following Steve Suo's stories in the *Oregonian*, which implicitly linked the rise of meth to the rise of the Mexican DTOs. Souder had lauded Suo, and had used his reporting as the foundation of his arguments before Congress that something must be done about meth, even veering wide of party lines by very publicly taking to task President Bush's drug czar, John Walters. Souder was, in that way, as informed and knowledgeable regarding meth as any member of the United States government. If he was unwilling or unable to see the complexities of the issue, I thought, who would be? When our time was up, I asked Souder, as I'd done at the beginning of the interview, if he saw any connection between immigration policy, small-town economies, the meth problem, and Big Agriculture as it existed in a place like Indiana's Third District.

Souder paused a long time before he said, "My constituents tell me we have two problems in northern Indiana: meth and immigration. As far as how they're connected, I don't know. I just deal with what I'm given. Like I say all the time, I'm just a weather vane."

CHAPTER 10

LAS FLORES

Shortly after Christmas 2006, Oelwein's Main Street looked like a movie-set version of its former self. Phase II of Mayor Murphy's revitalization was complete. The street, which had been ripped up six months before, was neatly and freshly paved. The updated, evenly graded sidewalks were cleanly plowed of snow. Saplings had been planted along both sides of the street, and though they were leafless in winter, they nonetheless promised new life in the spring. Above them, the refurbished streetlamps were hung with wreaths and wrapped in red velvety ribbon. No fewer than nine new businesses lined the sidewalks, all of them in long-empty storefronts, including Las Flores, the Mexican restaurant that had opened that fall.

Las Flores is equidistant from the movie theater on the north and the Do Drop Inn on the south, and is right across the street from Von Tuck's Bier Haus. One night I had dinner at Las Flores with Larry Murphy, Nathan Lein, and Clay Hallberg. It had been months since all three men had seen one another; life had gotten busy, and then suddenly the holiday season had descended, replete with its innumerable chores. The 2006 Christmas pageant, which had been the new and improved Oelwein's de facto coming-out party, had gone swimmingly, by all accounts. Now, life was settling once again into the slower rhythms of what promised to be a long, cold Iowa winter. At six P.M. on the night we met for dinner, the large digital thermometer in the Iowa State Bank parking lot said it was seven degrees, with a wind chill of twenty-four below zero.

I came into Las Flores with Nathan. We'd been pheasant hunting all afternoon in the cattail breaks and creek bottoms that bisect the land of a farmer known around town as Puffy. Clay and Murphy were already seated in a booth when we got to the restaurant. Keeping the indoor temperature tolerable, if not quite comfortable, seems to be a point of pride in northern Iowa in the winter. As such, it was cold inside the restaurant—not enough to see your breath, but enough so that Murphy and Clay, like the other dozen or so customers, still wore their parkas, albeit unzipped to the middle of their chests to expose heavy wool sweaters beneath.

Las Flores is the only outward sign, save for occasional sightings in the aisles of the Dollar General or Kmart, of the growing but largely invisible Mexican immigrant population in Oelwein. According to a local RE/MAX broker who specializes in rental properties, there are neighborhoods, particularly in the town's southwest quadrant, where Nathan lives, in which thirty or forty Mexicans share a few small two-bedroom homes. Most work at the John Deere plant over in Waterloo, though until January 2006 a few dozen had been employed by the now-defunct Tyson meatpacking operation in Oelwein. For well over a century, ever since the Pirillos and the Leos opened their bakeries and restaurants, immigrants in Oelwein have used food as an assimilative lever. Indeed, the mélange of immigrant cuisine and American curiosity is a principal socializing force in our culture, a fact that was once as true in San Francisco's Chinatown as it is today in small towns throughout the United States, as the number of Mexican immigrants has grown alongside a taste for tacos and fajitas.

The menu at Las Flores is enormous, as though trying to please both the locals and the Mexican workers. There's a selection of authentic Mexican food, which includes several fish dishes marinated in lime juice and sautéed in homemade sauces; a selection of Tex-Mex, dishes invariably ending with the word *gringo* (as in *taco gringo*); and a selection devoted solely to fajitas. That the fajitas section is at once the largest and the one with the fewest entries, a kind of billboard built into the menu itself, speaks loudly to the fact that, according to Eduardo, he sells a hundred "chicken sizzlers" to every *tilapia al ajillo*.

Murphy and Nathan and Clay all thought the change to Oelwein, at least as measured by food, was great. Overstating the case more than slightly, Murphy slipped into mayor mode while perusing the margarita list and said, "Where else in this county—or even in Iowa—can you get good Mexican, Chinese, and Italian food on the same block?"

Clay was smoking a Marlboro Light as he looked at the menu, tilting his head by degrees, trying to line up his eyes with the reading-glass half of his bifocals. Looking over the frames, he said, "Um, have you heard of Des Moines, Murph? If I'm not mistaken, isn't that in Iowa?"

"Even Greek food," said Murphy, pressing the point. He was referring to Two Brothers Greek Restaurant, a block north, whose windows had neon signs advertising steaks and pizza. Nowhere on the menu was there a trace of tsatsiki, taramosalata, or even a gyro.

"Since when does Salisbury steak count for Greek food?" said Nathan.

Murphy was unfazed, though his smile served as a slight crack of irony in his facade. "To me, it's just incredible the ethnic diversity in our little town."

"Scribe," Nathan said to me, "my guess is that Murph wants you to write that down."

Heritage in Oelwein is not something that is taken for granted; in a farming culture predicated on the changeability of seasons, history is in some ways what there is to hold on to. And yet the Irishman, the German, and the Norwegian sitting in Las Flores that night truly celebrated the influx of Mexicans into their town. It seemed only fitting, therefore, that Las Flores occupies the ground floor of one of the oldest and prettiest buildings in Oelwein. Four stories tall and made of hand-laid stone with a vaulted entryway, it's one of the most interesting as well, the street-level windows tinted nearly black, adding a sleek, modern aesthetic to the place. The restaurant itself is sixteen hundred square feet, enough to accommodate fourteen tables and nine booths. The smoking section seems to expand and contract depending on shifts in the clientele. The walls are fake brick from the baseboard to the sconces, and above that, synthetic adobe painted a pale yellow. Every few feet, and in no apparent pattern, hangs some kind of artisanal memento—a garish poncho, a gigantic sombrero, and a photo of a shoeless peasant strumming his guitar next to a burro. The cheesiness in no way undermines the authenticity. To the contrary, what makes Las Flores enduring—in an old building in an old American town—is in some ways the paradox of its novelty.

That Mexican immigrants stereotypically work hard, I was told, is considered the highest form of praise in Oelwein. That they are brown-skinned and speak a language which sounds fast in a town where people typically take their time formulating their sentences is, just as with the Italians in the early twentieth century, going to take some getting used to. There is respect, to be sure, though with predictable limits. As the real estate broker told me, "Not many landlords are lining up to rent to Mexicans." The feeling that the new arrivals are taking away jobs from the locals is up for debate, and does not seem—by my count, anyway—to be the flash point it is sometimes portrayed as being in newspapers across the country. On the other hand, the fact that the immigrants lack medical insurance, says Clay, is a tremendous strain on the already overtaxed local hospital. And then there is the question of the drugs, particularly meth. According to Jeremy Logan, meth is distributed by a few well-placed Mexican dealers who are increasingly busy ever since the Combat Meth Act went into effect.

Still, no one was on a witch hunt. Far from it. Everyone at the table—the doctor, the mayor, and the prosecutor—accepted that Eduardo, the owner of Las Flores, was probably an illegal immigrant without feeling the need to verify it as fact. As Nathan said, you wouldn't have to look very far into anyone's history around those parts, his own included, to find a similar story told in another time. He instinctively grasped what Representative Souder—for one—did not, which is that if you encourage people to come to your country, you cannot then hold it against them for showing up. As a prosecutor, Nathan simply didn't ask people's status. That way, he wouldn't be party to forcing someone out "through the gate," as he put it, "which is left perpetually and invitingly open."

One of the attractions at Las Flores is the sixty-four-ounce margarita, which is drawn from a clear plastic machine inside of which three large mechanical spatulas stir separate vats of red, green, and yellow slush. Murphy ordered strawberry, no salt, while Nathan asked for regular, extra salt. Meantime, Clay lit another cigarette. In front of him was a twenty-four-ounce Diet Coke in a brown plastic glass with crushed ice. Clay had been sober five months and counting—long enough to have had the Intoxilock removed from his truck.

Clay had also, though, been having trouble at Mercy Hospital, where he was chief of staff. After ordering tortillas and salsa, chimichangas, and fajitas, Murphy and Nathan listened as Clay launched into a critique of the hospital's owner, Wheaton Franciscan Health Care, which drew heavily on the anti-corporate formulations of Noam Chomsky—Clay's latest hero. Clay, a devout but non-church-going Methodist, was a fan of God in his specific way and suspicious of churches generally—especially the Catholic church. According to him, the Wheaton Franciscans, technically a nonprofit order of the church, had "systematized their disrespect for human life to such a degree" that Clay was either going to quit or be fired as chief of staff. What galled him even more than what he deemed the hospital's substandard equipment was the fact that, in order to save money, patients' tests were being sent by computer to doctors in Australia and India to be read and analyzed, with the results e-mailed back.

"I mean, what the fuck?" said Clay. "How 'bout no, okay? How 'bout, I'm not trusting my mammogram to some guy in Mumbai? It's not that they're not talented doctors," he went on, "it's that they're not here. Part of being a doctor is holding your colleagues accountable. If some guy in India misreads my patient's biopsy and the patient dies of cancer, do you think we'll get the guy from India deposed at the civil hearing that takes my license and sues me for all I'm worth?"

Clay stared at Nathan, who stared back impassively. As things around him heated up—Clay's temper, for instance—Nathan's heart rate seemed to slow considerably.

"Not likely," said Clay, finally answering his own question.

"Okay," said Nathan.

Murph said enthusiastically, "I'll be darned."

As Clay saw it, the hospital and insurance systems lacked critical oversight. For example, Wheaton Franciscan had recently begun placing physicians, most from India, in underserved areas across the rural United States. Like the Mexicans who worked in the slaughterhouses, the Indian doctors would work for less money than the American doctors. The trouble was, said Clay, few of the foreign doctors stayed for the entire two-year rotation, for the reason that the Indians' cultural milieu didn't mesh with that of places like Oelwein. These shortened terms, said Clay, drove the quality of care down and destabilized the staff. At Mercy, he continued, three doctors had left early in the past eighteen months, keeping the ER in utter turmoil. What's more, insurance companies used high doctor turnover as a criterion for raising premiums. Practicing medicine in Oelwein felt more and more difficult, said Clay, and morale was low.

Murphy nodded sympathetically. He said, "The insurance companies have a monopoly. What can you do?"

What Clay was considering doing was quitting. He'd been thinking about "freelancing," as he put it, by taking pay-by-the-hour jobs in rural emergency rooms.

"That's the only place I can do any good," said Clay. "I mean, who needs you more than an elderly lady with no insurance who comes to the ER at two P.M. on a Tuesday?"

"What's stopping you?" asked Nathan.

"My dad," said Clay. "This hospital—it's where Dad practiced for half a century. Our family practice *is* our family. This whole town, kind of, is our practice. I don't know how to just walk away from that."

"That's just the rub," said Nathan.

"Yes," agreed Murphy, "it truly is."

Still, the men had a lot to be happy about that December. One of Clay's two daughters had just had her first child out in Sacramento, California, where she lived with her husband. Nathan had won convictions against the twin brothers Tonie and Zonie Barrett—the former for first degree murder, the latter for conspiracy—in the June 2005 killing of Marie Ferrell. And Murph was getting good feedback on the improvements around town. The new library was a smashing success, and its patrons enjoyed two dozen computers with free high-speed Internet connections. Not only had Oelwein High School avoided bankruptcy, but 2006 was the first year in a decade that the student body had grown—by three students. Though the call center talks had stalled, Murphy and the city council had persuaded Northeast Iowa Community College to build a campus at the Industrial Park. The Regional Academy for Math and Science was also planning to move there, just west of the college. Murphy and the city council had decided to build a technology center on the remaining land as a gamble to lure more businesses, especially now that they could offer a new septic system. Finally, the second-largest ethanol plant in Iowa had recently been built seven miles west of town; this had resurrected some traffic on the local rail lines, allowing several Oelwein businesses to save significantly on transportation costs. Thanks to the plant, corn prices had risen by five cents a bushel. The hope was that things would just keep getting better and better.

Perhaps the most encouraging yardstick was that methamphetemine, measured by the number of labs that had been dismantled, had all but ceased to be an issue around Oelwein. In fact, the Cop Shop hadn't had a single call about a lab in nearly six months, dating back almost exactly to the week when ground was broken for the Main Street refurbishments. Things truly felt different around Oelwein since I'd first been there. In June 2005, it was not uncommon to see meth cooks in the headlights of your car late at night, riding around the town's more peripheral neighborhoods single-batching dope in bottles strapped to their mountain bikes. Just a year and a half later, the streets no longer felt unsafe, or like you weren't sure what would happen if you got a flat tire in the wrong place at the wrong time. Houses no longer blew up in the middle of the afternoon, and no one phoned in reports to the police about a strong smell of ether coming from a neighbor's garage. Even the Do Drop Inn felt vaguely (if somewhat lamentably) secure.

In fact, by Christmas 2006, Oelwein had come to represent the hopefulness of thousands of small towns across the nation that had seen major drops in the number of lab busts. The Combat Meth Act had been in place for six months, and national newspapers had largely stopped reporting on the epidemic; the rural United States was no longer portrayed in the sour, Lynchian light in which it had been cast since 2004. These were all reasons to celebrate, indeed, sitting in a booth at Las Flores as the snow began to fall outside the window.

The basic functions of the Combat Meth Act were to limit the amount of cold medicine consumers could buy in the United States; to allow the State Department to withdraw foreign aid from nations that fail to stop the diversion of pseudoephedrine and ephedrine to the illicit market; and to impose quotas on how much pseudoephedrine and ephedrine U.S. pharmaceutical companies could import. In a way, the Combat Meth Act accomplished what Gene Haislip, long since retired from DEA, had considered the most important aspect of the battle against meth for nearly twenty-five years: to monitor the importation and exportation of its precursors.

The quotas imposed by the Combat Meth Act set off a chain reaction of economic events that Haislip could have imagined only in his wildest dreams. Fearful of restrictions on pseudoephedrine, Pfizer, the world's largest cold medicine manufacturer and the maker of Sudafed, began using a chemical called phenylephrine to make 50 percent of its cold products. Phenylephrine, approved in 1976 by the FDA, cannot be made into methamphetamine. The switch caused the nine companies that produce the world's supply of pseudo to decrease their production, thereby reducing the amount of pseudo available for narco-traffickers to turn into meth. According to one of the last meth articles written by Steve Suo for the *Oregonian*, U.S. drug companies cut imports of pseudo by more than two thirds in 2006, to 275 tons from 1,130 tons the year before. The U.S. State Department convinced the Mexican government to halve imports of pseudo and to bar middlemen from the process, causing North America's aggregate imports of meth's principal precursor to drop 75 percent between 2004 and 2006. Suo also reported that, based on DEA statistics, meth's purity had fallen to an average of 51 percent, down from 77 percent the year before. The degradation in quality, Suo wrote, was a sure sign that far less meth was being produced. Mom-and-pop meth production was down not just in Oelwein, but everywhere.

Also in 2006, drug czar John Walters unveiled a plan that would expand drug courts, in which addicts are monitored by judiciary process for eighteen months and allowed to hold a job. (Nathan Lein, a longtime proponent of the drug courts, said their very existence was an admission that the standard procedure with drug addicts—putting them in jail for short periods and giving them little or no counseling—wasn't working and resulted in high recidivism rates.) Walters allocated money for nationwide anti-meth TV ads, the likes of which had shown great promise in a number of states, particularly Montana, where private citizens had funded such campaigns in 2005. Walters also promised high-level trafficking prosecutions by DEA. The very fact that he was trying—now that Congress had taken meth on—to catch up to the trend was itself a reason to feel good about what was happening nationwide. And worldwide: the United Nations Commission on Narcotic Drugs offered to broker deals between countries and pseudo manufacturers; and the International Narcotics Control Board, in Vienna, initiated plans to halt shipments of illicitly gotten precursors beginning in 2007.

All the good news was buoyed further by two reports that seemed to confirm meth's retreat. Every four years, the National Institute of Drug Abuse (NIDA) issues a report called the *National Survey on Drug Use and Health*. NIDA, an arm of the National Institutes of Health within the U.S. Department of Health and Human Services, is the de facto research arm of the Office of National Drug Control Policy (ONDCP), which is headed by the president's drug czar. As such, NIDA'S recommendations, which seem implicit in its research, guide legislative drug policy perhaps more than those of any other U.S. government institute. What NIDA reported just before the Oelwein Christmas pageant of 2006 was that meth use throughout the United States remained stable or dropped between 2002 and 2006. The nation's second-most-influential narcotics survey, Monitoring the Future, funded by the University of Michigan, reported something even more encouraging: meth use among high school students between 1999 and 2005 had sharply declined. Pointing to these studies as real-time indicators of the effects of changes in government policy, John Walters told the *Oregonian* in an August 2006 interview that the United States was "winning" the war on meth.

More surprisingly, Walters hinted something heretofore unimaginable: that the meth epidemic was over. "Was meth an epidemic in some parts of the country?" he said in his interview with Suo. "Yes . . . Is it the worst drug problem? Is it an epidemic everywhere? The answer is no."

But the questions that had to be asked that December night at Las Flores was why, if everything seemed so much better, had the number of meth cases that Nathan Lein was getting not declined? And why hadn't the number of meth-related complaints of Clay Hallberg's patients dwindled? The answers to those questions require an understanding of what exactly a drug epidemic is and how a report like the *National Survey on Drug Use and Health* gets made. But the most important aspect to understanding why Oelwein's meth problem seemed to have become "invisible," as Clay put it that night, was a recent shift in the narcotics market. As had been happening for twenty years, since the days of Gene Haislip, meth had not gone away or been eradicated. It had reassorted its genome.

Ask any drug epidemiologist the question "What is a drug epidemic?" and the answer will likely be, "I don't know." It may seem counterintuitive that a drug epidemiologist can't define the very concept for which the profession is named, but consider the difficulties of the related field of viral epidemiology. Say you ask your doctor these elemental questions: What is the flu? Where exactly does it come from? What exactly does it do? How does it do that? What can I do to confront it? What will be the outcome of that confrontation? The best your doctor can do is take the little that is known beyond a doubt about the flu; combine it with common sense, anecdote, and theory; and recommend a solution without any guarantee of success. The epidemiology of a drug is no different: it is unquantifiable in absolute terms.

Consider again the opinion of Dr. Stanley Koob, the neuropharmacologist at the Scripps Research Institute and a highly regarded drug addiction specialist. When he says that "meth is way up there with the worst drugs on earth," only part of that opinion can be proven. It can be scientifically measured that smoking a drug—as opposed to eating, snorting, injecting, or taking it anally—is the fastest delivery system to the brain. It is further supposed, though not proven, that the speed of delivery affects a drug's addictiveness. So, because meth can be smoked, it (like nicotine, but unlike alcohol) has entrée into the category of "most addictive." From there, Koob's statement veers into the realm of instinct mixed with common sense. The bulk of Koob's evidence regarding meth's "unique dangers" stems from his theory of the drug's social identity. In Koob's opinion, much of meth's danger lies in the drug's long history of usefulness to the sociocultural and socioeconomic concepts American society holds dear, many of which stem from the pursuit of wealth through hard work.

Now take national drug studies. Though the term implies technical exactitude, it is simply impossible to know how many people become addicted to any drug, methamphetamine included. It's impossible to know how many people are using a drug—addictively, regularly, episodically, or singularly. Furthermore, there is no set number or percentage of drug users that signals a drug "epidemic." It's this very lack of a quantifiable foundation that prevents any honest drug epidemiologist from being able to define a drug epidemic. Saying there is a meth epidemic is just as unverifiable as saying the meth epidemic is over. In this odd way, the newspaper columnists who, in reaction to Suo's reporting and the work at *Newsweek* and *Frontline*, had begun asserting in mid-2006 that there had never been a meth epidemic—that it was an invention, a myth—were partly correct.

The point is that we invariably come back to testing as a means of understanding drug use, even though assuming these tests lead to truth puts one on shaky ground. You simply can't prove something to be true or false if the means of confirmation are easily questioned. Consider how the *National Survey on Drug Use and Health* concludes every four years how many meth addicts there are in the United States. First, surveyors ask employers to give their employees a questionnaire on drug use. The survey asks employees whether they have done amphetamines (not specifically methamphetamines) in their lifetime, in the last year, and/or in the last six months. First, it seems unlikely that drug addicts will take this completely optional test; will answer truthfully if they do take it; and will even be at work in the first place—as opposed to home cooking meth. Further, since methamphetamine is just one of a broad class of stimulants in the amphetamine family, an answer of yes to a question about using one amphetamine can't be taken as an answer of yes to using another. And yet, for the study's purposes, anyone who says they've done any kind of amphetamine in the last six months is considered "addicted to amphetamines," and—in a way that is impossible to understand—a certain percentage of these responders is deemed addicted to crank. It's in accordance with this system that NIDA proclaimed—and John Walters celebrated—meth's demise in 2006.

But a drug's availability, according to Dr. Koob, is the key to its power. And whether or not the Oelwein police were busting labs, clearly there was still a lot of meth around town, since Nathan hadn't noticed a drop in his cases. Lab busts removed the drug's most obvious elements: the smelly homes, the fires, the sickened children. Removing labs, it turns out, isn't the same as removing the drug, or the problems for which that drug serves as some sort of answer. Where meth was coming from now; how it was getting to Oelwein; and why the Combat Meth Act hadn't stopped it—these were the new questions that had to be answered.

Sitting in Las Flores that night, I was reminded of a talk I'd had a year before with Phil Price, who had since retired as the special agent in charge of the Georgia Bureau of Investigation. At the time, Price was simultaneously investigating eleven execution-style murders of Mexican nationals, all committed in empty mansions in quiet Atlanta suburbs, all meth-related. In discussing the murders, Price had foreseen the Combat Meth Act's ultimate weakness, long before it was passed.

"Look," he'd said in his thick North Georgia accent, "I'll get in trouble for saying this, but the Combat Meth Act will only take the little bit of the meth business away from the dipshits with the Bunsen burners and the Budweiser chemistry set and give it to the only people who've known all along what to do with it: the Mexican DTOs.

"For a while," he went on, "people will applaud the government, and things will get remarkably better. But mark my words: it'll get worse from there. Because none of this is about a drug. It's about a system of government and an economy. The Combat Meth Act will only serve to highlight our immigration policy, and what a holy crock of shit it is. But no one will see that. All they'll see is a short-term victory against meth. By the time the crank comes flowing back," concluded Price, "the government and the media will be long gone, and we'll be stuck worse than ever."

PART 3

2007

CHAPTER 11

ALGONA

During the three and a half years I went back and forth to Oel-wein, I told myself that I was searching for the meaning of meth in small-town America. That is certainly true. But I think I was also looking for the meaning of a small town in my own life and in my family's history. And what, if anything, had changed so profoundly that when I would tell my father what I was seeing in Iowa, he was made to wonder if he would even recognize the place whence he comes.

Rural America remains the cradle of our national creation myth. But it has become something else, too—something more sinister and difficult to define. Whether meth changed our perception of the American small town or simply brought to light the fact that things in small-town America are much changed is in some ways irrele-vant. In my telling, meth has always been less an agent of change and more of a symptom of it. The end of a way of life is the story; the drug is what signaled to the rest of the nation that the end had come.

The truth is that, in the weeks I drove around Illinois, Kentucky, Alabama, Georgia, and Missouri, any town in which I stopped for a day or two would have satisfied the criteria as a setting for a book about meth—meth was a part of life in all of them. It's fair to say I focused on Iowa beginning in 2005 not because of the record number of labs in the state or because I was quick to develop a relationship with Clay and Nathan, but because Iowa is the place where my father's branch of the Reding family had lived since the mid-nineteenth century. As it turns out, my father's life fits into the conundrum of methamphetamine's link with the rural United States, not just because he comes from Algona, but because he worked forty-two years in the industry that I have come to see as a force behind the difficulties faced by places like Algona and Oelwein: Big Agriculture.

My great-grandfather Nicholas Reding came to Algona from the Franco-Prussian principate of Luxembourg in 1868. With him he brought his second wife (the first had died) and the fifteen children from his two marriages. After learning that the local schoolteacher would be educating his children in English, my great-grandfather became a teacher himself, founding his own school specifically so he could educate his children in German.

Louis Reding was the youngest of Nicholas's children, born in 1899. Louis spent his whole life in Algona, where he worked as a tractor partsman at the International Harvester shop. He died in 1979. Alice, my grandmother, was born in Lu Verne (pronounced "Laverne"), Iowa, twelve miles south of Algona. Alice was one of four children of a woman who must, by the fertility standards of the Reding clan, have seemed just a hair shy of barren. Alice was five feet tall; she worked as a teller at the Iowa State Bank for fifty-one years. She died in 1989, at the age of eighty-eight.

My father, Nicholas Reding, named for his grandfather, was born the youngest of four in November 1934; his sister Roz is the oldest, followed by twins, Jan and Joe. My father was small as a boy, with blond hair and dark brown eyes. During the Depression and war, it was often up to my father and his brother to kill pheasants, pigeons, or squirrels for supper. In the winter, they market-hunted jackrabbits, by which it is meant that they went out into the fields at night in the backs of trucks and killed the animals as they were temporarily paralyzed by the headlights. My father and uncle filled keg-barrels with the rabbits they shot, for this is how canneries in Sioux City and restaurants in Fort Dodge came about their meat during the rationed years in World War II. In the summer, they fished for perch and catfish in the East Branch of the Des Moines River— which flows 320 miles away, past the cabin in Ottumwa where Lori Arnold once lived.

My father went to Iowa State in Ames in 1952. He was seventeen. By then, his hair was well on its way to turning black; he was small, like his mother, and weighed just 110 pounds his freshman year. If it weren't for his three scholarships, he would never have been educated beyond high school. A baseball scholarship paid for his room, a chemical engineering scholarship paid for his board, and a Reserve Officer Training Corps (ROTC) scholarship paid for his books. There is a photo of him as a freshman, standing a head shorter than most other members of Iowa State's varsity baseball squad. That photo has always had a complicated effect on me. On the one hand, I feel a tremendous amount of pride that my father ever made it out of Algona, Iowa. On the other hand, I feel a comic sense of disbelief, for my father, standing on the end of a line of tall, strapping young men, looks impossibly young and small. It's surprising that he even made it through the brutal winters, never mind that he was able to swing a thirty-four-inch wooden bat at eighty-five-mile-per-hour fastballs without being blown over. What's more incredible still is the remarkable life he would go on to lead.

By his sophomore year, my father had grown to five feet nine and had gained thirty pounds—hardly the stuff of legend, but enough to be starting in center field for what at the time was a powerhouse of a collegiate baseball team. Iowa State was the runner-up that year in the College World Series—my father was the MVP. He set a National Collegiate Athletic Association record for the number of stolen bases in a game—six, including stealing home—that stood for many years.

At the end of the season, at the age of nineteen, he was drafted in the first round by the New York Yankees and the St. Louis Cardinals at a time when the rivalry between them was one of the most enduring and storied rivalries in sports.

My father, though, didn't believe playing sports was a reliable road out of poverty. Despite being drafted again by the Yankees following his junior year, he stayed at Iowa State to finish his chemical engineering degree. In 1955, he was offered a job with Monsanto, in St. Louis, Missouri. He arrived in the city with two shirts, two pairs of shoes, two ties, and one suit, and he moved into a boardinghouse. He met my mother at Monsanto, where she was working as a secretary. My maternal grandmother, Mildred Viola Nicholson, two decades removed from her years in Ebo, Missouri, took an immediate liking to my father. She saw a kindred spirit in a boy from the country who'd come to a grand and important American city in hopes of making his way. Mildred's first husband had left her, my mother, and my aunt, and Mildred had worked all her adult life as a single mother, first as a maid and then as a cook in a downtown cafeteria called Miss Hulling's. When my father became ill with influenza in 1956, my mother and grandmother took the bus every morning and every evening for three weeks to care for him at the boardinghouse until he was well again. My parents were married in 1958.

My father spent forty-two years working for Monsanto, retiring as vice chairman in 1998. In the decades he was there, Monsanto became an agricultural powerhouse, acquiring seed companies, patenting herbicides, and most markedly, pioneering the field of biogenetic crop engineering. So powerful was Monsanto that in 1996 it formed a joint venture with Cargill. It's in this way that the rise of Big Agriculture out of the small towns of the rural United States mirrors the story of my family and of my father's life. It's in this way, too, that the complexity and the overriding humanity of things becomes evident. Monsanto, in one telling, played a part in destroying the way of life in the small-town United States—the very place from which my father and my grandmother come. In another telling, Monsanto's industrialization of farming wasn't ruinous, but rather it revolutionized a remarkably difficult vocation through technology and science—in other words, Monsanto, along with Cargill and ADM and ConAgra, streamlined and modernized the raising of crops.

Initially, during the 1970s, the increased efficiency of American farmers proved a boon for small-town America. OPEC, rich with a surplus of so-called petro-dollars, was funding industry throughout the world—primarily in China, the Soviet Union, and Latin America—in the way the International Monetary Fund and the World Bank do today. Anxious to modernize their industry and infrastructure, these nations spent less money on food production, prompting U.S. farmers to—at the now-infamous behest of the secretary of agriculture—"feed the world" and "plant hedgerow to hedgerow." U.S. food production was pushed to record highs. By the close of the decade, though, the gas crisis had abated, OPEC was lending less money, and U.S. farmers who'd overextended themselves in order to grow grain to sell to Argentina or the Soviet Union had to foreclose on their land. The farm crisis of the early 1980s was born, and followed by a massive rural out-migration.

Rural sociologist William Heffernan has focused much of his work on the period from 1970 to 2000. Heffernan refers often in his work to the effect "the formation of the three major food chain clusters" had on American farming—and as a direct result, on rural America. One of the clusters that Heffernan identifies is Cargill-Monsanto. According to Heffernan, by 1996, two years before my father retired, Cargill—with the help of Monsanto and its stable of seed companies—controlled massive shares of almost every food-related market. It was among the top five beef and pork packers, beef-feedlot owners, turkey-farming operators, and ethanol producers. It was number one in animal-feed plants and grain elevators, and number two in flour milling, dry corn milling, wet corn milling, and soybean crushing. Cargill was also moving aggressively into the transportation business, namely river barges, railroad cars, and trucking companies, as well as acquiring grocery store chains. As a result of this centralization, says Heffernan, "most rural economic development specialists discount agriculture as a contributor to rural development." That's to say that, whether you're talking about Oelwein, Algona, or Ottumwa, Iowa, between 1980 and 1995, the lifeblood of those towns ceased to provide the same life that it had offered for over a hundred years—roughly since my great-grandfather arrived from Luxembourg.

Heffernan's analysis shows an astonishing sea change in a very short period. Just a quarter century ago, as Heffernan points out, "when family businesses were the predominant system in rural communities, researchers talked of multiplier effects of three or four." Meaning that each dollar generated by James and Donna Lein in Oelwein would exchange hands three or four times before leaving the community. Today, notes Heffernan, that number is down to one. Historically, farming communities were models of rural economic health, and mining communities like those in the Appalachians were an indicator of a crippling system of centralization. Today, farming and mining communities are indistinguishable, says Heffernan. Oelwein and Algona are statistically related to Elk Garden, West Virginia.

Much of the trip from Oelwein to Algona is on Highway 18. In an era of interstates, Highway 18 is a throwback, and little more than a well-kept country road running seven hundred miles from Mount Horeb, Wisconsin, across the Iowa and South Dakota prairie, all the way to Mule Creek Junction, Wyoming. Along its path, Highway 18 passes through twice as many Indian reservations (two) and national grasslands (also two) than towns of more than ten thousand people. In fact, west of Mason City, Iowa, it's generally twenty or thirty miles between gas stations, and an hour or more between towns that have their own high schools. It is truly one of the more nostalgic stretches of American road—one that seems frozen in time, though of course that's simply no longer true.

Ostensibly, I went to Algona to find my father's house and the makeshift baseball field where he and my uncle Joe used to play. Because the high school didn't have a ball field of its own, the Algona Bulldogs during the 1940s and '50s played all their games away. My dad said the provisional diamond was somewhere east along the railroad tracks, near where the pheasants used to sun themselves on cold days while picking at waste grain dropped from the freight cars headed to Chicago via Oelwein and Waterloo.

Riding around town with my father giving me directions by cell phone, I went to his childhood home, a three-bedroom wooden-shingled farmhouse built in 1919. He wanted to know every detail: the color of the wood and the roof; if there was still a porch; and if the mulberry tree was still in the front yard. After I gave him my report, it became apparent that the only thing that had been changed in nearly sixty years was the color of the small front porch—from green to gray. State Street, Algona's main drag, was also much as he remembered it, with the exception that the Iowa State Bank is no longer in existence, though the redbrick building that housed it still stands. Unchanged as well would appear to be the Reding habit for propagation stretching back to the first Nicholas Reding. According to the waitress who brought me a french-dip sandwich and cup of coffee at the town's café, her sister is married to one Reding and her cousin to another. "By spring thaw," she said, "you won't be able to turn over a single rock in this town without a Reding crawling out from under it."

After lunch, I called my dad again to help me find the old ball field. It was a fool's errand, for the prairie in every direction was under eight inches of snow, beneath which was a hard layer of ice. Still, I wasn't coming back to Algona any time soon, and I wanted to be near the place my father had once cherished, where he'd learned to hit and field and steal bases with Uncle Joe.

As I walked east along the tracks as they bordered Highway 18, it was clear and blue and frigid in the wake of the storms that had passed over the region in succession for a week. I could see, it seemed, forever, and forever seemed to be a sheet of white, frozen snow blown into topographical drifts. I have always found mountains to be beautiful. But I'm not moved by them in any way. The same is true of the ocean, and of beaches and large rivers. The Hudson and the Mississippi valleys are marvels of natural grandeur; they are magnificent, but not humbling. Prairie is humbling. The isolation—false as it may be, what with farmhouses every few hundred or few thousand acres—is at once exhilarating and terrifying. The sight of it that day, of all that open country, was gnawing at my stomach. The very idea that tiny Plains towns from Iowa to Montana are given names like Harvey and Melvin and Maurice, Dana and Bode and Britt—first names, familiar names—underscores the utter humanity of an attempt to exist in a place never meant to sustain our ill-fated and ultimately impossible desire for permanence. And yet here we still are, living and dying in Algona and in Cylinder, hunkered down in Fort Charles and Fort Dodge, having a french dip and walking down the tracks, looking forward to standing around the woodstove at night with Nathan Lein and his girlfriend Jamie Porter. The argument of some sociologists, namely that we should pick up and leave, call a spade a spade, clear out the towns of the Plains rather than artificially support them on farm subsidies, put the land into a national park and reintroduce the buffalo: this argument makes a certain kind of sense. Nathan Lein's parents wonder every night how they'll make it through another winter. And yet where else would we go? What, really, would we have ourselves do, if not this?

Even as I'm capable of criticizing my father's legacy, I'm incapable of feeling anything less than terrific pride in his accomplishments. His story defies sociology. It is an example of individual greatness of its own stubborn accord: the essential component of the American dream. Nonetheless, there are consequences. The best of intentions sometimes don't turn out like they're supposed to—just as methamphetamine, the miracle pharmaceutical of the 1930s, has today become a nightmare. Somewhere along the way companies grew to have no respect for the people whose lives their products perhaps intended to improve, refusing to provide workers with a decent wage or health insurance. Despite this, people fight to endure, just as they always have. And as they fight, some percentage of them will look to a drug that falsely promises help in that cause.

Walking along the tracks that day, I found it hard to believe that, just as my father had predicted, three rooster pheasants picked at waste grain in the frigid midday sun. Somewhere to the east, buried in the snow, was the ball field.

CHAPTER 12

EL PASO

By the beginning of 2007, the Combat Meth Act had been in effect for six months. As Phil Price, now a former special agent in charge of the Georgia Bureau of Investigation, had predicted two years earlier, the laws making it harder to buy cold medicine had indeed reduced the number of Beavis and Butt-Head labs across the United States. The numbers of addicts, however, hadn't changed. This meant that those who had relied on home-cooked dope—15 to 25 percent of users, according to 2005 DEA estimates—were now doing business with the DTOs, meaning that 95 to 100 percent of the meth consumed in the United States came from Mexican-run labs. The DTOs had quickly adjusted to the difficulty of importing large amounts of pseudoephedrine into Mexico by purchasing it from a growing number of middlemen—mostly in China but also, increasingly, in Africa. This, in turn, resulted in increased production of the drug.

Also as Phil Price had predicted, the U.S. media by mid-2007 had completed an autopsy of the drug epidemic that, according to drug czar John Walters, was now all but over. Excluding the work of Steve Suo and a few others, the media's rabid coverage of meth in 2005 and 2006 had treated the drug as a small-lab phenomena. Now that small-lab numbers had dwindled from Arizona to New Jersey, state politicians, magazines, newspapers, and evening newscasters took this reduction as the sole indicator that the epidemic was under control or cured. Seen another way, meth just wasn't as interesting to report on once it could no longer be cast as a fundamentally American morality play whose acts were once carried out ad nauseam in trailers, kitchen sinks, and bathtubs across the nation. In many cases, the postmortem became a witch hunt, as bloggers and newspaper columnists called into question whether the meth epidemic had ever existed in the first place. Nowhere was this suspicion more candidly stated than in a March 2006 article in Portland's *Willamette Week*, the rival paper of the *Oregonian*. Titled "Meth Madness: How The Oregonian Manufactured an Epidemic, Politicians Bought It and You're Paying," the article functioned as a compendium of questions regarding Steve Suo's and the *Oregonian*'s integrity. Furthermore, *Willamette Week* accused state and federal officials of using the meth story for their political gain.

The gist of the criticism, as summed up by the *Willamette Week* article, was that meth, as a media phenomenon, had been propped up by numbers and statistics that seemed questionable, if not specious. For instance, *Willamette Week* took to task a report entitled *Multnomah County Meth Tax* written by an economic research firm called ECONorthwest. The report, oft-cited by Suo and both Oregon and national politicians—and ultimately imitated by other firms in other communities like Benton County, Arkansas—claimed that every household in Multnomah County paid the equivalent of $350 annually to compensate for the community problems caused by meth. That's to say that every household in the densely populated area, which includes Portland, was paying the rough equivalent of their yearly state taxes to cover the rising costs of increased foster care, overtime staffing of police precincts, property damage, and missed work time attributable to a surge in meth use.

The *Willamette Week* article contended that the statistics on which the report was based were a mix of fact and anecdote, and therefore the study itself was preposterous. For instance, a Portland police chief couldn't explain how he'd come up with the statistic that 80 percent of arrests in his precinct were meth-related. Nor, said the article, could the idea of a "meth tax" be taken seriously when it includes the cost of "meth-fueled property damage" that cannot be conclusively linked to the drug. According to *Willamette Week*, the *Oregonian's* reliance on "bad statistics and a rhetoric of crisis . . . has skewed the truth [and] rearranged governmental spending priorities, perhaps without justification."

Newspaper columnists from the *Wall Street Journal*, the *New York Times*, and the *Miami Herald* agreed. John Tierney of the *Times* lamented that, thanks to meth, politicans had "lost sight of their duties." Glenn Garvin of the *Herald* called the *Oregonian's* coverage "nonsensical." Craig Reinarman, whose criticism of the Reagan administration's response to the crack epidemic was put forth in the book *Crack in America*, worried that the exorbitant meth coverage by papers like the *Oregonian* had further directed money to law enforcement and prison, and "away from the underlying sources of people's troubles," as he told *Willamette Week*. No one was more critical of the nation's meth coverage than Jack Shafer of Slate.com, whose weekly columns tried to disprove every study on which the concept of a meth epidemic had stood. Among Shafer's favorite targets were the estimated hundred million dollars annually that meth supposedly cost the state of Indiana, and a National Association of Counties survey that found meth had sent more people to local emergency rooms in 2005 than any other drug.

It takes a considerable lack of irony for one newspaper to loudly and dramatically accuse another of histrionics. Nevertheless, *Willamette Week* made one extremely valid point: drug studies and statistics are inherently flawed, insofar as the supposedly quantitative data is based largely on hearsay, observation, and common sense— which, depending on where you stand, may or may not seem common, and may fail altogether to make sense. It's unfortunate, though, that *Willamette Week*—along with most of the other critics, Jack Shafer of Slate.com included—relied on equally unstable ground for their metrical evidence. What the paper and Shafer pointed to were the NIDA and University of Michigan reports, which found, via a deeply faulted system of their own, that meth use had remained stable or dropped in the United States between 2004 and 2006. Basically, one quantitative analysis proved to be as invalid as the other.

Meantime, as *Willamette Week* tried to disprove ECONorthwest's findings by referring to the University of Michigan report, it seemed to be important to understand the true effect of recent changes in the meth market fostered by the passage of the Combat Meth Act. What would the law—along with an absent media—mean in Lori Arnold's hometown of Ottumwa? As an answer to that question, I was reminded of two trips I'd taken there the year before.

On Halloween night of 2005, I'd met a former Mexican drug trafficker, along with his handler, in a small conference room at the abandoned commuter airport outside Ottumwa. The trafficker asked to be called Rudy. Now twenty-four, he was born in Ciudad Juárez, Mexico, then moved with his mother and brother across the border to the Juárez's sister city of El Paso, Texas. There, Rudy and his brother joined a gang and began dealing cocaine at the ages of thirteen and fifteen, respectively. By sixteen, Rudy was traveling from Juárez to El Paso with up to fifteen kilos of cocaine in a backpack. The Rio Grande between the two cities is dry for much of the year, said Rudy, and largely unguarded away from the busy international bridges. Rudy and his brother would pick a promising spot, descend into the riverbed, and climb up the other side. When they were discovered, Rudy and his brother would return to Mexico, have a soda to pass the time, and then try to cross again from a different spot a few hundred yards or a couple of miles away; they were always successful, he said.

Eventually, Rudy and his brother began working for a *comandante* of the Mexican federal police, predominantly transporting marijuana. Then one day his brother was in a car accident in Mexico and lost a load of dope, leading to his murder. Rudy was able to identify the body only by a tattoo on his brother's calf—his brother had been shot so many times that his face was gone. Afraid for his life, Rudy agreed to take a hundred-pound load of methamphetamine from the Mexican border up to the Ozark Mountains. This was in 1999. According to Rudy, he had no idea what meth was, or even what he had delivered to the white men with long beards who met him in the wooded hills outside Rogers, Arkansas. From there, Rudy took a series of meatpacking jobs, first in Missouri and then in Iowa. All the while, he dealt meth, which was either sent to him one to five pounds at a time in the mail or given to him in bulk by traffickers to distribute at the packing plant.

Rudy called the DTOs' infiltration of meatpacking plants "the perfect system." The first thing you do once you cross the border, he said, is to steal someone's driver's license. Or you buy a stolen license at the meatpacking plant. (When Rudy said this, his handler—a sergeant in the Ottumwa Police Department named Tom McAndrew—laughed, and added that at least once a month, a confused first-generation Mexican American in California, Texas, or Arizona will call the Ottumwa police wondering why there is an outstanding warrant for his arrest in Iowa, a state to which he has never been.) Moreover, said Rudy, traffickers work long hours in the packing plants, just like everyone else, in an attempt to go unnoticed. As he put it, U.S. law enforcement is used to drug dealers who are flashy and don't work. Mexican traffickers used this strategy of blending into the general population of immigrant workers to very quickly develop markets as far north and east as Michigan and Pennsylvania. The DTO's domination and expansion of the meth market was so streamlined, in fact, that when Rudy went back to El Paso two years after his first delivery to Arkansas, crack and coke were no longer the smugglers' drug of choice; crank was.

Eventually, Rudy was compelled by a speeding ticket and resultant immigration investigation to work as an informant for what was formerly the Immigration and Naturalization Services (INS), but since 2001 has been the Immigration and Customs Enforcement (ICE)—a department of the Office of Homeland Security. ICE agents told Rudy that he would be rewarded with a green card if he could help them indict and convict enough "coyotes," as the human traffickers who bring groups of illegals across the border are called. Rudy agreed, but he played both sides of the fence: many coyotes also smuggle drugs, so Rudy used his connections at ICE to lessen his competition for the El Paso meth market. When ICE agents balked at their promise to give Rudy a green card, he left Texas and headed once again for Iowa. He'd heard that the Cargill Excel plant in Ottumwa was hiring, and he assumed the police and sheriff's department there would be highly unsophisticated compared with DEA in El Paso.

Rudy got to Ottumwa in 2002. How exactly he came to be an informant there he won't say, though it was through a deal for some violation, whether for dealing meth or lacking papers. What is clear is how desperately Rudy is needed in Iowa. Tom McAndrew is the director of the Southeast Iowa Inter-Agency Drug Task Force, an umbrella agency including state, local, and federal antinarcotic agents. It was McAndrew who, as an undercover cop, busted Lori Arnold in 2001. Today, McAndrew calls Rudy the most overused informant in Iowa, pointing to the fact that Rudy, in addition to working for DEA, gets "farmed out to every police and sheriff's department in the state, not to mention a couple other states when the need arises." It's for good reason. According to people at DEA, a critical difference between the Colombian and the Mexican dealers is that the Colombians have to rely on Americans to distribute and sell their product. Not so with the DTOs, who rely on a vast network of Mexican traffickers and dealers who are hard to track. The language barrier alone—particularly in rural areas where there may be many immigrants but few English-speaking ones willing to work against their own people—makes it difficult for DEA agents to penetrate the drug organizations. And according to Rudy, even native Spanish speakers would still need to have the proper connections to Juárez or El Paso or Matamoros to gain access to information. Talking to Rudy made it easy to see how the DTOs' insularity—enforced with the threat of violence against a distributor's family members who remain in Mexico—made him so formidable.

According to McAndrew, Rudy was one of only three Spanish-speaking informants working in a state rife with Mexican DTO operatives. As we spoke that night, McAndrew kept going to the lone window in the little room at the commuter airport and peering out into the darkness from behind the curtain. The reason McAndrew had finally agreed to let me talk to Rudy, he said, was to underscore what McAndrew and his men—along with the rest of Iowa law enforcement, whether DEA agents in Des Moines, Bureau of Narcotics Enforcement agents in Cedar Falls, or cops in Oelwein—were dealing with, and what limited recourse they had with organizations that had a militaristic level of organization, efficiency, and increasingly, violence. In the end, Rudy was good enough that he could, as McAndrew said, "bring in as many five-pound deals as we [could] handle." But he was never going to infiltrate high into the traffickers' organizations. They were too closed. In a way, it made McAndrew long for the days when Lori Arnold ran things, before the DTOs took over. McAndrew had fit right into Lori's milieu.

Pointing at Rudy, McAndrew said, "This is it, man. Not that I don't love you, buddy. But you and me against them—that's pretty funny."

In a May 12, 2008, *New Yorker* article, Malcolm Gladwell observes that world-shifting ideas, far from occurring to just one person at a time, crop up in something more akin to clusters. Alexander

Graham Bell, Gladwell points out, is credited with inventing the telephone, though Elisha Gray filed a patent for the same invention on the same day. Calculus was discovered independently by Isaac Newton and Gottfried Leibniz; the theory of evolution was formulated by Charles Darwin and Alfred Russel Wallace at approximately the same time. For Gladwell, "the sheer number of multiples could mean only one thing: discoveries must, in some sense, be inevitable."

Lori Arnold had certainly had an enormous impact on Ottumwa in her day, as well as on a good deal of the greater Midwest. But who knows how many others had spearheaded drug routes in the rest of the country—with or without the help of a superlab hidden on a horse farm. Though he didn't quite have Lori's vision, Jeffrey William Hayes of Oelwein was essentially trying to do the same thing. Had a few things gone differently, he might well have been the Lori Arnold of his time. Oelwein and Ottumwa might have reversed roles as planet and satellite in the meth solar system. The story of multiples is surely the story of meth, both in the case of Lori Arnold in Iowa and the Amezcua brothers in California, along with an unknown number of contemporaries.

"Good ideas," concludes Gladwell, "are out there for anyone with the wit and the will to find them." Once found, good ideas reinforce one another. This is one way of describing Rudy's presence in Ottumwa, along with however many others who have landed there with the idea of going into the crank business: Lori built it, and the rest came.

It says a lot about what Ottumwa has become that Tom McAndrew, despite fifteen years working there, has never moved his family to Ottumwa from Kahoka, Missouri, seventy miles away. He would fear, he said, for the welfare of his wife and daughters. The night we all met at the commuter airport, Rudy concurred, saying, "I used to think El Paso was the worst place in the world. Now I think this is."

It's cliché to suggest that the undercover cop and the drug

dealer are but one chromosomal mutation from being the same person. And yet in McAndrew and Rudy—the country boy and the street thug, whom McAndrew describes as "just a big old softy"— there was every reason to see basis in this stereotype. Rudy loved the rush of bringing McAndrew and DEA small-time Mexican meth dealers. Rudy's job was essentially, he said, to "go around Iowa, making connections." Being in danger was like drug for him. For McAndrew, the cat-and-mouse game he played with dealers was also like a drug; he just loved busting dealers, plain and simple.

The two men needed each other in ways that were readily apparent: McAndrew needed Rudy's connections and Spanish skills; Rudy needed McAndrew's supervision to work off his violation and stay out of jail. They both nodded knowingly and completed each other's sentences during the two hours we talked that Halloween night. They were two of a very limited number of people in a vast, underpopulated area doing this one specific thing: infiltrating drug rings. So while they were wary, untrusting friends, they shared a curious kind of respect. McAndrew clearly didn't like Mexicans, and Rudy clearly didn't like whites. And yet, as with the cobra and the mongoose, where would they be without each other? The dynamic between them was most clear in something that McAndrew said that night while we drove back to town: he wondered if Rudy's eventual career turn, once he'd turned in enough low-level dealers to McAndrew and DEA, would be to go back into the meth business. "That's what I'd do," McAndrew had said.

While we were at the airport, Rudy talked at length about the mistrust between native Ottumwans and the immigrants who came in ever larger numbers. McAndrew said he understood, but added drily that he didn't feel welcome in town, either, given how many Mexicans there were. McAndrew and Rudy both laughed. Then McAndrew grew deadly serious. Recently, he said, Mexican meth traffickers had begun following his men around. Just a few weeks before, two off-duty agents with the Iowa Bureau of Narcotics En-forcement had gone into a pharmacy on Main Street and were fol-lowed by two young traffickers. The agents were told to stop investigating a particular meth case. If they didn't, said the traffick-ers, the officers' wives and children would be killed. To prove they meant business, the traffickers related the ins and outs of each fam-ily member's daily routine: they'd been watching. (The violence did not include only Mexican drug traffickers. A few months before that, a meth addict had walked down Main Street with a shotgun, shoot-ing at shop windows, lights, and bystanders for ten minutes before McAndrew's men killed him. McAndrew himself had recently been run over by a car during a crank bust.)

Rudy had seen it all before in El Paso. He'd seen what happened in a trafficking war, and how, when things got serious, the DTOs sent in "the scariest people you ever saw—people who do things like what they did to my brother." (Coincidentally, the month be-fore, the new police chief of Nuevo Laredo, Mexico, was gunned down by traffickers just four hours after being sworn in.) Ottuwma would be fine, said Rudy, as long as nothing happened to make the DTOs want to further consolidate the market or fight over turf. "If that happens," Rudy said, "watch out." At that, McAndrew once again stood and looked out the window.

Ironically, ignoring the DTOs is in some ways to the advantage of local police and sheriffs' departments of the rural United States for the reason that confronting them would almost certainly result in failure. In Oelwein, chief Jeremy Logan had been enormously suc-cessful in the fight against local meth production. When I asked him what he'd do about the DTOs, he said flatly, "Who knows." Barring instances like the ones in Ottumwa, where traffickers threatened the local police, those in the employ of the major narcotics networks largely work unseen within the small-town immigrant community.

As Rudy noted, part of the DTOs' success is because their vendors go unnoticed, work long shifts, and remain highly mobile. Phil Price had once noted that the traffickers' subtlety works nicely for everyone involved. "If Joe Blow torches his mom's house," he said, "you have to respond. But if smart traffickers are quietly moving hundreds of pounds, totally out of sight, you don't really have to pick that fight. You're a small-town cop and federal help is two hundred miles away, in the state capital. You're probably smart not to look too close."

How Ottumwa would deal—or not deal—with what was quickly becoming a newer, more violent phase of the meth epidemic was on curious display one sweltering July night, as Tom McAndrew oversaw the last of three exercises designed to train the Wapello SWAT team how to respond to a meth lab, along with the often-well-armed men who work at them. It was eleven o'clock, and we were sitting in the dark amid several hundred acres of chest-high corn adjacent to the Des Moines River. I was pretending to be a meth cook, along with McAndrew, a local pharmacist, and a fireman from the nearby town of Eldon. Armed, like the SWAT team, with paintball guns, and protected by motocross helmets, we were to resist arrest as vehemently as we could once the SWAT team made their move on our position. We weren't sure when that would be, and waiting to be attacked had everyone on edge. Especially since the day's two previous exercises—one in an old barn, another at a former batch site in the woods—had gotten increasingly aggressive. We were all supposed to be acting. But the heat and the isolation had conspired with the adrenaline, nearly leading to two fistfights. The fourteen-man SWAT team took the training seriously, bearing down in full body armor, their paintball guns designed to look like automatic weapons. The tackling and cuffing took place at full speed. If one of us "killed" one of them, it was taken as a very real failure.

Now we'd been waiting for two hours in the heat of the river bottom while the unseen SWAT team belly-crawled toward our position through the corn. As we sat around a fire we built in the small clearing where our imaginary lab was, the adrenaline and fear keening through our bodies grew tempered by fatigue. So McAndrew, seated in a lawn chair with his paintgun across his lap and his motocross helmet propped on his forehead, began telling stories.

The first story was about a famous Ottumwa meth cook, who was thirty-five years old and lived in a nice three-bedroom house with his twenty-year-old girlfriend. This was back in the late 1990s, when McAndrew's team was raiding an average of one meth lab every four days. (One task force member, Doug Hurley, personally helped to dismantle fifteen hundred meth labs in the first nine years he worked in southeast Iowa.)

What McAndrew and his men found in the kitchen of this particular house was a typical "user lab": an electric heating pad, some chemistry glassware and tubing, a small machine that popped cold pills one sheet at a time from their aluminum-backed packaging, a few kerosene containers full of anhydrous ammonia, and some Coleman lantern fluid. It was enough to make three to five grams of crank at a time. Or, if done wrong, to blow up the house.

In the living room, said McAndrew, there were three old-fashioned porcelain bathtubs full of human excrement. Mounds of excrement, McAndrew said, neatly piled as though the shape—measured by the proportion of length to width to height, like Mayan or Aztec ruins—were of utmost importance.

"This wasn't just shit," said McAndrew. "It was architecture."

Kept neatly in manila folders were hundreds of photos. These, too, fit together with what McAndrew, in his quiet drawl, called "some kind of a hell of a deal." Roughly, the cook and his girlfriend would get high on meth, which they liked to do intravenously. Then the cook would instruct his girlfriend to insert a store-bought enema into his sphincter. Next, to keep the enema from coming out, she inserted pigs in a blanket, small hot dogs wrapped in dough sold frozen in bags at the grocery store. According to his scientifically detailed notes, the cook's record was to have one full pound of pigs in a blanket in his anus at one time. Another time his girlfriend inserted into him seven blowgun darts, a lit cigar, and a large dildo, which McAndrew described as being as big around as a Coke can. According to his journals, the man was capable of going up to two days without defecating. When he could no longer hold all this inside himself, it was off to one of the bathtubs. He could, if he took enough methamphetamine, begin the entire process all over again following just a few hours' sleep.

McAndrew said such bizarre scenarios were not uncommon back when home-cooked crank still accounted for a quarter or so of the Ottumwa meth market. The real point of the story, though, is that McAndrew sees no difference between the man with the user lab and the traffickers who follow his men. McAndrew isn't the type to choose his battles or to walk away from a fight. He and his men had handled the local meth market and its users just fine. Now, though, they were confronting something different, and it wasn't clear McAndrew saw how poorly equipped he might be.

By midnight, McAndrew was nearly done telling his story, pausing every few minutes to look out into the darkness beyond the fire. The pharmacist and the fireman were quiet. In the sullen silence they seemed to be wondering where in the world they were. Not because they were in a cornfield waiting for the SWAT team to attack them, but because they were in Iowa, and it no longer seemed recognizable. When the pharmacist asked what happened to the meth cook, McAndrew's story ended, in a way, with the man being sentenced to six years, and with him getting out of jail in nine months.

In another way, the story ended like this: with the enormous boom of a concussion grenade, followed immediately by the SWAT team racing in from all directions, weapons raised, wearing full body armor and night-vision goggles, screaming, "Police! Police! Get on your knees!"

Unlike the day's two previous scenarios, they did not wait for us to shoot first this time.

CHAPTER 13

DISCONNECTED STATES

Thomas P. M. Barnett and Moisés Naím are two post-cold-war thinkers who have come to prominence recently. A reading of their work suggests a framework for understanding the changing manner in which Ottumwa and Oelwein fit into the world—and ultimately, how meth has become such an inherent part of life there. Barnett is a professor and researcher at the U.S. Naval War College. One of the anchors of his worldview, as put forth in his book *The Pentagon's New Map*, is the idea that nations can be divided into two types: the "functioning core" and the "non-integrated gap," or "disconnected" states. The former—the G8, plus Mexico, Brazil, Taiwan, Australia, and other similar industrialized nations— play by one "rule set" predicated on global political and economic integration. The latter—and for Barnett this includes most of the world's nations—are a collection of rogue states, battered economic and political shell states, dictatorships, and otherwise wayward entities. This non-integrated gap relies on a separate rule set predicated on the black market and the movement of goods and services that are a threat to the stability of the functioning core.

The global drug-trafficking business is by nature disposed to operate outside the bounds of law, politics, and traditional economics.

Though, as the meth trade has shown, this doesn't stop traffickers from functioning in tandem with, or from preying on, government policy and stable financial systems. One might say that the makers and distributors of narcotics function as a disconnected state, which nonetheless exerts tremendous influence within the borders and cultures of nations without regard to whether they're functioning or disconnected—globalized or marginalized. And just as methamphetamine from the non-integrated gap state of North Korea travels to the core nations of Japan and Australia, so too does pseudoephedrine from the core nation of India get shipped to Mexico (another core nation), where it is made into crank which is sent to the United States (perhaps *the* core nation). This happens through a loose network of market forces that combine the ideas of connectivity and division deep within the same borders. The state of Michoacán, Mexico, is an example, as are the cities of Nuevo Laredo, Juárez, Nogales, and Matamoros, where even the Mexican army holds no sway.

But what about inside the United States? What about California's Central Valley; or the so-called Methlehem section of tiny Oelwein, Iowa; or the tinier still town of Benton, Illinois? What about Algona and Lu Verne and Congressman Souder's poultry-rich Third District of northeastern Indiana? How connected, really, are these places to the rest of the United States, and to the world? In some ways, the link is clear. There is a very good chance, for example, that most of what you ate today came from the Central Valley, whether eggs or beef or dates or oranges or lettuce. The chicken you had last night stands a better-than-average chance of having come from somewhere within a hundred miles of Fort Wayne, Indiana.

In another way, though, many of the towns of the rural United States are quite disconnected from the rest of the nation. Poverty rates are higher, fewer people have achieved secondary levels of education, and substance abuse is far more prevalent than in urban America. It's worth noting that the reason your dinner moves an average of fifteen hundred miles to get from its source to your plate is because the source—or sources, really—is determined by companies like Tyson and Cargill and ConAgra based on where they can pay the cheapest labor costs. Barnett posits that when one piece is no longer part of the system—that is, when it is disengaged from the standard rules—everyone is vulnerable. Oelwein may look very different from Independence, but Oelwein's problems none-theless affect its neighbor. Oelwein's vulnerabilities are Iowa's vul-nerabilities, and America's.

Naím, the editor in chief of *Foreign Policy* magazine and the former minister of trade and industry of Venezuela, is saying much the same thing as Barnett is in his book *Illicit*. Rather than a nation, the victim in his paradigm is more likely a car manufacturer in De-troit who suffers from Chinese knockoff parts, or Hollywood tak-ing a hit from the black market DVD trade in the Golden Triangle of Brazil, Paraguay, and Argentina. For Naím, when everything and anything can essentially be stolen before it ends up in the hands of consumers, no one can be truly inoculated from the "system" of chaos. Now, instead of Hollywood DVDs or cars, think of jobs in Oelwein and Ottumwa, Greenville and Gooding. When those towns are in trouble, so too are Scarsdale, New York, and Ladue, Missouri—the second- and fourth-richest cities in the nation, re-spectively. The proof is in the meth that ends up in New York or St. Louis after stopping at a small, rural transhipment point.

Were Naím or Barnett an epidemiologist, it stands to chance they would gravitate toward the study of RNA viruses, like the flu. The power of the common flu relies in part on what is called *antigenic drift*, meaning that, as humans develop antibodies to ward off in-fection, the virus mutates its proteins so that the antibodies can no longer bind to the viral surface. Basically, you make a lock, and the virus makes a key. When the key turns, you get sick. What hap-pens once in a lifetime, on average, is that these same RNA viruses "reassort" themselves. That is the fear with H5N1, commonly referred to as bird flu, which places like the Centers for Disease Control and the World Health Organization are carefully monitoring. The fear is that this particular strain of flu will "figure out" how to adopt (or co-opt) the genetic attributes of the same regular old infection that makes large numbers of people in the world vomit and feel puny for a few days or a week each year. By rearranging, or reassorting, its RNA, H5N1 could theoretically use the common flu to make the jump from chickens and ducks to humans. Once a human falls ill with both flus, the two viruses would be able to replicate in the same cells at the same time, resulting in an *antigenic shift*. The key to unlock your immunity, if you will, would be passed along with every sneeze and cough on every airplane and in every office around the world in a matter of days or weeks. As a UCLA professor writes in his opening lecture for a class on viral epidemiology, "THIS IS NOT GOOD!"

Drug trafficking is a lot like the common flu. It's long been guaranteed to mutate periodically within a fairly closed system. Drug traffickers stay around by making keys to government locks, at times before the locks are even thought of. This is what happened when the DTOs began moving to meth production via pseudoephedrine in anticipation of—as opposed to as a reaction to—Gene Haislip's legislation in 1996. But drug trafficking, says Naím, has gotten a lot easier in the last twenty years. Or at least a lot harder to follow. Traffickers, like an RNA virus, affect antigenic drift all the time, and infections come and go as epidemics every decade: LSD and PCP in the seventies, cocaine in the eighties, crack in the early nineties, and crank ever since. All a drug needs in order to mutate is a body politic; the shift occurs where that body is weakest—where unemployment is high and poverty is rife, and people are disabused of their marginalization, or their "disconnectedness" from the "core." The places where this occurs are not just the rogue states that Barnett imagines—the Yemens and the Tajikistans and the Ecuadors of the world. The "core" has holes of its own, in Ottumwa and Oelwein, in Cylinder and Algona, and in El Paso.

Naím writes that since "the early 1990s, global illicit trade has embarked on a great mutation. It is the same mutation as that of international terrorist organizations like al-Qaeda or Islamic Jihad . . . All have moved away from fixed hierarchies and toward decentralized networks; away from controlling leaders and toward multiple, loosely linked, dispersed agents and cells; away from rigid lines of control and exchange and toward constantly shifting transactions as opportunities dictate. It is a mutation that governments in the 1990s barely recognized and could not, in any case, hope to emulate."

When I read that, it reminded me of one of the fears I heard voiced many times while researching this book: that drug traffickers will someday team with terrorist organizations. Or, at the very least, to exploit the same weaknesses in the social fabric that the Arellano Felix Organization and the Gulf Cartel have so successfully exploited. In truth, this has already happened at least once.

In 2001, Tony Loya—who'd run Operation Snowcap from Guatemala back in 1987—retired from DEA and took a job as the director of the National Methamphetamine Chemical Initiative (NMCI). His job was to track the meth business on behalf of the Department of Justice and to anticipate the DTOs' next moves. Loya noticed that gas stations that sell soda, cigarettes, and basic pharmaceuticals like cold medicine—or what Loya calls "stop-and-robs"—were buying enormous amounts of pill-form pseudoephedrine. In addition, the gas station owners had special machines that could pop entire rows of pseudoephedrine pills from their blister packs in the way that a garlic press squeezes the meat from the skin. In the Central Valley, agents found dump sites littered with thousands of empty blister packs near dismantled labs.

Once Loya noticed this, he began investigating whether the same thing was happening in other areas of the country. It was: convenience stores in New Jersey were doing the same thing. As it turns out, the Jersey stores were owned by Yemeni nationals who were not only importing bulk cold medication; they were illegally importing powdered pseudoephedrine and routing it to trafficking organizations. When DEA moved to close down their businesses, the Yemenis moved to Canada, mostly to Toronto and Montreal, where there were no laws governing the importation of bulk pseudoephedrine. There was nothing Loya could do.

By 2002, DEA agents had informed Loya, who cultivates law enforcement contacts the world over, that high-level Mexican traffickers were going regularly to Detroit. Loya knew from other contacts that production of meth in the Central Valley was expanding exponentially, and reasoned that the Mexicans were courting the Yemenis by meeting them in Detroit, close to the Yemenis' home turf. On a hunch, Loya authorized nighttime surveillance of remote roads at Canadian points of entry. Where there typically wouldn't have even been any cars at night, he said, the video caught images of dozens of eighteen-wheelers. When searched, several of the vehicles were found to have loads of pseudoephedrine hidden in the fender wells.

Soon, said Loya, in an indication that the relationship between the DTOs and the Yemenis was becoming stronger than ever, the Yemenis began traveling to see their Mexican partners in the Mexicans' backyard: Las Vegas.

"They'd have these big dinners," said another former DEA official who ran wiretaps on the dinner meetings. "Lots of wine—very lovey-dovey. Then we'd get the tapes back from our wiretaps, and the Mexicans would call their friends back in California and say, 'If it weren't for the money, I'd kill these heathen Moor sons of bitches.' And the Yemenis are in their hotel rooms on the phone with Toronto saying, 'If it weren't for the money, I'd kill those stinking Catholic infidel sons of bitches.'"

The wiretaps also revealed that the Yemenis were funneling

hundreds of millions of dollars to the terrorist organization Hamas. It was just luck, said Tony, that he was able to put together the clues.

In the end, any moves against the DTOs were just a minor irritation, for the real connection between drugs and terror is seen in Barnett's concept of "disconnected" states and Naím's "invisible border." The DTOs simply reassorted themselves, moving production from the isolated farmlands of California's Central Valley to the Mexican state of Michoacán, for the reason that, as another former DEA agent described it, "the further you get from the limited bandwidth of control surrounding the seat of government, the more autonomous and lawless things get." Michoacán is several states removed from Mexico City, the country's capital. The former DEA agent went on, "We won't even send agents to Michoacán—they'd be killed immediately. Even Mexican federal people can't get in there. It's like its own nation within Mexico, in the same way that all major trafficking points—Juárez, Nogales, et cetera—are like city-states. There's no way to control them centrally." That lack of control extends north of the border, all throughout the poor, disconnected parts of the United States. In Ottumwa, Tom McAndrew is trying to figure out how to keep his men from having their families killed.

Two weeks before meeting Rudy, I'd been in Georgia and Alabama in the wake of Hurricane Katrina. I'd gone there because, according to Tony Loya, record amounts of meth had been flowing into the area from the East Texas border during the past few months. There had been an increase in drug cartel violence around the sibling towns of Laredo and Nuevo Laredo that had made every major American newspaper's front page off and on for weeks. The Mexican government, in reaction, had sent in the army. The drug lords, in countersuit, had redoubled their attacks on one another. To that end, they had begun employing a gang known as the Zetas, former American-trained members of the Mexican special forces.

One morning, I'd spoken with Sherri Strange, then the DEA special agent in charge of the Atlanta office. According to her, the meth market in her seven-state area was so good that many of the Zetas had gone into business for themselves, armed with their expertise in surveillance, weaponry, and counterintelligence.

"The DTOs hold Atlanta," said Strange. "And they're here in a way that, to me, after twenty-five years being on the street and in charge in various locations, is frightening. We used to have Mexicans—and excuse the term, I'm only talking about a few but, I'm sorry, all the big players are Mexican—that were pretty minor league. They were just guys trying to make enough money in a year to go back home and retire. Now, in the last eight months, there's a sea change. We're getting traffickers who are as highly trained as we are in intelligence gathering, evasion techniques, weapons. They're scary. I can literally walk down the street—and this happened here a while back—and just know what's going on. You see them, if you know what to look for, and you just think, 'Oh my God.'"

Later in 2005, I went to meet Alex Gonzalez, an officer with the Hoover Police Department, in Alabama's poultry-rich northern tier. An interdiction specialist, meaning that he pulls cars and trucks over and searches them, Gonzalez and his partner are also part of the vast web of people who keep Tony Loya apprised of what's happening on the fringes of the narcotics world. Describing the relationship he has with the traffickers, Gonzalez said, "We'll get a load one day, a big one, maybe a hundred pounds of crystal headed to Atlanta. Or maybe $1.2 million in cash headed back to Mexico. And that night the traffickers call you on your cell phone and say, 'Nice job, man! That was a big bust!' It's like we're friendly, almost—joking with each other. Then they ask about your wife, and it gets very creepy; they want you to know how much they've got on you. They say, 'Too bad while you were taking the five hours to deal with that hundred pounds, we got another thousand pounds past you.' The hundred pounds were just a decoy."

He went on: "They watch us watching them. Their 'counter-intelligence' is so superior to our 'intelligence'—and I can't stress enough what a bullshit word that is—that it's just no contest. You taunt each other, like it's a game, but it's a game they always win.

"What's not a game is that, if drug organizations can not only get major shipments past us every day, but can know how *much* they got past and can *laugh* at it—if they're watching that close—what're the terrorists doing? I'll tell you what they're not doing is advertising. It's not a game to them, I wouldn't think. And what if they go into business together? They've done it before. Then what?"

CHAPTER 14

KANT'S REDEMPTION

My last trip to Oelwein was in mid-December 2007. As the plane flew west from New York, an ice storm worked its way east. I met the weather at O'Hare Airport, which closed for most of a day; that was where I spent the night. By late the following afternoon, the glare off the frozen fields along Highway 150 was dizzying, and the sleet turned to snow and back to sleet again. It snowed the whole week I was in Oelwein; the high temperature was eighteen degrees. This was only the beginning of a long winter. By April, Fayette County would get nearly eight feet of snow. Drifts at the Leins' farm would be forty feet high where the wind, with nothing to stop it for what seemed like a thousand featureless miles, had piled it up to the roof of the house.

On the first morning of that last trip, Nathan and I got in his white diesel Jetta (it now had 222,000 miles on it, 45,000 more than when I'd first met him) and headed to court in West Union. Nathan was dressed in his customary gray suit and white shirt. His hair was carefully gelled, and he had on his class ring from Luther College. Jamie had once again gotten a job contracting with DHS, and was no longer bartending in Strawberry Point. Things around the house were much better for it. Better still, most of Jamie's cases were down in Independence. This meant she didn't run into clients' families, or even the clients themselves, while out and about in Oelwein. And she and Nathan didn't have to worry about influencing each other's views of people whom, for instance, Nathan might be prosecuting, even as Jamie was attempting to persuade the court not to take their children away.

It's a thirty-minute drive from Oelwein to West Union. When it's three degrees Fahrenheit, with a wind chill of twenty-seven below, it takes half that time for the Jetta's heat to kick in. As we drove, Nathan and I looked for pheasants along the side of the road, coming out of the draws and creek bottoms to peck at waste grain fallen off the farm trucks. When we saw them—in pairs and threes, their green and red heads iridescent in the harsh, slanting light— Nathan made a note of whose field they were on. That way, we could come back in the afternoon and ask the farmer for permission to hunt on his property. At one fence crossing, we saw an entire covey of birds, prompting me to whistle and slap the dashboard with excitement.

"Uh-uh," said Nathan. "Amish."

The Amish didn't let non-Amish hunt on their land, and vice versa. Not that there was any real antipathy between the two groups in and around Oelwein. Rather, there were rules of engagement, which served to highlight the differences between the Mennonites and the rest of the community. Even when the Amish came to town and participated in the wider world, they invariably managed to set themselves completely apart. The night before, I was at the Kum and Go gas station when an enormous blue van pulled in. No fewer than fifteen Amishmen, none of whom were technically allowed to operate gas or electric machinery, poured out of the van, which had five rows of seats. The first day of deer season had—in accordance with the semi-religious aspect of the sport in northern Iowa—ended at sundown. The Amishmen had hired the van and driver to take them to a piece of state land called the Volga River Wildlife Management Area to hunt that day; attached to the back fender of the van was a heavy, grated cage that could be used for hauling equipment, but in this case was stacked with four gutted whitetail bucks. All fifteen Amishmen, including elderly men and boys in their teens, each with a beard and no mustache—or in the case of the boys, a dusting of peach fuzz along their jaw—walked single file into the Kum and Go to eat microwaved burritos and drink steaming black coffee from Styrofoam cups. Despite the violent cold, they wore collared white shirts, navy blue suits of thick wool, and rubber knee-high boots. In order to comply with state hunting regulations they each had pulled a hunter-orange stocking cap over the crown of their straw hat and fastened it with safety pins. When the Amish left the gas station, everyone in line watched them. Then someone said they were Yoders.

"No they ain't, either," said the cashier. "Them are Bontragers, no question."

Covey of pheasants or not, asking the Amish for permission to hunt wasn't going to happen. Not that it was of any consequence, for the principal motivation behind going hunting was less to hunt and more to spend time with Nathan, whom, as had happened with Clay Hallberg, I'd long before come to think of as a friend. On the drive to West Union that morning, Nathan and I, prompted by the fact that I'd gotten married two months before, talked about his relationship with Jamie. Nathan said it was hard to imagine himself getting married. Thinking about it was a little bit like imagining death, or eternity: when he closed his eyes and looked into it, the darkness closed in all around. It was better to keep his eyes open.

"I don't know if I can trust anyone like that," he said. "Or, frankly, if I can be trusted with someone's heart."

Nathan said his father still asked about Jamie, despite the fact Nathan had not brought her to the farm in nearly a year. His mother, though, said Nathan, never breathed a word about Jamie. While his father's good-natured inquiries felt to Nathan like the faintest kindling of familial warmth and acceptance, his mother's silence was like a bucket of cold water, Nathan said. Eventually, Nathan began ignoring his father's questions altogether, leaving them to smolder and die beneath the weight of his mother's coolness. It was not hard to imagine the three of them in the tiny farm kitchen, bundled in wool, taking a quick, standing dinner on a brutal winter night before going back into the barn to help the ewes lamb out. Briefly, they would all look at the green, peeling linoleum floor to which his father's questions had silently fallen. Nor was it hard to see how, eventually, Nathan's father would surely stop asking about Jamie.

As far as Nathan was concerned, this was fine—at least until he figured out some other way to deal with it. When I wondered aloud what that way might be, there was a long silence while we both pretended to look across the frozen plain for pheasants. Finally Nathan said, "Jamie doesn't complain, but I know it's hard for her."

Nathan was fully aware that he was crippled, as he put it, by an irrational fear of conflict. He knew Jamie was not going to wait around forever. She had turned thirty-one in 2007. She wanted to get married and have children, and she wanted to do those things with Nathan Lein and no one else. They'd been living together close to eighteen months. Jamie wanted to be included in his plans about the farm. Yet, still she ate dinner alone in Nathan's house on the nights he was at his parents' place, or else she tried to work late herself so they'd get home at the same time. Sometimes she didn't know what she was doing, coming home to a house that wasn't hers, sitting there alone waiting while the man she wanted to have a family with ate dinner with his family. Then again, she didn't know what else she could do. To say that it was hard for Jamie—and for Nathan—doesn't quite give the situation its due.

"I'm sure that eventually," said Nathan, "something will give. Till then, here we are."

With that, we pulled into the courthouse parking lot, the Jetta's tires making a sound like crinkling paper on the frozen crust of the snow. It was eight A.M. sharp. With no overcoat on, Nathan stood behind his car for a few long moments, with his briefcase on the ice-slicked trunk, going through his papers as though the cold were of no concern.

The Fayette County Courthouse, in West Union, was built in 1905. Inside, there is a marble atrium, and three stories above it, an enormous round skylight of green stained glass. Everything is clean and polished, including the granite drinking fountains, which are the size of a tollbooth. The staircase is marble, and Nathan and I walked up to the third floor, past mothers and fathers in work pants and parkas sitting with their children on comfortable benches in the high-ceilinged hallway outside the juvenile courtroom. Beyond this was an old oak door with a plaque that said LAW LIBRARY. On a bench beside that door sat two young men in orange jumpsuits, their hands manacled to chains on their waists, and from there, to cuffs on their ankles.

"Howdy," said one man.

"Back again," said Nathan, as though he were talking to someone who'd just left a store and then returned, having forgotten something on his shopping list.

The Law Library is where the three Fayette County assistant prosecutors and the various private and state defense attorneys have their coffee and go over the day's cases with one another. The Law Library, with its twelve-foot-high bookshelves of polished cedar, hardly has a tense atmosphere, in part because very few cases are actually tried in Fayette County. Much of what happens is confined to the workmanlike procedurals of plea bargains, parole renewals, and county-jail incarcerations. Add to this that many of the attorneys have been coming here five mornings a week for one or two decades—and will continue to do so until they retire—and the result is a measure of familiarity that would be unattainable in, say, Miami-Dade County. Streamlining one's strategy with an opponent not only gets everyone out of court sooner; it is also simply a matter of course, and a benefit of the attorneys' personal fluency.

From the window in the courtroom, three stories high in a building that sits on a slight rise in the prairie, one can see the First National Bank and Steege's drugstore across the street, and beyond them, over the tops of the surrounding houses, the thirty or so rolling miles stretching east between West Union and Mississippi Lock and Dam Number 10, near the confluence of the Wisconsin River. Along the way, there are Elgin and Gunder, St. Olaf and Farmersburg, Froelich and McGregor. Halfway to the river, the land bucks and jumps, the river valleys tighten as the grade increases, and there is a proliferation of timber and coal. Twelve thousand years ago, an iceberg the size of Wisconsin flattened most of Iowa, and as it receded, deposited scree and lime along what would one day be called the Mississippi. For a time, this tiny area of Iowa was called Little Switzerland, so lush and fertile did the hills appear to the Prussians and Austrians who settled those valleys in the 1850s and '60s.

First on the docket that morning was the man in shackles who'd said hello in the hallway. Though he looked twenty-five, he was in fact thirty-eight. He had blond hair, a blond beard, blue eyes, and a nose like a falcon's beak. He entered his plea of guilty with a good-humored tinge of a Minnesotan accent.

He was a familiar sight in the Fayette County Court, and he'd been, like Roland Jarvis, in the clink off and on for years. Several months before, he'd been put on probation for driving under the influence of an illegal substance, in this case meth. A week ago, he'd been picked up after driving erratically up in Winneshiek County, northeast of Fayette. Now he claimed not to know that both driving and leaving the county violated the terms of his probation. Nathan had grown weary of him. Sipping his coffee half an hour before, Nathan had said to the judge, who sat just a few feet away from the attorneys in the Law Library, filling out papers: "I can't stand it when someone patronizes me."

"Me neither," the judge had said without looking up. Then Nathan said he wanted the maximum sentence of three years. The judge and the defense attorney agreed. What they all knew was that because of overcrowding in the Iowa prison system, the man would be out in six months.

In the courtroom, it was a matter of going through the formalities of reading to the man the charges, the meaning of his plea, the basis for sentencing, and the philosophical tenets on which rest the power to incarcerate a human being in the state of Iowa. From the bench, the judge started by reading all of this. Then he recited the rest from memory while filling out paperwork, only occasionally glancing up at his charge. The judge had a white beard and white hair, and he'd recently retired. He and his wife were planning to drive their camper to Florida, but the county had asked the judge to come back to work until his replacement could be hired. He'd agreed, but his patience was short. He'd just turned seventy, and he was tired of the cold.

When he was done with the sentencing, the judge looked up and said to the defendant, "You can't expect me to believe that you, as something of a professional in the goofing-up department, didn't know what probation means. Can you?"

"No, sir," said the man. "I can't."

The judge shrugged and shook his head lightly. Looking back down at his mountain of paperwork, he said, "Well, good luck."

Clay Hallberg had labored during much of 2006 and part of 2007 to shore up Oelwein's critically thin addiction-counseling alternatives. He'd succeeded in helping to convince the Iowa Child Health Specialty Clinics to open an office just two doors down from the Hallberg Family Practice. Staffed with four women, all of whom were capable of offering help to children whose parents were addicted to meth, the clinic had quadrupled the available assistance in a town that—though it had come a long way in three short years—still had little recourse for addicts and their families. But it was a start, and by playing a role in getting the clinic to Oelwein, Clay felt involved in his town's revival. It was also a means by which Clay alleviated the guilt he felt for resigning as chief of staff at Mercy, and for his increasing desire to shut the doors of the seventy-year-old Hallberg Family Practice.

Clay had been sober for over eighteen months. It lent him, he said, increasingly clear insight into things, some of which was quite painful. Part of that insight was that he'd been, as he put it, cutting his nose to spite his face regarding medicine. So instead of fighting two battles he couldn't win—namely, against the insurance companies and against what he saw as immoral hiring practices at Mercy Hospital—he'd rolled up his sleeves and gotten back to basics, working on a contract basis in a couple of rural emergency rooms. The money was good, the excitement level was high, and the rewards were immediate. Rather than having too little time to treat someone living through the prolonged hell of meth addiction or cancer, Clay could concentrate on just getting someone through the afternoon, or keeping him alive till morning. It was the medical equivalent of the Alcoholics Anonymous philosophy that had saved Clay's life: one day at a time.

Despite these developments, in the harsh, fluorescent reflection of Clay Hallberg's continuing sobriety, his life did not look the same to him as it had when he'd been drinking. Some aspects were worse than they'd ever been, said Clay. His blood pressure had gotten so out of control that he began fearing for his well-being. What was becoming clear to him in his sobriety, too, he said, was that his marriage needed some serious attention. Or rather, it had long ago to him begun needing attention, and he was just now able to see this. The man who promoted Whorfian linguistics and the fluid communicative harmonies of music had found he'd lost the ability to speak meaningfully to his wife of twenty years. When they talked, he said, they made no sense to each other.

One evening after dinner at Las Flores, Clay and I went across the street to Von Tuck's Bier Haus. More than any other place in Oelwein, Von Tuck's captures the town's desire for upward mobility by taking the drinking tradition of the northern Midwest and elevating it to a level of finery unseen anywhere else in town. Even a sober doctor can feel at home there. Top-shelf whiskeys line Von Tuck's polished bar, it's not loud, and the bartender is nice even if he doesn't know you. It was here, while drinking a Diet Coke and chain-smoking Marlboro Lights, that Clay described his most recent epiphany.

"I'm a bastard, okay?" he said.

I waited a moment, thinking there was more. There wasn't.

"That's it. That's the deal: I'm a shit, and now I can stop."

This insight wasn't visited on him in a blinding flash of light, said Clay. There was no collision, the likes of which had killed his mother three years ago. This leap of understanding did not, like the Clydesdale, bolt unseen from the highway ditch in the middle of the night, crushing the vehicle of Clay's intellect, shattering the emotional windshield through which he'd long viewed himself. It was not a euphoric realization, not like taking all his neurotransmitters and putting them in a shot glass and swallowing them at once. Biochemistry, hydrology, genealogy, physics, Egyptology—the truth was so much more real to him than any of that had ever been.

His blood pressure, he said, had gone way down. "I'm like a fucking lizard, it's so low," he said. He was focused in the ER, not worrying about making mistakes, or about trying to save people who hadn't even walked in off the street yet.

"I drove myself to drink," he said. "I probably drove everyone around me crazy. Either way, it doesn't matter. I'm not anyone but me. When you're a shit, you think you're other people. You think *for* other people. All I have to do is not that. The rest'll work out."

He lit another cigarette. "The thing is, I could never believe that. I didn't know how. But now I do."

A few more businesses had opened in Oelwein by that December, including Lou Ann's Quilt Garden over by J & L Sports, across from the building where Marie Ferell had been bludgeoned to death by Tonie Barrett back in 2005. Lou Ann ran quilting classes out of a building that she and her husband bought, spurred on by the promise of tax breaks that the city council had passed the year before. Now Lou Ann not only had her shop but also rented the two apartments above it. Her quilting retreats were booked three years in advance, mostly by middle-aged women who went with Lou Ann to Minneapolis or Chicago or Kansas City to quilt, see movies, and eat at good restaurants for a few days at a time. The Quilt Garden made for some nice cross-traffic with the nearby Morning Perk, which had expanded its coffee and breakfast business with an adjacent knitting and collaging shop.

Out at the Industrial Park, the Oelwein campus of Northeast Iowa Community College and the accompanying Regional Academy for Math and Science (RAMS) were nearly complete. Classes were scheduled to start in the fall of 2008. With the call center still hemming and hawing about whether to set up shop in India or Oelwein, Murphy had begun construction of a Tech Spec Center, as it was called, just east of the RAMS building. Meantime, the old 160,000-square-foot Donaldson factory, across the street from the Cop Shop, had two brand-new occupants after being empty for nearly two decades. One was a wind turbine company called Sector 5; the other was a battery manufacturer called East Penn. Between them, they employed nearly one hundred Oelweinians at hourly rates of fifteen to twenty-four dollars, which is way above the county average.

In reward for his efforts, Larry Murphy had been elected to his

fourth mayoral term on November 2, 2007. Murphy's renewal efforts were far from done; if anything, his conviction had redoubled,
and he was more consumed than ever by his town. Next on his
agenda was to expand what he'd come to call the "downtown
streetscape" to twelve blocks from the present seven. This would
include more sewer and water improvements, new plantings and
repaired streetlights, and converting more abandoned buildings
into attractive new commercial spaces. Murphy wanted trails in
the parks and two city-run indoor swimming pools to help his
"community wellness" agenda. He also wanted the twelve-block
area to have more efficient geothermal heating and cooling, in order to cut energy costs. He wanted to begin several more housing
initiatives, which was still a euphemism for razing abandoned and
low-income rental properties. To this end, Murphy was pressuring
Nathan to run for city council. Land ordinances had, under Murphy's direction, been enforced by the police. If Nathan became coun-
cilman, Murphy would have an ally in supporting his initiatives.

The idea that Nathan would run for city council was obviously
another step toward grooming him to "someday run this town," as
Murphy once told me. Nathan was undecided. For one thing, he
insisted that he was an intensely private person and that politics
would never suit him for that reason alone. For another thing, Nathan liked to say that he disliked almost everyone he met, though
to see Nathan smile his way through a crowd is to be certain that
quite the opposite is true. In fact, his insistence on playing the can-
tankerous outsider is precisely what would give Nathan a chance in
the April election and beyond, if he—as Clay Hallberg posited—
ever decided to run for state congress.

It is worth noting that Nathan's is an inherently rural sensibility,
insofar as he cultivates a quiet dissatisfaction with the outside
world from a self-conscious remove. The defensiveness in his insistence that he "doesn't like people" is as palpable as the yearning in
his habit of saying, "This is just Oelwein; it's not New York." Watch

Nathan work a meet-and-greet at Von Tuck's Bier Haus in the pre-election season as he weighs his desire to run for city council, and you'll know that, far from not liking anyone, he likes everyone, and wishes not to be made vulnerable for it. It's his longing for approval and inclusion that makes him distrustful.

Here Nathan's behavior is allegorical. A decade ago, Oelwein was the butt of one of Jay Leno's jokes on *The Tonight Show*. In the intervening decade, meth came to signify the distillation of poverty and disenfranchisement in America to which Leno spoke, which is to say it came to signify the rural United States, and ultimately, the fullness of its outsider status. Oelwein was the standard bearer. In the wake of this, the town's—like Nathan's—posture is a careful balance of pride and defensiveness.

Not long after Jay Leno's joke, Larry Murphy began trying to find a place for Oelwein in a new world. It took Murphy a considerable amount of time to build consensus for his first, giant step, which was to regain some balance—via large-scale economic reforms—against the unmovable weight that a drug had come to represent. The town's fight for balance can be seen everywhere—in the downtown improvements and the dark streets at night in the Ninth Ward, and in Nathan's and Clay's and Jarvis's and Major's private lives. Jarvis had ruined his life for inclusion in the glamour of all that Oelwein wasn't in the late 1980s and early 1990s: the Corvettes and the money and the promise of what people like Lori Arnold and Jeffrey William Hayes seemed to offer. Major had nearly ruined his life a decade later for inclusion in the Family. Clay Hallberg, in reward for having come home, wanted inclusion in his father's world, in which a town GP didn't have to fight the hospital and the insurance companies. In a way, it seems that, like all these people, the rural United States has been fighting for balance since the early 1980s and for acceptance in a nation intensely divided between the middle and the coasts. In the last decade, meth has become an apt metaphor for the division. And those conflicts even exist within Oelwein, where meth once again provides the lexicon:

either you are a shitbag tweaker or you aren't. And while there is no reason to be unfriendly about it—no reason, that is, not to exchange pleasantries on the way into court—every time Nathan put a tweaker in jail, it pushed the balance slightly more in the right direction.

In November 2007, Murphy had organized what he called a Community Burial Ceremony of Gloom and Doom. What was contained in the coffin carried by a procession of townsfolk were the symbolic remnants of Oelwein's economic and social helplessness. What Murphy wanted to make clear, however corny it seemed, was that people should no longer take suffering as a precondition of their lives. Murphy wanted people to fight, and to be aggressive and prideful about the rebuilding. As far as what the change in one town might do relative to the direction of the rest of the country, Murphy and Nathan and Clay were all too aware that what happened in Oelwein was just a drop in the bucket. There was a feeling akin to that of a city-state under siege. Oelwein was repelling the invaders, but that didn't mean they were going away. The lack of good jobs was certain to remain, drug traffickers were likely to keep gaining a foothold, and the population would dwindle, whether or not corn prices stayed high and the local businesses all switched to geothermal heating.

As Nathan and I talked about this one evening, I asked him if he'd consider running for mayor once Murph was no longer in office. We were in his garage. The fire in the stove was out, and we were cutting kindling to get it going again.

"Yes," said Nathan, "I would."

It was one of the only times in two and a half years at that point that I heard Nathan speak of the future with an utter lack of equivocation. Larry Murphy had changed things, indeed.

CHAPTER 15

INDEPENDENCE

One night on that last trip to Iowa, I drove down to Independence to see Major. When I arrived, he was babysitting his son Buck, who was now four years old. Major was still living with his parents, Joseph and Bonnie. That they trusted Major enough to go to a party that night was a great improvement since the summer of 2005. Back then, fresh off a horrible three years during which Major and his girlfriend would break into Steve and Brenda's home to steal what they could in order to sell it to buy more meth, Major's parents were afraid to leave him alone for even fifteen minutes. Now his parents were once again considering something they thought they'd never again have the chance to do: take one of their beloved fishing trips to Canada next summer.

When I got to his parents' house, Major was drinking a beer and chewing tobacco as he prepared Buck's supper of microwaved tomato and cheese pizza. Buck, once the child with the highest hair-follicle count of methamphetamine in the history of the state of Iowa, was watching TV from inside a fort he'd built by anchoring one side of a blanket beneath the couch cushions and the other side beneath heavy books on top of the coffee table. On both sides, he'd stacked cardboard bricks from the floor to the blanket-roof to make walls. Buck peered at the television out of a hole he'd left in the bricks. On TV, Bugs Bunny attempted to outwit Yosemite Sam, who in this version played the part of a French chef hell-bent on fricasseeing rabbit for dinner. Presently, Buck destroyed the fort he had created and marched into the kitchen.

"What?" said Major.

"Dinnertime," said Buck.

"Because you're the boss?"

"Yes," said Buck. "And boss hungry."

As Buck sat on the couch and ate, Major updated me on all that had been going on. Words like *sex* and *beer* and *meth* had to be spelled out, since Buck was in the stage where he repeated everything he heard, and was beginning to ask questions with difficult answers. All in all, said Major, Buck was doing very well. Developmentally, he was still ahead of the game. What two years before had been a personable habit of making eye contact and smiling shyly had morphed into a practice of holding one's gaze while asking a question—"Who you?" he'd asked me when I walked in— and then maintaining eye contact while the answer came: the habit of a boss, for sure.

What had not changed since I'd last seen him, said Major, was the fear that one day, out of the blue, Buck would develop some kind of problem that was a direct result of Major's heavy meth use. The idea of this—and that it might, no matter how many strides Major made in his life, become a sudden and crushing reality—grew inside Major like a benign tumor that could, at any moment, metastasize into an inoperable cancer. The very notion that innocent, tiny Buck might be victimized by his father's past was still enough to make Major want to go and finish himself off with one last, superlatively freeing crank overdose.

Research regarding the long-term effects of meth exposure in children was, as it had been in 2005, still inconclusive. University of Toronto pharmacology professor Dr. Sean Wells told me, "It'll be two decades before there are any firm findings," since "long-term effects cannot be studied in the short term." For Buck and Major, no news was good news. But the same lack of information also allowed Major's imagination to reinforce his sense of guilt. It was a cruel fate for someone like Major, who so badly wanted to be liked that he had easily fallen under the sway of the Sons of Silence, to whom he still referred as the Family. Major was alone with his self-loathing, which at times extended to Buck, the bearer of his father's sins, the vessel holding the despicable remnants of his parents' all-too-present past.

Major said he still felt far from accepted by people in Independence. With the help of meth and the Family, he said he'd put himself at a far remove from most of American society, and this at times only further tempted him to return to his old life. The help Major got from his parents was remarkable, though their relationship continued to be fraught with difficulties. Buck's mother was still meth-addicted and still living with the Family. Major knew it would be his undoing to have any contact with her, but he missed Buck's mother horribly. Who else, really, could even begin to understand his situation?

Major was still on probation, still attending mandatory Narcotics Anonymous meetings, and still working a construction job to which he was always having to find a ride; his license would remain suspended for another six months. The good news, he said, was that he *had* a job, and that each day he stayed clean, he was a step closer to being free of meth forever (he hoped) and to getting off probation. Once he could drive again he hoped to find a house for himself and Buck and maybe to pick up his studies at the community college where he'd left them for dead six years ago. One day, he said, he still hoped to become a machinist.

The bad news, said Major, was that he lacked anything in which to believe. He was working hard—at staying clean, at raising Buck, at making money. But without meth, Major found it impossible to feel, as he put it, "happy." It was precisely the dilemma that Clay Hallberg had seen so many times in patients like Roland Jarvis. Even when Major did the right thing, he couldn't quite believe in its rightness, for that thing didn't satisfy him—meth did. The first time I spoke to Clay on the phone, he'd said that an entire generation of people was suffering from this, and that meth was less the culprit than the perfect metaphor. To get back to normal—that is, to begin once again to derive meaning from the humdrum facts of life— might take years. Clay's own recent epiphany was essentially that intellect cannot substitute for instinct—knowing is not feeling. In the same way, Major's self-admonishment that he ought to be grateful is no substitute for the neurotransmitters—and the feeling of well-being they create—that he can no longer produce. In the meantime, the gravitational pull of meth, with its pyrotechnic promise of biochemical ecstasy, could be overwhelming. Major, standing in his kitchen on a Saturday night, seemed to be searching aggressively, almost violently, for order, even as he was resolved to the fact that he would not find it. I asked him if he was ready to revert to his given name, Thomas, or if he still preferred his nickname.

"It's not a nickname," he said. "It's who I am."

The first time I'd met Major we'd gone on a glorious July day to an isolated park a few miles outside town, at Major's request, to play Frisbee golf. The course was laid out in the woods, and each "hole" was a large metal basket set at certain distances, from a hundred yards to several hundred, from each "tee," which was nothing more than a mowed patch of grass amid the trees. After playing, Major instructed me to take a shortcut on the way home. As one gravel section road led to the next, with green, chest-high corn obscuring the horizon in every direction, it was obvious we weren't headed back to town but, rather, farther into the country. Major asked me several times if I knew where I was, knowing well that I did not. He clearly enjoyed the control. Eventually, he told me to pull in the driveway of an isolated farmhouse, which turned out to be the current residence of the Family. There, the Sons of Silence leader, Bob, was living with his daughter—Buck's mother—and presumably batching meth in the barn, just as he'd been doing when Major was sent to jail.

Only a few days before, Bob had called Bonnie and Joseph in the middle of the night to say that he was coming to kill them and Major, to burn their house down, and to kidnap Buck. And yet, at the first chance Major had, he'd concocted an elaborate plan to play a game of Frisbee golf in an isolated park in order to be driven back to the life he both loathed and longed once again to live. When I pulled out of the driveway, Major pleaded for me to take him back, then refused to tell me how to get back to town. He berated me, threatened to have me killed, and pounded the dashboard as I drove. Major pulled out a cell phone, called a girl he used to know, and promised me that if I'd take him back to the Family, he'd get the girl high and she'd do anything I wanted. It took an hour of driving around aimlessly before I finally got him back home.

By that stretch, Major had come a long, long way. He still prayed for Buck's mother to come back to him, but only if she were clean. He still dreamed of the Family when he slept at night, and had to fight the occasional urge to rejoin them, but it was no longer a daily battle he waged with himself. In order to see more clearly still how far he'd come, one has only to think of Roland Jarvis, for example, or even Lori Arnold, who was due out of federal prison for the second time in June 2008.

The last time I'd visited Jarvis, oddly, was the only time I'd ever seen him outside his mother's house. He was sitting in his mother's front yard in a lawn chair, wearing his customary flannel shirt and heavy warm-up pants despite the heat, idly chatting with neighbors walking by on the sidewalk. That, though, seems to have been a high point. I'd tried to contact Jarvis, but to no avail, which I took to be a bad sign, given how welcoming he'd been during two years' worth of my trips to Oelwein. No one seemed to know where he was or what had happened to him. Clay Hallberg, his doctor, hadn't seen him in months. It was as though Roland Jarvis had been suddenly swallowed up by the musty living room floor of his mother's house.

Yet here was Major, twenty-seven years old (Jarvis would turn forty in December 2007), staying clean, holding a job, seeming to enjoy the sight of his son, who, so far, needed no transplants and no special education. Gone were the days when Major was so high that he mistook a nickel for baby food. (Buck nearly choked to death on the nickel, while Major, fearful he'd be put in jail if he took the child to the hospital, drove Buck to his parents' house and had them take Buck to the ER. Once there, Buck had emergency surgery to remove the nickel from his trachea.) No longer did Major seem to have the energy for the monologues describing how enemies of the Family were duct-taped to chairs and given lethal amounts of intravenous methamphetamine, their bodies thrown to the hogs. By December 2007, Major had lost his enthusiasm for the Sons' white supremacist espousals, which, ironically, he'd always spewed to an inaudible beat—as though, even as he raged against blacks, one of his beloved Wu-Tang Clan riffs played in his mind. Compared with Roland Jarvis, Major had triumphantly entered an entirely new realm.

Major's hope was nonetheless tentative. For one thing, he was attempting to stay clean of meth while refusing to stop drinking. (When I asked him about this, he asked if drinking was illegal. I shook my head. To which Major added angrily, "Then I rest my case.") Just how close Major was to losing the ground he'd gained was made clear in a story he told me while Buck, drowsy with his belly full of pizza, climbed inside his newly rebuilt fort, ostensibly to watch more Looney Tunes, and fell quietly asleep.

The previous night, Major said, he had put Buck to bed and walked in the agonizing cold to a favorite bar eight blocks away. Between the time he'd spent with the Family, the time he'd spent in jail, and the time he'd spent essentially hiding in his parents' home, afraid that any social contact would lead to a relapse, most of Major's friends had moved on in one form or another. Many had left town looking for work, or had married and taken jobs that kept them out of the bars at night. The rest, not unreasonably, were afraid to get involved with a former neo-Nazi meth dealer. But that night, Major had run into a girl with whom he'd gone to high school, and on whom he'd had a long-buried crush. As they talked and drank, Major became aware that not only were his adolescent feelings still fresh, but that she, too, had long had feelings for him.

The sudden awareness that his mind was at ease was almost dizzying, since he'd been constantly preoccupied for so long. Life, Buck, his parents, his past—for a sweet, short time, thoughts of all these things dissolved away with the pitchers of beer and the warm, dark room. He was drunk and happy, reconnecting with a part of his life that was free of the burden of his recent entanglements. He and the girl laughed about how, back in high school, Major, who'd never done drugs of any kind until after he'd graduated, had actually given a speech to the student body on the evils of methamphetamine.

Then, ecstatically, Major and the girl took advantage of the low light in the corner booth to engage in the kiss that had been nearly a decade in coming. As he kissed her, though, Major snuck glances at the big windows at the front of the bar. He knew he had to leave, even though the warmth of her body held him fast. It was going on midnight on a Friday, and the police would be out cruising. They all knew exactly who Major was. None of them, he felt sure, truly believed a man like him could ever get clean, and they would be gunning for him. He had eight blocks to walk—a loner on quiet, frigid streets, standing out like a criminal. Which, legally, he would be: being drunk in public (and Major was most certainly drunk by now) would constitute a violation of his probation. Should he be caught, he would get three years in jail, no questions asked. He'd completely run out of strikes.

Finally, Major told the girl he had to go, pushing his way out of the booth. He'd thought about getting the girl to drive him home, but he knew that would be foolish. She was drunk, too, and if the police pulled her over—which was likely—he would go to jail just the same. He thought briefly about driving her car himself. Eight blocks wasn't that far, after all, and Major was nothing if not an expert at driving drunk. But he decided against this, too, knowing that public drunkenness would get him jail time but that another driving violation would mean he'd lose his license for good. So Major kissed the girl good-bye, went out the door alone, and started walking.

At first he kept to the edge of the sidewalk. Then, he said, he pulled his parka hood over his head, shielding his face. He thought about Buck and his penchant for building forts, and how a small boy convinces himself that to be unseeing is magically equivalent to being unseen. For a block, Major walked with his hood pulled tight and his head down. Then he threw the hood back. He was getting panicky now, and he started moving along the snow-covered lawns, nearer to the houses, drawn by the shadows of the awnings and the frozen, screened-in porches.

Soon Major was panting beneath a tree, in the throes of what felt to him like a paralyzing, vomitous meth withdrawal—a full three maddening years since he'd smoked his last foil. All the paranoia came crashing back on him, knocking the breath from his lungs with a force like a wall of water. His vision tunneled, and he began sweating. His heart raced as he puked on the frozen snow. When he was done, he started running—jumping fences and looking behind himself in utter terror in a mad dash to make it back home to his child and his parents, driven suddenly by a desire not to escape, but to get caught. He wished to hear the sirens that wouldn't come. To have looked back and seen the police would have been a relief. Anything would have been better, Major said, than the invisible force that bore down on him from behind.

EPILOGUE

HOME AGAIN

In June 2008, I moved to St. Louis with my wife, having lived away from my hometown for eighteen years. During the first week I was there, the *St. Louis Post-Dispatch* newspaper ran daily stories about a two-state murder rampage. First, as the killer was in the midst of his spree; then as he was apprehended; and finally, as the details of his situation made themselves clear. The murderer's name was Nicholas Sheley, and he was from Rock Falls, Illinois, about eighty miles east of Oelwein. In the three hundred or so miles between Galesburg, Illinois, and Festus, Missouri, near St. Louis, Sheley beat or bludgeoned to death eight people in five days. The whole time, he'd been high on crank.

In addition to the Sheley story, the *Post-Dispatch* ran several pieces during my first two weeks home about meth manufacture in Jefferson County, Missouri, which is just outside St. Louis. Jefferson County had become famous in 2005 for having the highest number of meth labs in America, as measured by the number dismantled each year. Missouri led the nation with 2,788 labs busted in 2005, and Jeff County, as it's called, had an astounding 259 of them—nearly twice that of the next leading Missouri county of Jasper. Given that most police officers with whom I spoke figure they dismantle only one in ten labs at best, that's as many 2,600 labs at work in rural, bucolic Jefferson County back in 2005. According to the *Post-Dispatch*, after a brief but precipitous fall in meth-lab busts during 2007, once the Combat Meth Act had passed, Jeff County was on track by June of 2008 to have 200 labs dismantled by year's end: a clear indication that the batchers were back.

The feeling I had while reading the stories of Jeff County and Nicholas Sheley reminded me of the feeling I had when I first started researching for this book, in May 2005. As I drove around Iowa, Illinois, Missouri, Kentucky, California, Georgia, and Alabama that summer and fall, there was a genuine sense of shock and fear in the towns I visited. People were confused by the thought that, somehow, just down the street or on the other side of town, a drug that could be made in a sink was making people do crazy things. Not long before I met Phil Price, the former special agent in charge of the Georgia Bureau of Investigation, he'd had to arrest a good friend of his—forty-five years old, a father of three, and a new meth addict. Price, backed by the SWAT team, had talked his friend of two decades out of a motel room in rural Canton, Georgia, where the man had taken his own nine-year-old son hostage. It doesn't take many stories like this to make people question what they know about one another and about themselves.

The notion that the small-time crank business was back in full force was vexing to me as my wife and I settled into our new neighborhood. It was also frightening. One of my principal motivations for wanting to write this book is that my wife, who grew up in a small town in rural New York, is a recovering alcoholic. I have thought on a thousand occasions: What if meth had been as easily available when she was a teenager as it is now? What if crank, instead of booze, had been her drug of choice? It's reasonable to suggest that I'd have never met her. Now she was pregnant with our first child. The notion that nothing had changed—for James and Sean in Greenville, for Jeff County, for the place in which I would soon raise my family—was more upsetting to me than it had ever been. Like the mothers and fathers I'd met in Canton and Benton and Oelwein in 2005, I wanted to know what kind of world my child would inhabit, and how things had gotten to be this way. It was as though I was back where I had started three years before.

According to DEA, the Combat Meth Act was supposed to have effectively killed the home-brewed crank business. According to the nation's drug czar, meth was dead. If we were to worry at all, it should be about the DTOs, not batchers in Jeff County. So why had the epidemic shifted in the one way that could not have been predicted? Now that meth making had come back home, as it were, people were once again comparing the drug to some kind of supernatural evil, just as had been common in 2005 and 2006. People were starting to panic all over again.

In order to put things in perspective, I called Tony Loya. An hour-long conversation with him not only confirmed that meth's genome had reassorted itself once again; it suggested something like a reversion to 1996, after Gene Haislip had finally succeeded in passing a law monitoring the use of powdered pseudoephedrine. Meth seizures that year went down, along with purity, signaling the first major DEA triumph over the drug's spread. Of course, the victory was pyrrhic, once traffickers switched to the pill-form pseudo that drug lobbyists demanded remain unmonitored. The watering down of Haislip's 1996 law is what opened the door to the single most destructive period of meth's recent history, culminating nine years later, in 2005, with the highest rates ever of both domestic and international production of the drug. Now it was becoming clear that, in the wake of the Combat Meth Act, a new and destructive era of the meth epidemic was already under way.

Loya is five feet six and slightly built. The first time I met him, in a secure room at the Federal Building in San Diego, he appeared behind photochromic gold-rimmed glasses and a deep tan to be in exorbitantly good health for a man of fifty-nine. Loya had the looming and insistently charismatic presence of a Vegas entertainer. He's been a government employee for thirty-nine years: first with the California Bureau of Narcotics Enforcement (BNE), then with DEA for twenty-five years, and now with the National Methamphetamine Chemical Initiative. He is thoroughly a company man, preternaturally slow to criticize the government or any government agency. He considers American industry "the reason we lead the world" and advocates the fiscally conservative desire for small government and limited regulation. Recent developments, though, had truly stretched many of Loya's convictions.

What was clear the day that I talked to Loya on the phone— nearly three years to the day after first meeting him in San Diego— is that he in some ways has found himself playing the role of Gene Haislip. Loya was one of architects of the Combat Meth Act. He also had unprecedented success in persuading the Mexican government to outlaw pseudoephedrine imports into the country in 2007, thereby depleting the amount available to the DTOs. Loya is proud of his work. He is also growing weary, four decades after going to work for a government that, as he put it, "seems ever willing to give new life to the same damn problem it purports to solve." He went on, "Every decade, we get a chance to put meth on the mat once and for all. And we always fail."

According to Loya, the failure of the Combat Meth Act is, like the failure of Haislip's 1996 law, the direct result of lobbying related to the pharmaceutical industry. The guiding philosophy behind the Combat Meth Act was to lessen domestic crank production by monitoring the sale of cold medicine nationwide. According to Loya, DEA gave Congress three stipulations for doing so successfully. One, the means of monitoring would have to be federally mandated, as opposed to being left up to individual states. Two, pharmacies would need to track cold medicine sales via computer, rather than through handwritten logs. Three, said Loya, DEA insisted that pharmacists' computers would need "stop-buy" language built into their monitoring programs—meaning that if a customer who has already purchased the monthly maximum of Sudafed tries to buy more, the computer will automatically prompt the pharmacist to disallow the sale, or "stop the buy."

This time, it wasn't Allan Rexinger's Proprietary Association that objected to the key elements of a piece of antimeth legislation; it was the National Association of Retail Chain Stores, which represents, according to Loya, the five major pharmaceutical drug chains in the United States: Target, Wal-Mart, CVS, Walgreens, and Rite-Aid. The organization's acronym, Loya noted sardonically on the phone that day, is NARCS.

While the Combat Meth Act was being debated in 2006, lobbyists on behalf of NARCS argued that a "stop-buy" clause in the legislation would make pharmacists and retail employees into policemen. Why, for example, NARCS asked, should CVS employees have to tell a customer that he can't buy something? Rather, NARCS said, the data should simply be made available following the sale to local police, at which point the police could do as they saw fit. The stores would be willing to comply, but they should not have to do so at the potentially unfair loss of sales.

The counterargument, as Tony Loya characterized it, was this: "Does refusing the sale of alcohol and tobacco to minors amount to 'policing'?

"Yes," Loya went on, "it does. And the drug chains have been doing that without complaint for years. So what's the difference if they have to tell a few people that they can't buy more than a certain amount of Sudafed? But the lobbyists insisted that any attempt whatsoever at keeping track of sales is a threat to their financial health. It's just not true."

In the end, Congress rejected the "stop-buy" language. More important, Congress resisted DEA's pleas that the law's interpretation be federally controlled. Instead, Congress decided to make the Combat Meth Act more of guideline than an actual mandate, leaving specific interpretation to state governments. This, according to Loya, effectively laid the law bare to the powerful NARCS lobby. Meantime, the law's leading advocates and negotiators—Republican Congressman Mark Souder and Senator Dianne Feinstein, Democrat of California—declared the legislation a groundbreaking blow to meth.

Loya characterized the failure of the Combat Meth Act in terms that would have been all too familiar to Larry Murphy back in 2005. States, he said, just like towns and counties, are businesses. Poor states like Missouri, just like poor towns like Oelwein, are loath to risk straining relations with chains like CVS and Rite-Aid. Back when Larry Murphy made the decision to rebuild his town by rejecting businesses that weren't good for the community, he reconciled himself to the risk that Oelwein could become poorer still, and that he would be blamed. Oelwein gambled and won in 2005 and 2006. Missouri, faced with an implicit threat to its already teetering economy from NARCS, chose to play it safe, refusing to adopt DEA's "stop-buy" language in its interpretation of the Combat Meth Act late in 2006. At the further behest of NARCS, Loya said, the state legislature allowed pharmacies to rely on handwritten logs of cold medicine sales, thereby saving chains the need to buy new computer programs. A year and a half later, Missouri once again has the highest per capita crank production in the United States.

"Here we are," Loya said, "the most technologically advanced nation in history, and we have thousands of people writing hundreds of thousands of names in notebooks. We pass a law, and then we basically tell these huge companies that they're not responsible for complying. It's stunning."

In reaction, the cottage meth industry has become more efficient than Loya ever imagined. Beavis and Butt-Head labs have become more like midlevel operations, he said. Smurfing has become an industry in its own right. Having developed not just local but also national distribution chains, Smurfers drive from state to state and region to region buying cold medicine and selling it to increasingly productive and organized networks of batchers. Locally, Smurfs pay pharmacy employees to ignore the fact they are stealing cold medicine.

"CVS or Walgreens employees," said Loya, "make more in two

minutes of pretending not to notice theft than they make in a week of standing behind the counter. It's a no-brainer." As a result, Loya said, lab numbers are still down compared with their all-time highs in 2004 and 2005, but production is way up.

What's more, Loya's sources indicate that cocaine seizures along the Mexican border are at a twelve-year high, noting that the last time cocaine was so heavily consumed was in 1996, when Haislip's law briefly depressed the DTOs' meth market. Loya attributes the increase in cocaine seizures this time to his own hard-fought success with getting the Mexican government to limit pseudo imports. What Loya fears, though, is that local meth producers will keep the market alive while the DTOs, flush with money from a booming cocaine business, will have time and capital not only to recover from a temporary setback, but to become even stronger.

"I mean," Loya said, "I'm stuck in a time warp. It's twelve years ago all over again, with the Mexicans biding their time with cocaine till they can figure out a way to get back the part of the meth business we just took away. Will they go to Canada for pseudo, or North Korea, or Colombia? Who knows. My guess is Canada. What's certain is they'll go somewhere. Because the addicts are here. The money is here. The Smurfs are keeping everyone high while the Mexicans reorganize."

Loya noted that the DTOs will never abandon the meth business—no matter how good the cocaine market—since, with meth, the DTOs control manufacture, distribution, and retail. Meth is a peach of a business. It's also possibly, as Patricia Case once noted, "the most American drug." Coupled with the American mania for work, it's as though meth's ever-reassorting genome is a part of our own. As Loya's friend Bill Ruzzamenti, another former DEA special agent in charge, once said to me, "Meth truly will never go away. It can't. It's too big a piece of what we *are*."

While Loya waits to see what the DTOs will do next, he continues to privately negotiate with pharmaceutical companies and the retail chains that sell their wares, in order, as he put it, "to make them see what's at stake." The hope is that if NARCS will take the pressure off state legislatures, they might amend their meth laws to look more like what Loya and DEA had in mind all along.

"You know," said Loya, "I'm sympathetic to big business. I'm not trying to make things hard for them. I just say to CVS via the lobbyists, 'Look, your clerks are in cahoots with crooks. We're going to take them down, and you'll look bad. Do you really want your company to look like a criminal organization?'" Loya paused. "I say that, and I try to stay calm while freaking houses are blowing up in Jefferson County. But I can't stay calm anymore. So then I just yell."

A few days before we spoke, Loya told me, he'd had a meeting with the vice president of NARCS. Loya listened while the man reiterated that clerks and pharmacists in the employ of CVS and Rite-Aid aren't police officers. They should not, said the NARCS vice president, be expected to tell customers that they can't buy cold medicine. If someone was shoplifting, the man wanted to know, would the clerk apprehend, cuff, and jail the shoplifter? No—he'd call the police, as he should. And anyway, he went on, the pharmacies aren't legally obligated to do anything more than what they're doing. Drugs and drug manufacturers are police business, not theirs. The Combat Meth Act makes that very clear, he told Loya.

"After all these years, and all these meetings, and all these conferences," said Loya, "I started to do something that I've never, ever done: I started to get up and walk out. Midsentence. It was like I just . . ." Here Loya paused. His first street buy, as a twenty-year-old agent with the California BNE, in San Francisco in 1968, was meth. He's been contending with it ever since. "It was like," he went on, "something finally broke."

But Loya didn't get up to leave. He remained seated. Then he stopped listening. He let the vice president talk, and he tried not to hear a word of what he said, instead summoning all the patience he could muster from the deepest reaches of his soul. Finally, said Loya, the man's mouth stopped moving. That's when Loya started to explain, one more time.

In April 2008, Nathan Lein was elected to the Oelwein city council. He won, said Clay Hallberg, in a landslide. The Ninth Ward, where Nathan lives in a small white house across the street from a former meth lab, is no longer just his home—it's now his charge, too. In May, Major graduated from community college in Independence with a degree in machinery repair. Bob, the leader of the Sons of Silence, was arrested along with his daughter—Major's ex-girlfriend, and the mother of his son, Buck—for manufacture of methamphetamine with the intent to distribute. Bob and his daughter await sentencing. Buck's half sister, Caroline, is in foster care. Buck begins kindergarten in the fall.

Lori Arnold was released from the medium-security federal work camp for women in Greenville, Illinois, on June 3, 2008. She moved to Chandler, Arizona, to live near one of her brothers. One week later, she took her first mandatory urine analysis, to test for illegal substances in her system. She failed, and was sentenced to five years' probation.

The last time I called Roland Jarvis, in July 2008, he was sitting in the living room of his mother's two-bedroom house. It had been more than three years since we had watched *Goodfellas* in that same room and Jarvis began unwinding the strands of his two-decade struggle with meth. I was glad to hear his voice, after my calls had gone unanswered for over twelve months. At one point, I had heard a rumor that he or his ex-wife had committed suicide.

"No," he said, "no one's committed suicide."

Aside from that, it was strikes and gutters, as some people say in Oelwein: ups and downs, goods and bads. Jarvis's middle son had finally received a new kidney and was doing well. Jarvis's mother, though, would be headed back to jail soon, this time for driving drunk. His two daughters were doing well, too; one had graduated from Oelwein High that spring. He'd been fishing with them at the town lake just the other day.

"Same old, same old," said Jarvis.

I asked him if he was clean.

"Not really," he said. "But I'm still here."

When we hung up, I thought about a trip I'd taken in the summer of 2005. I was still looking for a town to write about then. I'd been to Oelwein twice that summer, spending about a month there. I'd been driving a lot, too, dropping into towns I'd read about in newspapers, asking people to talk to me about meth. I spent a lot of time in emergency rooms, in courtrooms, and in county jails. One weekend, I drove five hundred miles from Kentucky to Iowa, then back again. The problem is that I wasn't sure what I was looking at, exactly, or even what I was looking for. So like everyone else, I went to California.

I started out in San Diego, where I met Tony Loya. Then, for a week, I drove around the Central Valley, finally ending up in San Jose. Along the way, I tried to insinuate myself into every town with a motel vacancy. The Central Valley was just as Steinbeck had described it: hot, flat, and dusty, the cool, distant mountains a promise, or maybe just a mirage. It felt like Iowa in the summer, or the Dakotas, or even Missouri. I didn't know what I was looking at when I saw how some of the canals in the most isolated parts of the valley ran red. Later, a DEA agent told me that, in addition to providing water for the most prolific farm country in the nation, the canals were dump sites for red phosphorus from meth superlabs hidden among the orange and pecan groves.

At the end of that trip, I took a late-afternoon flight from San Jose to JFK Airport, in New York. Three hours after takeoff, looking at a map in the back of an in-flight magazine, I reckoned us to be over eastern South Dakota, heading for Iowa. At that point, the plane would have been at the nadir of its arc, where it would remain for a short while before beginning the long, smooth descent.

With the sun slanting low in our wake, the land was awash in the refracted warmth of the day's dying light. In the glow, and from thirty-five thousand feet, it was impossible to see the little towns below.

At that height, too, we were caught in the temporal netherworld that is specific to late-afternoon and evening transcontinental flights. The curvature of the earth was clearly visible. Ahead, to the north and east, the air was blue and dark. Behind, to the south and west, the air glowed red. It was truly as though the night were pushing itself across the vast contours of the land, driving the day before it. Below us, though, in Sioux Falls and in Algona, the light, along with the notion of possibility, remained.

Fifteen minutes later, even the largest of the land's features began to fade as the plane moved east. My mood soured. I didn't want to go back to New York. Instead, I yearned to return to Missouri for the first time in years. We were too far north to see St. Louis, so I searched for the Mississippi among the tiny, sparse points of light visible against the opaque land. At least the river, I thought, might give me some fleeting connection to my home.

Moments later, I found what I was looking for in the growing darkness. With my eyes, I followed the glowing river north, knowing that one of the tiny clusters of light must be Oelwein. Suddenly I knew what I was looking at, and where I needed to go.

ACKNOWLEDGMENTS

Of all the people to whom I'm indebted for help in making this book possible, the people of Oelwein, Iowa, are at the top of the list. Without their willingness to let me into their lives, and to stay embedded there—at times annoyingly, I'm sure, like a tick—*Methland* would have never been. Nathan Lein and Clay Hallberg's intelligence, candor, and abiding sense of humanity make them truly remarkable people. I'm also deeply obliged to Mayor Larry Murphy for letting me watch at close range as he whittled away at Oelwein's troubles. In a time when the word "hero" has been overused to the point that it's lost all meaning, Larry serves as a reminder of what a hero looks and acts like. Thanks also to Jamie Porter, Jeremy Logan, Tammy Hallberg, Tim Gilson, Charlie Hallberg, Alan Coffman, Jan Boleyn, and Mildred Binstock.

There are other Iowans, too, to whom I owe my deepest gratitude. Chief among them are the addicts, former addicts, and traffickers who have let me use their stories in the making of this book. It takes tremendous courage to open one's life to public scrutiny, especially a life that has in some ways been defined by crime. In that capacity, I'm grateful to Roland Jarvis, who spoke with me over the course of nearly four years in the hope that others would not fall prey to the addiction that has monopolized his life for two decades. Thanks to Lori Arnold for the many letters she sent me from federal prison. Her willingness to talk—and to act as a sounding board for my own understanding of meth trafficking in America—was crucial to the making of this book. Many thanks also to the Cooper family—Joseph, Bonnie, Buck, and Thomas, a.k.a. Major—who, along with Judy Murphy, were elemental in my understanding of how meth affects not just parents and their children, but communities. And finally, thanks to Jeffrey William Hayes who took the time to write hundreds of pages of letters to me from Leavenworth Prison.

Tony Loya has been battling the country's meth problem for thirty-seven years. Like Larry Murphy, Nathan Lein, and Clay Hallberg, Tony is an indisputable—if unheralded—hero. He was also invaluable in providing insight into the trends that have defined the meth epidemic since 1972, the year he made his first drug buy as a young agent with the California Bureau of Narcotics Enforcement. If anyone will ever succeed in curtailing this epidemic, it will be Tony.

A number of state and federal narcotics agents, police officers, and sheriff's deputies helped me a great deal, at times leveraging their careers to do so. In that regard, I'm deeply indebted to Bill Ruzzamenti, Craig Hammer, and Rich Camps in California; Sergeant Tom McAndrew in Iowa; Sergeant Alex Gonzalez in Alabama; and Phil Price and Sherri Strange in Georgia. Thanks also (wherever you are) to Rudy, the meth dealer turned federal informant whose life story was as enlightening as it was chilling.

Anton Mueller at Bloomsbury is an outstanding editor. Over the last two years, I wrote the first half of *Methland* four times before finally getting it right. Or at least before shaping it into the form in which it now stands. Though I was—to put it politely—less than enthusiastic each time Anton read my latest effort and instructed me to start over, I'm glad now that he held his ground. An editor with patience, a strong stomach, and an enduring passion for his author's book is a rarity these days indeed, and one for which I feel extremely fortunate and grateful.

Thanks also to my agent at ICM, Heather Shroder. She not only sold this book at a time when no one seemed interested in the meth epidemic, but she also guided it through a potential disaster when the initial publisher, Houghton Mifflin, merged with Harcourt Brace. Had Heather not found a new home for me and my book at Bloomsbury, I'm not sure what would have become of us.

No one was more valuable in the making of this book than my mother and father. The genesis of *Methland* dates to 1999, and was defined for five years by one failure after another—all before I ever began writing. My parents' willingness to believe that I would succeed despite repeated setbacks stretches the bounds of comprehension. Through it all, they refused to do anything less than support me wholeheartedly. It seems only fitting that, while reporting for this book, I got to see for the first time the small town of Algona, Iowa, where my father was born and raised, and which he left over half a century ago. Everywhere I went in Iowa, in fact, and among the many people I met, I caught sight of the forthright generosity of spirit that defines my parents.

Most of all, I'd like to thank my wife, Kelly, who helped me at every stage of this process. It was she who encouraged me to write a book proposal for *Methland* in 2005. Later that year and all through 2006, the only thing that made being away from home for weeks at a time any easier was knowing that Kelly would be there when I got back. She was patient and kind while I wrote *Methland*, and thoughtful in her criticism as it neared completion in 2008. As a wife, a friend, and a mother to our child, she is everything and more that I could ask for.

Finally, I'm indebted to the two residents of tiny Greenville, Illinois, who inspired this book. I met them—a white meth-addicted felon and a black army sergeant recently home from Afghanistan— in a bar in November 2004. Over the course of several nights, it became clear to me that two people who were so different on the surface were in fact united by circumstances beyond their control. One of the facts of their lives was the huge sway methamphetamine held over their town. I'll never forget the moment when, in talking to them, I saw this story for what it is. In gratitude and in hope, *Methland* is dedicated to them.

A NOTE ON SOURCES

Much of *Methland* is a retelling of events as they were related to me over the course of four years by the people of Oelwein. *Interview* isn't really a word that applies here. During the weeks and months that I spent in town, nothing was ever spoken into a tape recorder, or written in a space below questions plotted on note cards. Rather, the people in this book shared the stories and the facts of their lives with me at the same time that we shared the day's events. We cooked dinner and watched movies, drove back and forth to the grocery store, shoveled snow, and did chores around the house. They graciously permitted me to play pool and hunt pheasants with them, go to parties and to work, eat with them in restaurants, stop by the post office on the way to the doctor, and call on neighbors. The telling of past events unfolded simultaneously with the living out of present circumstance, thereby—I hope—adding a depth and texture that is otherwise unattainable.

In the absence of a tape recorder or video camera, I was forever excusing myself to write notes whenever there was an appropriate moment. Each night, I'd take these handwritten notes and expand them into scenes, while the memories remained fresh. Outside Oelwein, too, I employed this same live-in reporting strategy whenever possible. In Independence, Iowa, the former addict and meth cook

Thomas, a.k.a. Major, preferred to talk while playing Frisbee golf, in which the players throw plastic discs of different shapes and weights (heavier ones are "putters," while lighter discs, because they fly farther, are "drivers") toward a basket affixed to a tree. When Major and I played, it allowed him to escape, however briefly, from the scrutiny of his parents, with whom he lived. So, too, did Major's parents seem to appreciate any chance to leave their home, where they were not only overseeing the informal, inpatient rehab of their meth-addicted son, but where they were also helping to raise their grandchild, Buck. When I talked to Major's parents, it was normally over lunch or a beer, preferably in a place where they could both smoke. Seeing them briefly outside their home made clearer still the complexity of their circumstances.

A slightly different protocol guided my interaction with two former meth traffickers: Lori Arnold of Ottumwa and Jeffrey William Hayes of Oelwein. Over the course of three years, Lori and Jeffrey William, as he prefers to be called, sent me hundreds of pages of letters from the federal prisons where they were serving lengthy sentences. The letters detailed not just the ins and outs of major meth production and distribution in their respective hometowns, but also the ups and downs of their lives in prison. Even though Jeffrey William hardly appears in this book, his letters were nearly as vital as Lori's in providing context and detail to the rise of the modern meth epidemic—and moreover, to the causal link between the industrial meth trade in California, Mexico, and the rural Midwest that he and Lori helped to initiate. In the end, their letters are also stories that frame a particular time in the history of rural America.

In order to give specific shape to the careers of Lori, Jeffrey William, and Major, I drew heavily on reports issued by the U.S. Office of National Drug Control Policy and the National Institutes of Drug Addiction. I also depended on international, regional, and local methamphetamine assessments published regularly by the Drug Enforcement Administration. In addition, several people made accessible to me information not available publicly, mostly outlining the history and present role of major Mexican meth traffickers, along with the link between these trafficking organizations and terrorist organizations. Among the people whom I interviewed formally on at least two occasions were Bill Ruzzamenti, the director of California's Central Valley High-Intensity Drug-Trafficking Area; Tony Loya, the director of the National Methamphetamine Chemical Initiative; Sherri Strange, special agent in charge of DEA's Southeast Region, headquartered in Atlanta; and Phil Price, former SAC of the Georgia Bureau of Investigation. In May 2006, I attended a meth summit between Mexican and U.S. officials, including the attorneys general of both nations, in Dallas. In interviews there, one government official spoke openly—in return for anonymity—about what he saw as the "direct and conscious link between failed U.S. immigration policy and the meth epidemic."

My contention that the economic downfall of the rural United States is attributable in large part to the consolidation of the American food business is based on a wide range of sources. Many of those sources are the farmers and meatpacking workers of Oelwein and Ottumwa, Iowa. Along with dozens of newspaper articles written since the beginning of the farm crisis in the 1980s, these men and women helped form the foundation of my thinking on the subject. Also of particular importance was the work of two rural sociologists: William Heffernan at the University of Missouri, Columbia, and Douglas Constance at Sam Houston State University in Texas. I drew heavily on Dr. Heffernan's paper—written along with Drs. Mary Hendrickson and Paul Gronski—titled "Consolidation in the Food and Agriculture Business," which essentially synthesized three decades of research, the bulk of Dr. Heffernan's well-documented career. The input of Dr. Constance, on the other hand, came via long e-mails and phone conversations.

The work of several other sociologists was fundamental in the making of *Methland*, whether or not I had reason to cite their work in the text. Three documents of particular interest were Dr. Patricia

Case's "A History of Methamphetamine: An Epidemic in Context," Dr. Craig Reinarman's book *Crack in America*, and Dr. Karen Van Gundy's paper "Substance Abuse in Rural and Small Town America," written at the Carsey Institute at the University of New Hampshire.

Numerous scientists contributed greatly to the information in this book. To them I owe my understanding of meth's chemical properties, of the specific behavioral and psychological repercussions of meth addiction, of the biochemical effects of meth on the human brain, and of the psychological effects of a drug epidemic not just on individuals, but on communities. Much of the information that I accessed is available publicly, though several people in particular sent me papers in progress and also took time to speak with me about their ongoing studies, be it in person, by e-mail, or on the phone. These include Dr. Perry Halkitis at New York University, Dr. Rick Rawson and Dr. Tom Freese at UCLA, Dr. Sean Wells at the University of Toronto, and Dr. Linda Chang at the University of Hawaii.

The number of archived newspaper articles on which I drew directly or indirectly while writing *Methland* fills two file drawers. These articles come from papers as geographically and demographically disparate as Allentown, Pennsylvania's *Morning Call* and the *Fresno Bee*. Taken of a piece, the articles form one of the deepest strata on which this book rests. Of particular importance was the three-part series "Unnecessary Epidemic" written by Steve Suo in the *Oregonian* in October 2004. Equally crucial were several pieces written between 1999 and 2003 in the *New York Times* and the *Los Angeles Times* detailing immigration violations at meatpacking plants, particularly those that followed the story of a federal indictment against Tyson in 2001. Pieces and series in the *Chicago Tribune*, the *San Francisco Chronicle*, the *St. Louis Post-Dispatch*, and the *Atlanta Journal-Constitution* played important roles as well.

In the end, though, nothing is as important in *Methland* as the people. The newspapers, the science, and the research papers serve only to corroborate what I saw and what I was told by the residents of Oelwein, Iowa. They were the ultimate source of this book, which in its simplest form is an exercise in fitting one small American town into a broader framework of crisis. Everyone who appears in *Methland* does so by choice and with full knowledge. Without them *Methland* would be empty indeed.